Fremd bin ich eingezogen
Fremd zieh ich wieder aus
Der Mai war mir gewogen
Mit manchem Blumenstrauss.

(A stranger I arrived here
A stranger I depart
May was kind to me
With many a bouquet of flowers.)

❧

Wilhelm Müller
text to the first song of Franz Shubert's "Die Winterreise"

Contents

Foreword

BY ZUBIN MEHTA

I have always considered myself one of the many fans of Hans Hotter, having admired him from the top balcony standing room for years at the Vienna Staatsoper singing a variety of parts from Pizzaro to Scarpia and the entire Wagner repertoire in which he was at the height of his career.

His innate understanding of each role, not only musically, but also in the most detailed dramatic presentation, made him surely a conductor's dream. A dream, alas, that I was never to profit from as he had already retired by the time I was important enough to ask for his services. I did, however, have the unique idea of asking him to do the Sprecher's role in Arnold Schoenberg's *Die Gurrelieder,* which he performed with me on several occasions both in America and Europe. This adventure has already been described in his autobiography, and therefore I won't go into more details.

Another facet of this incomparable artist is the contribution he made to develop singers of the next generation like James Morris, Dame Gwyneth Jones, Thomas Quasthoff, Hermann Prey, and Robert Holl, who have made important careers.

We are all fortunate that thanks to the numerous recordings that he has taken part in, so many generations will benefit enormously from his artistry both in the world of opera and, of course, his beloved lieder.

Foreword to the German Edition

BY DIETRICH FISCHER-DIESKAU

Mounting the vanguard before a book of memories written by a role model is a source of great joy. When I first heard Hans Hotter's voice singing Brahms's lieder on the radio back in the thirties, long before I came into personal contact with him, I was instantly fascinated by his round, sonorous tone, and no less by his sensitive, supremely artistic approach to the delineation of this music. This impression took on greater depth when I became acquainted with his first recordings of selections from the *Ring* (along with Martha Fuchs and Margarete Klose).

It became quite clear to me from a number of experiences, first and foremost in Bayreuth when I witnessed his incredible dramatic intensity, that he ranked among those few personalities on the operatic stage who assume a special position, one that has a rejuvenating and inspiring effect on the performing style of an entire era. The mere fact that he was already commemorating his two hundredth stage performance at the German Theater in Prague back in 1932, yet not taking his leave of the boards until just a few years ago, gives us some idea of the remarkable time span during which this artist—probably the most important Wagner interpreter of his generation—practiced his craft.

What he has to say about his collaboration with conductors like Clemens Krauss (especially in world premieres of Strauss operas) or Wilhelm Furtwängler, Hans Knappertsbusch, Arthur Rother, and so many others combines with his fortunately sizable catalogue of phonograph recordings to attest to the vast expanse of his artistic work. Time and again, Hans Hotter's convincing interpretations of so many diverse roles were essential to defining and evaluating the work of several stage directors who have since become famous. I hope that Hotter's elucidation of his work here will have a meaningful impact on further developments, especially as he himself was also active as a director. Anyone who ever witnessed his Wotan—and from then on was unable to identify anyone other than Hotter with this role—has an opportunity here to benefit from his recollections of a goodly number of other characterizations he created in his virtually endless ability to move from one personality to another.

One would need a separate homage to do justice to all that the art of recital singing owes to this musician par excellence. Let it simply be stated here that without Hans Hotter we would surely never have had the musically "streamlined," purified recital performance style we take for granted today (notwithstanding the incursions of old habits we unfortunately have to endure from time to time). This man with his incredible resonance sources was capable of moving effortlessly from the gentlest pianissimo to the most overpowering fullness of tone, which enabled him to express everything the classical and romantic eras gave him to utter, ranging all the way to the remotest, most unfamiliar treasures.

Hotter also reports on things he has learned from his teaching of young people, an activity that occupied a not insignificant part of his life, and from which so many of today's major names have greatly profited. To this day, the question of "succession" has not fallen silent. No, there will never be a successor to a personality or a voice like this one. Let us be grateful that we now possess his own account of his life and work.

Preface and Acknowledgments to the Translated Edition

BY DONALD ARTHUR

On February 20, 2001, a blue-ribbon audience studded with senior music critics and operatic cognoscenti gathered at Munich's hallowed Prinzregententheater to witness what might arguably have been called the most remarkable opening night of the current season, or any other season for that matter. Granted, neither the work performed, a student performance of an operetta, nor the smooth but unspectacular production nor the majority of its performers rated much notice at all—let alone from such a distinguished audience in a city that had experienced the world premieres of such seminal works as Mozart's *Idomeneo,* Wagner's *Tristan, Meistersinger,* and the first two *Ring* operas, Richard Strauss's *Friedenstag* and *Capriccio,* and Mahler's grandiose Eighth Symphony, not to mention a veritable phonebook-sized list of presentations of other major musical and theatrical works. The special attention was riveted exclusively on a single member of the cast in a small cameo part, who made his first entrance toward the end of the piece. Ironically, this same "bit player" had figured significantly in two of the more prestigious aforementioned world premieres and literally hundreds more definitive performances, both here and throughout the world.

Der Opernball is a bit of lightweight froth with a standard drawing-room comedy plot revolving around the usual extramarital intrigues in an upscale setting, in this case a grand ball at the Paris *Opéra*. It had been selected to commemorate the centenary of its prestigious venue, first dedicated in August 1901, with its royal namesake, Prince Regent Luitpold, in attendance. For this reason, the setting had been moved from Paris to Munich, and an extra character had been written into the script in the person of the prince regent himself, who welcomed guests to the theater and then reappeared at the end of the evening to reprise the big hit tune. For this occasion the August Everding Theatre Academy housed in the Prinzregententheater had decided to ask one of Munich's top homegrown operatic icons to play the part, and ninety-one-year-old Hans Hotter, more than a decade older than

the historical character he was portraying, agreed to perform on this opening night and in four successive performances—his final public appearances
in a theatrical setting. (He would ultimately step into the spotlight one last
time, two and a half years later, in the final year of his life, when he accepted
the Wilhelm Pitz Medal from the German Society of Stage Choruses at the
Bayreuth Festival chorus hall on August 10, 2003.)

Many in the audience on those evenings couldn't help wondering why
such an illustrious artist had agreed to grace the boards in a student production. He certainly didn't need the money, and the fee was insignificant
in any case. His many recordings were still best sellers and continued to
guarantee his prominence, and he was a far cry from a limelight addict, willing to hobble onto any stage for yet another shot of applause; he contemp-
tuously called that *Leichenfledderei* (corpse abuse). He just knew that if
someone of his stature were to add his name to the proceedings, it would
act as a drawing card to give some deserved exposure to the anything but
untalented youngsters in the cast, who were now far more likely to be seen
and heard by influential spectators than would have been the case had the
young singers been the only attraction. This was pure Hans Hotter: a typical act of basic human decency from a man who, while he knew he had paid
his dues, also humbly regarded his Olympian career as largely the product
of encouragement from persons in high places and the grace of destiny.
These were strokes of fortune that were only meaningful to him if he passed
them along. And so he emerged from a well-earned retirement for one last
romp with the kids.

While he otherwise may have withdrawn from active involvement in the
theater to his pleasant villa in the south of Munich, Hans Hotter was anything but idle. Good friends and members of his close family came and went,
old colleagues would drop by to swap memories and hear the anecdotes he
told so masterfully, and he would grant press and media journalists interviews on a vast number of musical and theatrical topics. Once in a while, he
would venture out to attend a concert or provide encouragement to a pupil,
which was the story when he attended a dress rehearsal of *Die Walküre* at the
Bavarian State Opera, where Mihoko Fujimura, a mezzo-soprano he had
first taught on one of his visits to Tokyo, was taking over the part of Fricka.
A few months after his Prinzregententheater appearance, in the autumn of
the same year, he got very busy and active working on this book, on which
I had the great honor and distinct pleasure of collaborating.

The whole project came about through a series of such unlikely coincidences that both of us found ourselves quoting the old theatrical hypothesis that if this story had been told in a stage play or film script, any producer
would have rejected it flat out as too far-fetched for any audience to believe.
It wouldn't even have passed muster as a plausible opera plot.

Pref.1.   The Wilhelm Pitz Prize is a highly coveted award presented only to the most distinguished artists of the Bayreuth Festival by members of the festival chorus in memory of their first chorus master, the legendary Wilhelm Pitz. When Hans Hotter received the award on August 10, 2003, with the full chorus applauding him, it marked this great artist's final public appearance.
Photographer, Karl Heinz Lammel; photo courtesy of the *Nordbayerischer Kurier.*

It all began in August 2001 with two different lunches on two different continents a few thousand miles apart, neither of which involved Hans Hotter directly. Lunch number one took place in Boston, Massachusetts, where I had come for the sole purpose of making the personal acquaintance of several individuals who had made possible the original English-language edition of Astrid Varnay's memoirs *55 Years in Five Acts — My Life in Opera.* Throughout our work on that book, Astrid and I had communicated from Munich exclusively by letter, fax, e-mail, and on odd occasions by transatlantic telephone. Neither of us had ever actually seen William Frohlich, the director of the press, or his ultraprofessional staffers Ann Twombly and Sarah Rowley face-to-face, and so I decided to take advantage of a get-together with my Boston family to have lunch with people who, sight unseen, had actually become friends. In the course of a casual discussion on potential projects, I mentioned a book I had read in German by my former singing teacher, who had long since become a household name in the English-speaking world. I suggested I might perhaps translate a couple of sample chapters and submit them to the scrutiny of my dining companions. Without making any commitments, Bill Frohlich kindly agreed to appraise the results, and so we left it at that, and I went on to the next leg of my U.S. journey, to my hometown of New York.

The following day, I was on my way up the stairs of an apartment building in Greenwich Village to visit Valerie Glazer, an old friend of Astrid Varnay's dating back to Astrid's pre-debut standing room days at the Metropolitan Opera, when Valerie appeared on the landing to tell me to hurry up; Astrid was on the phone from Europe "and this call is costing her a fortune." When I arrived at Valerie's phone, Astrid said that she had just received a call from Hans Hotter, whom I occasionally helped with his English correspondence, although he spoke the language with remarkable fluency. Hans, she said, had been trying to reach me about something—he hadn't specified what. Astrid's female intuition had told her I would probably be getting in touch with Valerie at some point in my New York trip, but nobody could have guessed I would have started up her long staircase at the very moment she called.

I promptly telephoned Hans, who reported on the other luncheon meeting, a chance encounter in a café in Salzburg during the festival season, where, because most of the other tables were already occupied, a German friend of Hans's resident in Oakland California—Rüdiger Naumann-Étienne and his wife Annette Campbell-White—had been asked to share a table with a gentleman from New York, who later revealed himself to be Ara Guzelimian, the artistic adviser to Carnegie Hall. In the course of conversation, Mr. and Mrs. Naumann mentioned their friend Hans Hotter, and Mr. Guzelimian casually inquired if there might be some kind of authorized biography of that great artist for English-language readers. The question precipitated a phone call to Hans in Munich, in which Rüdiger generously offered to subsidize the effort should it prove necessary, whereupon Hans called Astrid, Astrid called me at Valerie's, I called Hans back, and he asked if I would like to translate his memoirs for English-language publication, and might the Varnay publishers be interested in his book, whereupon I replied: "As a matter of fact, I was just . . ."

I told you this story was fairly implausible.

It should be added here that Rüdiger and Annette have subsidized the project with far more than just money. They have helped, counseled, and encouraged all parties involved throughout the creative and editorial process, helping us smooth over some of the rough spots in the course of collaboration.

In fact, many of those snags proved to be blessings in disguise. The most important holdup on the project came about when I submitted the sample chapters. The people in Boston, Bill Frohlich and his advisers, said the book was interesting "as far as it went," but that, considering in how many ways Hans Hotter had virtually redefined and ennobled the interpretation of much of the music he performed, there needed to be more depth in the description of his creative and re-creative process.

Beyond this, the publishers, while acknowledging Hans's total abomination of the Hitler regime (of which he made no secret in the German book), questioned the lack of detail on what it was like to be such a prominent artist during the terrible years between 1933 and 1945. They asked why a man with his prestige, who could have easily established a career anywhere in the world, chose to remain in Nazi Germany. They felt it was essential to incorporate more of this historical background in what would ultimately be a major prime source reference work.

While I agreed with that judgment, I was frankly a little reluctant to approach Hans with these questions. I was aware that his advanced age and frail health might have prompted him toward a "take it or leave it" attitude—in which he would have been totally justified. In the depths of my cowardice, I finally decided to broach the subject in a fax message dispatched across town to the other side of Munich. Less than an hour after the fax arrived in Hans's study, he was on the phone to tell me the German book had left out many of his observations at the behest of his editor at the time, who felt this might limit the book's popular appeal. The editor had also asked him to soft-pedal the references to the Third Reich, urging him to concentrate on his professional life and leave the political frame of reference for the historians. When his German-language memoirs came out, though, they were roundly criticized on both these counts by some readers, and he felt the reactions in Boston in fact confirmed their appraisal. In short, Hans said, "Let's go to work!" And so we did, rewriting the entire book.

For well over a year, Hans and I met on regular occasions, reviewing my translations of his German text and recording hours of conversations to fill the lacunae as we discovered them, amplifying the original copy by two full chapters and sizable references to a number of topics at several strategic intervals throughout the book, including considerable detail on several operatic characterizations and a healthy contribution on what does and does not count in musical education. And included at last is a full description of how he had been offered an opportunity to get out of Germany in 1937, and why he felt honor-bound to decline.

Hans also let me sit in on a number of conversations with friends like Franz Klarwein (the cousin and namesake of the famous tenor) and with colleagues and descendants of colleagues, chatting about their memories of his years on the stage. He also allowed me to be present at tapings with interviewers like Marek Kalina of Radio Free Berlin; the Pulitzer Prize–winning journalist Manuela Hoelterhoff from New York; and his onetime biographer, the distinguished London-based music and travel writer, Penelope Turing. In these talks I was generously allowed to make notes of what he told those far more experienced questioners for inclusion in this volume. His own highly knowledgeable daughter, Gabriele Strauss, often joined us and added salient points to our conversations—as did her husband, Richard, probably the world's top expert on the life and works of his illustrious, eponymous composer grandfather, whose influence on Hans Hotter's work had been definitive.

Most of these conversations were accompanied by the spectacular meals prepared for the occasion by Hans's housekeeper, Libuše Kousal, a former Czech actress, who also shared theatrical memories with us from her native Prague, a city that had played a formative part in Mr. Hotter's early career.

As work went on, the greater part of my time was still perforce occupied with meeting deadlines for my freelance translation work and commuting to a number of studios all over Central Europe, where I did voice work. Meanwhile Hans's health was beginning to decline badly, and some of our work on the book had to take place in conversations between my apartment and his hospital rooms. To pile Ossa on Pelion, hardly was he out of those woods when surgery to correct a spinal injury had me *hors de combat* for more than two months. Nevertheless, determined to win our merit badges for tenacity, we plugged on, completing our work during the summer of 2003.

This task could not have been accomplished without a great deal of help from many friends and counselors, and one of Hans's last instructions to me involved expressing personal appreciation to this honor roll. To cite a single example, he had remembered having learned the role of Amfortas in *Parsifal* from an American conductor on the staff of the Breslau theater, but couldn't pinpoint the name. The distinguished American tenor Loren Driscoll, a former star of the Deutsche Oper Berlin, who now heads the Union of German Theatrical Performers in that city, checked the archives of the organization, found the roster of the Breslau theater back in the thirties and came up with the name of Weldon Gales. Then an Internet reference to an article in the *Detroit Free Press* revealed Gales to have been the first conductor of the Detroit Symphony. An e-mail to Jeanne Salathiel at the music division of the Detroit Public Library produced the details of his life along with photographs of the long-forgotten maestro. Other helpful archivists were Peter and Friederike Emmerich from the Bayreuth Festival Press Office, Francesca Franchi and Bobby Woodward from London's Royal Opera House Covent Garden Archives, John Pennino and Robert Tuggle at the

Metropolitan Opera Archives in New York, Richard Wandel of the New York Philharmonic Symphony Society Archives in New York, Dr. Thomas Siedhoff from the press office of Bavaria's August Everding Theatre Academy and the staff of the Franklin D. Roosevelt Library in Hyde Park, New York, who confirmed our presumption that a letter from President Roosevelt to Hitler, vastly misquoted by the latter's propaganda goon, Joseph Goebbels, had never been written with that content in the first place.

Many useful facts and observations were also provided by the dean of New York music pundits Martin Bernheimer, who had once taken voice lessons from Hans Hotter; the late Rabbi Morrison D. Bial, who had been an aspiring singer before entering the clergy and continued to be a life-long operagoer and expert on the subject; Stewart and Sarah Brown, founders and heads of Testament Records in England who have released and rereleased a number of operatic and recital CDs featuring Hans Hotter; the great Marilyn Horne, and the executive director of the Marilyn Horne Foundation, Barbara Hocher and her staff; Professor Michael Kater of Toronto, one of the world's top experts on the history of the performing and creative arts in Central Europe during the Nazi years; Maestro James Levine, who had been present as a teenager at my first meeting with Hans Hotter at the 1960 Aspen Festival, where he also accompanied many of Hans's lieder classes, and his brother and family historian Tom Levine, who clarified a couple of details Hans and I had both forgotten; the late Robert Lochner, a distinguished American chronicler who lived history in the Germany of the pre- and postwar years, his knowledgeable widow, Ann Lochner, and their equally savvy polyglot daughter Anita Lochner; Laurence and Kiyomi Lueck of the Wagner Society of Hawaii; Dr. Robert and Estelle Roth, old friends and musical experts; the preeminent coloratura soprano, Rita Shane, who shared memories of her own performances with Hans Hotter. Daniel F. Tritter was more than generous with operatic, historical, and legal expertise. Other friends and colleagues have contributed in ways too many to recount.

Special thanks are due, regrettably posthumously, to the late Helga Hotter, Hans's wise and charming wife of many decades, who assembled every critical review of his work and huge collections of photographs from all phases of his life, and who also left us the effervescent memory of some fairly pungent career-related one-liners. Hans once described her as someone "who could be candidly critical of anyone and anything, yet never hurt anyone's feeling with her directness"; this book would have been better had we been able to draw from her insights, perceptions, and total recall. More than once we hypothesized on how Helga might have phrased something.

Astrid Varnay, my first ghostwriting victim and my literary conscience ever since, has read and commented on every word of this manuscript and has been invaluable in every phase of its creation. Our special thanks to her and her mantra: "Look it up, Donald," which has become the maxim of all my work.

As work continued on the book, the original publisher, Northeastern University Press, joined the prestigious University Press of New England family, providing this book with an added list of friends. My thanks to Dr. Phyllis Deutsch, Richard Pult, Ann Brash, Betty Waterhouse, and the rest of the team in Hanover for their meaningful input.

Shortly after he received the Pitz Prize, and long after we both believed the book to have been "put to bed," Hans asked me to invite my friend Alan Titus, that year's Bayreuth Wotan, who had attended the ceremony in Bayreuth, to join him and his daughter for an informal coffee hour in his living room. The conversation at that get-together got Hans thinking about the long monologue Wotan sings in the second act of *Die Walküre* and why, if improperly interpreted, it can seem so grindingly tedious when it is in fact key to all of Wagner's creativity. A subsequent hospital stay, his last, gave Hans time to think about that conversation, and in between sessions with various attempts to resolve his worsening diabetic condition, he began making mental notes on one last insertion into the chapter that treats that topic. When his physicians finally realized there was little more they could do for Hans other than make him as comfortable as possible in his final weeks, he used the time he had left to discuss the thoughts he had formulated while still on his sickbed. At this juncture, his walking disability had become so severe that he was no longer able to descend the short flight of stairs to his living room, and so we met in what had been converted to a bed-sitter. Physically he was very weak and clearly suffering horribly from the pain involved in the simple task of walking from his easy chair across the room to the lunch table. But there was nothing frail about his thought processes as he expostulated his profound vision of that essential musical passage and what it meant to the chronology of the dramatic arts. I then wrote everything up and inserted it into the text. As he had done with every other word in the English edition of his memoirs, Hans checked through the manuscript, made valuable suggestions, corrected misapprehensions on my part, and finally read and approved the revision.

A week or so later, Hans telephoned to ask if there was any further work that needed doing on the book before turning it over to the publishers. In actual fact, there was one open issue, but one that our combined efforts had thus far failed to resolve: the title of the book. In German, Hans had called it *"Der Mai war mir gewogen"* as he explains in his own preface. This title is laden with meaning for the reader conversant with the German language and its literature, especially the song literature. Taken from the first poem by Wilhelm Müller, which Franz Schubert set to music in his monumental song cycle *Die Winterreise* (the winter journey), it shows the poet in deep winter reflecting back on how favorable everything seemed to him back in the month of May. Now, in the late winter of his own very long life, Hans reflected on the fact that, for all the hard work he had invested in his artistic career and the deprivation to which he had been subjected by the harsh winds of history, good fortune had basically always been in his corner, happy coincidences came along invariably at points in time when he could make the best use of them, and fortune smiled through most of his life, for which he wanted to express his gratitude. The German quote did it perfectly for the German reader, but he didn't want a literal translation of the German quote as the title of his book in English. First of all, "May" is a girl's name in English, and the obvious prurient overtone of a possible double meaning was not at all to his taste, beyond which this wasn't a phrase people would recognize instantly and be able to relate to his career as he told the tale.

Surely, he asked, for anybody raised in the English language, there must be some literary quote that will say the same thing. Sure, we all replied, but every time anyone came up with something it was invariably nixed as not being in keeping with what Hans really wanted to say, and in the bargain, totally unrelated to his own artistic productivity. "Destiny's Child" was the name of a rock band; "With a Little Bit of Luck" came from a Broadway musical that had nothing to do with Hotter, although he like the song; and so it went. All the quotes, Shakespeare, biblical, and poets, major and minor, never quite shed light on this combination of hard work, endurance, and gracious fortune that enabled Hans Hotter to become the paradigmatic figure he had been for so many years. And so I decided to leave the issue unresolved in view of Hans's severely weakened condition, telling him simply that I believed we had done our job creditably and could turn product over to the readers in good faith. To which he replied, in a relaxed and not unhappy tone, "Then I can rest."

"Sure, buddy," I replied with affectionate impertinence, "on your laurels"; and we agreed to stay in touch. As matters developed, months of reflection, brainstorming, and soul-searching by myself, Hans's friends and the good friends of this book in New England still failed to turned up anything we could all feel Hans might be able to relate to, and when we did make suggestions, the reasons they were turned down by the others made sense to everyone. And so it was decided simply to call this book generically *Memoirs* and let Hans's story speak for itself without any far-fetched literary allusions, which might confuse more than they would enlighten. In that phone call with Hans, I left the issue unresolved, knowing somehow that the second shoe might never drop, nor ever have to.

A day or so after my last conversation with Hans, Richard Strauss called to prepare me for the inevitable—as a matter of fact, he told me, much as wanted to hallmark one thought, one that will recur frequently on subsequent pages: that my entire life—especially my professional life—has been blessed by the benign glow of an especially favorable star. Things happened, people entered my life, all of which, without any manipulation on my part, had a profoundly beneficial effect on my destiny. That is why I feel that "May was kind to me."

Hans Hotter

Chapter 1

"But I have no desire whatsoever to go to Hamburg. I don't want to go back to Germany at all what with all the things happening over there. Vienna and its opera might tempt me . . ."

"Where do you get the idea he won't show up in Vienna, too, this Mr. Hitler? You mark my words; he'll show up here in Prague, as well, soon enough. No, no, you have to make your career in your fatherland. That's where you belong now. They've got so many good operatic ensembles where a young singer can develop slowly and gradually and make a name for himself. Take it from an old, experienced theater cat, who wishes you well. But if the Hamburg Opera wants you: don't sign for a penny less than eight hundred marks, because you can get that here from me, too."

This conversation took place in the director's office at the German Theater in Prague in March 1934. Seated opposite me was my highly esteemed director, Dr. Paul Eger, who had convinced me to come to the Czech capital exactly two years before. Back then there had been another important conversation between the two of us: it took place in Berlin. The State Opera there had invited the twenty-three-year-old, long and lanky baritone, who, in the second year of his career as a member of the Breslau Opera,[1] was just taking his first baby steps on the stage, auditioning with the intention of being engaged by that prestigious house.

The clever Dr. Eger somehow got wind of that intention and managed to intercept me on the way to the Opera House Unter den Linden; he then used the full persuasive power of his Central European charm to lure me into his home. Although I knew nothing more about him other than the fact that he then headed the Deutscher Bühnenverein—an association of theater directors in the German-speaking countries—I can distinctly remember the impression that clever, quick-witted theater pro made on me. Of course, at the time I was sadly lacking in experience and familiarity with the ways of the world. So I was basically just following my instincts.

---

1. Breslau, the capital of Silesia, is today the Polish city of Wrocław.

Today, more than a half century later, I am convinced that the course of an artistic development is not solely dependent on talent and suitability. The decisive factor is meeting the right people at the right time, individuals capable of guiding you in the right direction. Inasmuch as, when we're young and impulsive, we are—God knows—not always capable of recognizing certain things, we need the fortunate circumstance of an encounter with someone with a "good nose" for those factors at the right moment to come to our aid. In the course of this narrative, I will have many a tale to tell of such propitious encounters.

In any case, Paul Eger turned out to be one of those key personalities in the guidance of my professional career. With wise, forceful words he made it clear to me that an engagement at the Berlin Opera at that point in time could be inopportune—if not downright damaging to my further development: "At that outstanding opera theater, you would either be prematurely given assignments you can't do justice to yet, or you might not get enough to do, and then you'd find yourself perilously cast adrift in a big city. Now, sing whatever you were planning to audition at the State Opera for me."

Destiny took its course. My voice seemed to please him, and a two-year contract was signed. Eger picked up the phone and had somebody connect him with the director's office of the State Opera: "Unfortunately, my dear colleague, I have to inform you that Hans Hotter, who was just about to audition for you, won't be coming because he has just signed a contract with me for the German Theater in Prague."

After hanging up the receiver, he casually remarked, "Now I can tell you: I knew you had every chance of being engaged there. But you're still so young, dear friend. I sincerely believe and hope you'll soon be singing at the State Opera anyway." "Soon" turned out to be four years later at a guest performance as Jago in *Otello* under the direction of Victor de Sabata.

"Do you have any debts?" was the next, rather perplexing question from my new director: "Come on now, a young singer like you must owe somebody some money . . . how much is it, then?"

"Well . . ." I stammered uneasily, "actually, I do . . . yes, of course, I owe my singing teacher some money . . ."

"How much?"

"Just a minute, around five hundred marks."

"You can have that from me right now."

So saying, he walked over to the desk, took out the money and put it in my hand—a small fortune for me. "Give me a receipt for this; you can pay me back in Prague during the second year of your contract."

When I reminded him of the loan at the beginning of the 1933–34 season, he said testily, "You must be mistaken. I don't remember any advance," and tore up the receipt from Berlin right before my eyes.

It was many years later that I finally realized how right I had been to turn down Berlin in favor of Prague back in 1932. Amazingly enough, the thought of having been railroaded by Eger never entered my mind—that's how convincing his arguments must have been at the time. "Look here, my dear friend" (to this day, his words still ring in my ears) "the vocal material you just presented to me, together with your whole appearance make it quite clear that you'll soon be on your way to the dramatic repertoire, including the Wagner roles. At your age—how old are you now?"

"I just turned twenty-three."

"Great God, you've still got so much time. At your age," he continued, "a development like this is unusual, if not downright perilous. A singer shouldn't start doing the so-called heroic baritone roles as a rule until he's in his midthirties. Take advantage of this stroke of fortune and come to Prague for two years of training. I'm convinced you won't remain under my wing for very long. I can't pay you the salary Berlin was offering you, but I can offer you something you may some day thank me for on your knees. In my house, you'll be primarily singing smaller parts, and once in a while you can try your hand at something a little more ambitious. As fate would have it, a couple of guest artists in your future voice category will be coming to me in Prague: Rudolf Bockelmann, Jaro Prohaska, Alfred Jerger from Vienna, Theo Scheidl, perhaps even Friedrich Schorr from Berlin—all experienced, first-class dramatic singers. Sit in the artist's box as often as you can and watch their performances, and come to their rehearsals, too, so you can watch these artists at work and learn from them. There's nothing better for a young singer in his development phase."

Those were golden words, and I really took them to heart in those two years. And everything happened exactly the way my fatherly friend had planned it for me.

In the autumn of 1932 I began my engagement in Prague, and a short time later I became a member of the group there. Besides the opera company, there were separate ensembles for drama and operetta, but without any boundaries. We were all members of one big family.

As usually happens, however, in big families, there were little quarrels or even a few dirty tricks among the artists. They may not have been very tragic and generally fit more into the category of schoolboy pranks than serious artistic activity. Let me tell one particularly funny story, because it has gone into the annals of the Prague Opera in those days. It is the "dog's head story." The leading character is a young Pekingese. One of our singer colleagues had given him to his girlfriend. As he was famous for telling long-winded stories in excruciating detail, we all had to listen to the incredible tale of the purebred Pekingese and what a most unusual animal he was. The unique quality of this dog was that he might grow bigger and bigger as time

went by—but his head would always remain the same size. This prize example had been especially imported to Prague directly from China.

We were in the middle of a *Meistersinger* performance, when we sprang
one of the aforementioned "pranks." It should be mentioned here that this
dog fancier was also a notorious hypochondriac, and someone who, after
he had sung, would invariably ask his colleagues, "Was I good?" As we expected that question at the end of the act, we quickly agreed on the answer
we would give him. And soon the first of us was asked, "Well, tell me, how
was I?"

"Quite good, actually. Tell me, you're just getting over a cold, aren't
you?"

"Me? Why do you ask?"

"Oh, it's nothing. The people out front won't notice a thing, but of
course we can hear it."

"But that can't be. I'm in terrific voice . . ."

"But I tell you, it's nothing. I'll guarantee you the people in the house
will never catch on."

And off he went to ask the next one, "You just heard me in the first act.
Did you notice anything about my voice?"

"What do you mean? Everything was just fine. Oh, well—of course I did
notice that you must have had a little cold, but that's over. Now and then it
still sounds a little scratchy."

Nervous and upset, he turned to yet another one, "Listen, please tell me
honestly, did you notice anything about my voice in the first act?"

"Your voice? Sounded just fine—a couple of high notes did sound a little
like you're getting over a little cold, but you'll see. Nobody will notice a
thing in act two."

Our perturbed puppy owner disappeared in the direction of the dressing
room, and shortly afterward we could hear him vocalizing in there. Somebody stuck his head in the door. "Don't drive yourself crazy. Just rest your
voice. My teacher always says: 'don't keep fooling around with it—it'll go
away all by itself.'"

Another colleague joined them, "What are you so nervous about?
Everything's just fine."

"But now I really am nervous. I thought I was in especially good form
today."

"You are. Now, just calm down and get ready for the second act. Tell me,
how long have you two had that Pekingese?"

"The two of us? A little more than a year, why?"

"I saw your girlfriend with the dog yesterday in a coffeehouse. Actually
I didn't want to say anything, I thought I might have been mistaken."

"Mistaken? About what?"

"About the dog. But our colleague, Franzl, the bass, he noticed it."

"Noticed what?"

"First you don't notice a thing, but both of us, Franzl and I, thought, for a two-year-old dog, he's actually pretty big."

"Big? In what way?"

"Like I said, first I thought I was wrong, but Franzl said it. too, the dog's head—you said his head stays small, didn't you?"

"Of course his head stays as small as it is. I already told you all about that . . ."

"Yes, but that's just it. Both of us think the dog's head has gotten bigger lately, more massive . . ."

"Not a chance."

"Well, of course, we could both be totally mistaken."

"Franzl doesn't know a damn thing about dogs. Besides, I've got it from the breeder in China—in writing!"

"In what language?"

"Why do you ask? In English, I think. What difference does that make?"

"None at all, of course. But please don't get so upset. This whole business isn't worth it."

"Of course this has me upset. And it is worth something to me, considering how much I paid for that lousy mutt . . ."

"What are you yelling and screaming about?" said a third colleague, joining the fray. "Save your voice, you've got two more acts to go."

"Listen to me. You know that Pekingese I gave my girlfriend?"

"Of course I know him. Who doesn't? You've told us so much about him."

"Now then, tell me quite honestly: did you notice anything about the dog?"

"Me? How come? Well, I hadn't seen him for a couple of weeks. Then yesterday I was in the coffeehouse with my wife, and we met your girlfriend with her dog, and my wife said: 'Fiffi's developing . . .' That's its name, isn't it? Fiffi?"

"Yes, yes," came the reluctant response from the other side. "What did your wife say?"

"He's developing nicely! Ever so sweet! A regular tough guy. He's got a really powerful big head."

The dog owner sank into his chair in visible exasperation. His beloved colleagues had now acquired something resembling compassion for him and wordlessly left the dressing room. During the next two acts he hardly uttered a word, as he struggled, visibly strained, through the rest of his role, having plenty of vocal trouble toward the end. Normally a singer who enjoyed taking one bow after another, he hardly appeared before the curtain at the end, then went straight off to his dressing room and left the theater without giving a single autograph at the stage door. As quickly as he could, he made his way to the nearby theater café, stormed over to his girlfriend waiting for him there, grabbed the dog out of her hands and gaped at the animal's head.

"What's wrong with you?"

"But they all said his head was getting bigger!"

"Stuff and nonsense! They were just pulling your leg. That's what you get for bragging all the time."

The singer stared straight ahead with a look of desperation in his eyes—livid with himself and the malign world of his colleagues.

On another occasion, I was involved in what we all considered a harmless little gag, yet one that would have both positive and negative repercussions on my life depending on who happened to be running various countries at the time. I had developed a small reputation in my circle of friends for my ability to imitate various people's voices, ranging from some of our friends, colleagues, and bosses at the theater to one or two political figures, including Adolf Hitler, who had taken over my native Germany at the end of January 1933. When the news of my Hitler imitation got around, one of my colleagues from the drama section asked me to take part in a vaudeville skit for a review being planned as a special New Year's Eve event at the theater. The sketch he had written showed an interview between a local radio reporter, played by the author of the sketch, and a Teutonic knight in shining armor, portrayed by yours truly, whose responses to the reporter's questions were larded with quotes and misquotes from some of the speeches Hitler had recently given. The audience, few of whom took the menace of Hitler all that seriously at the time, howled with laughter and we were happy to have joined in the fun.

Unfortunately, this was not the end of the story. A few days later, I was summoned to the German Embassy in Prague, where a diplomatic official gave me a severe dressing-down for making fun of the Führer, even threatening to confiscate my passport and telling me in no uncertain terms that the possibility of continuing my career in Germany would be highly unlikely after this disrespectful performance on my part. Fortunately, some friends from Munich, Professor and Mrs. Nonnenbruch, were living in Prague at the time, and they put in a good word for me at the embassy, whereupon the authorities there agreed to table the matter. I discovered several years later that they hadn't quite kept that promise, a decision that ultimately proved to be a positive development as world history took its course in my own little corner of the world.

The opera house gang all got together outside the theater either in that coffeehouse, the Wilson, or in the Blue Grotto, right across the street from the stage door—in the latter place generally toward the end of the month, because you could get a cup of coffee on credit there, and we often found ourselves a little short just before payday. In Prague, the Austrian custom of going to the coffeehouse had also become a part of everyday Czech life. This gave us singers a chance to make contact outside the usual operatic circles with some of the acting luminaries of the time, such as Alexander Moissi, the young Paula Wessely, Ernst Deutsch, Curt Goetz, and many others. I remember with great pleasure some performances Leo Slezak gave in an operetta role (I've forgotten which one). During that period I also heard Michael Bohnen and was able to witness Richard Tauber performing his starring role in *Dreimädlerhaus*.[2] What impressed me the most about Tauber was his incredible vocal technique. I can still remember a recording of Richard Strauss's *Freundliche Vision* on which he demonstrates a masterly example of breath control. I saw Tauber—it must have been in 1933—several times in the artists' box at some fairly average opera performances. One evening we got into a conversation, and I asked him in passing what interested him about these performances. He replied, "I like to listen to my singer colleagues over and over again—so I have a clear idea what *not* to do."

In 1947 I met Tauber again in London, where he had gone into exile during the Nazi era. It was a happy encounter with a tragic finale, as I will relate later in this book.

Back to Prague: besides the powerful presence of Paul Eger, there was another personality in the house to whom I owe a great deal. I'm talking about the musical director of the opera, Georg (later George) Szell. The input I received from him in the course of our collaboration was priceless, and throughout my musical-artistic development it became the mainstay of a new understanding of music for me. Only a very few people later exerted such a strong influence on my artistic maturation process. Hungarian-born, of Czech extraction, he was a total musician, who had learned his craft from the ground up. Like many of the great conductors he radiated great calm from the podium, a prerequisite to authority. It is known that Toscanini, who in 1941 invited him to conduct his NBC Symphony in New York, had a very high opinion of Szell. The story goes that he said he knew no musician who had better ears than Szell.

Szell once demonstrated this gift to me in an astonishing way in Prague. Right at the beginning of my Prague engagement there was a new *Meistersinger* production. Back then I sang Master Nachtigall, before later portraying Fritz Kothner, Hans Sachs, and then Veit Pogner. When you have a rel-

---

2. The operetta about the life of Franz Schubert, scored to his melodies. It is generally known in English as *Lilac Time*.

(a)

(b)

(c)

1.1a, b, c. Photomontage: (a) Monterone in *Rigoletto* (1932); (b) Masetto in *Don Giovanni* (1933); (c) the Herald in *Lohengrin* (1934). All of my roles in Prague, large and small, were challenges and learning experiences, often with major colleagues in the leading parts.

atively small assignment in a long opera like *Meistersinger* and have lots of free time, you occasionally come up with some pretty silly ideas. So it happened that at the dress rehearsal I suddenly hatched a plan, directly at the end of the opera, while the chorus, the orchestra, and all the soloists are volubly intoning a C major chord, to slip in a moderately loud B-flat, in other words a whole tone below the C. The rehearsal was over, and the whole cast waited on stage to get their notes from the stage director. I found myself in a state of somewhat weary, bored passivity and was listening only half-heartedly to what the stage director was saying, when I suddenly heard a voice behind me say, "If you think I didn't hear that rubbish with the B-flat you're sadly mistaken."

I turned around in horror and found myself staring directly into the face of Georg Szell, who looked right past me without expression. My speechlessness was not so much prompted by the fact that he had heard it, but that he had even heard who it was!

Szell cut an elegant figure. He was highly educated and also had a delicious sense of humor. Beyond that, I was impressed by his extraordinary skill at the keyboard—a rare trait among the great conductors. The thing I most admired about him was the way he handled younger singers: with endless patience, never unpleasant or disagreeably loud. He helped us in the development of our personalities by urging us, especially when it came to forming our artistic taste, to develop an opinion of our own and especially to find the courage to make it known. If he liked someone, his confidence in that person was boundless. When one day the man singing Pizarro in *Fidelio* was taken ill on the morning of the performance, he talked me into taking over, although I had never sung the role and had a somewhat shaky command of the music. Musically and vocally, he helped me over all the pitfalls. The thing that really had me worried was not so much the vocal challenges but the dialogue, the spoken words. Singers with dialogue in an opera are always on somewhat shaky ground. And on top of that, Pizarro's dialogue is often rather stilted. For example, he has the following line: "Besteigen Sie sofort mit einem Trompeter den Turm." (Climb the tower at once with a trumpeter.)

Immediately before the beginning of the opera, I had a quick walk-through rehearsal with the assistant director. I was just about to say that line when a gentleman from the chorus walked by and said, "Be careful you don't say: *Climb up the tower at once with a suitcase.*" The effect was horrible. Anybody who has ever had anything to do with the theater knows how dangerous these mischievously fabricated "fluffs" can be. With the help of God and Szell, the performance came to a happy conclusion, but in the more than three hundred *Fidelios* that followed that first one in Prague over the course of the following years, the curse of that ominous line is always upon

1.2.   Maestro George Szell was a great musician but a stern
taskmaster in Prague. Many years later, we made music
together again in Cleveland.

me in that terrible second before I have to say it. Szell, however, guided me
through both this performance as well as the long series to follow.

Unfortunately we lost contact for a while in the wake of political developments. Not for another twenty years, when I was singing at the Met in
New York, did he bring me to Cleveland, where he had conferred world
renown on the symphony orchestra in that city. We celebrated a renewal of
our artistic collaboration and our friendship and regaled one another with
memories of the old, unforgotten days in Prague.

For a young native of Munich, who thus far, apart from Troppau and Breslau, had never gone beyond the borders of his Bavarian homeland, my time in the Czech capital was a real taste of the "big, wide wonderful world." In the early 1930s, Prague was one of several European cities in which two separate cultures had thrived side by side for ages. A political football throughout the centuries, the province of Bohemia, with Prague as its capital, was tossed back and forth between Slavic and Germanic sovereignty almost from its beginnings, ultimately being absorbed into first the Holy Roman Empire and then the Austro-Hungarian Empire under the rule of the Hapsburg dynasty, a dominance that ended with the conclusion of the First World War in 1918, when Czechoslovakia became an independent nation. It is perhaps interesting to note in this context that the cultural admixture was particularly robust, with such great literary figures as the German-language authors Franz Kafka, Rainer Maria Rilke, and Franz Werfel more or less contemporaries on the Prague cultural scene with Czech-language writers like Jaroslav Hašek and Karel Čapek.

The centuries-old mixture of Czechs and Germans and the only slightly faded glow from the recent era of the Austrian empire laid the foundation for a lively and totally friendly rivalry in culture and society. Musical life, with concerts given by local and foreign artists, was on an impressive level. Besides the German Theater, there was also the Czech National Opera, a top-ranking institution, which, apart from the standard repertoire operatic fare and some local operettas, also devoted its attentions to the great classics of the Czech repertoire. I can remember my great delight at performances of the very popular *Bartered Bride.* Another of Smetana's works, virtually unknown outside the country, remains engraved on my memory: *Libuše,* a national festival opera which is set during the earliest history of the Czech nation. In the story, a prophetess predicts that a great nation will arise from the Czech soil. At these words, the entire audience would rise to its feet—for the uninitiated listener an extremely impressive event.

I would never have been exposed to the Czech side of cultural life in Prague had it not been for a happy coincidence that developed into one of the most important friendships of my life. Back in Troppau, where my career began, I made the acquaintance of a local high school boy, some two years younger than myself, who moonlighted as an assistant director at the theater there. His name, depending on whether you spoke to him in Czech or German, was either Pavel or Paul Eckstein. In the intervening years, Paul had moved to Prague to study law at the prestigious Charles University there, completing his doctorate in law there in 1935, while taking private music lessons on the side. Both as a student and as a young lawyer, he spent every free moment enjoying the performances in the German Theater, the Czech National Theater or one of the drama theaters or concert halls.

Shortly after I began my first season in Prague, two years after the end of my Troppau engagement, he got in touch with me and we renewed the friendship. Paul soon became an integral part of a small group of close friends with whom I enjoyed getting together socially, and it was he, with his universal cultural background, who introduced me to the Czech side of Prague cultural life. Often, after performances at one theater or another, we would meet either for rollicking joke-telling sessions or serious conversations on a variety of topics, mostly centering on the arts. Paul was a brilliant raconteur and boasted an enormous collection of Jewish jokes, which he told with the expertise of a seasoned cabaret comedian. Often one or another of his friends would chide him, suggesting that in view of the virulent wave of anti-Jewish sentiment that had fallen upon the German-speaking world since the advent of Hitler in Germany back in 1933, it might be somewhat unseemly for a Jew like Paul to indulge in Jewish humor. Paul replied laconically that he certainly found nothing wrong with that sort of thing: as in most Jewish jokes, it is the Jewish element that emerges on top of the situation when the punch line comes around. There was more, however, to Paul Eckstein than just a grand collection of funny stories: an incipient renaissance man, his cultural background was vast and universal, and our conversational waters often ran very deep indeed.

Very often these conversations would run on to the moment when the last streetcars brought us from the taverns where we hung out to our various dwellings. And it was on these streetcars that yet another one of Paul's passionate interests and great talents came to the fore. He was absolutely fascinated by electrical equipment, especially devices that transported anyone or anything from one place to another. This fascination with electrically driven transport had taken on such proportions that he made it his business to become acquainted with many of the streetcar drivers; often, when the only passengers on the last car of the daily schedule were the members of our little art-loving clique, some of the drivers would even let the budding attorney practice his skills on the car by driving us home under the regular driver's careful supervision. He developed great proficiency as a streetcar driver, a talent that—in a bizarre and macabre way—would ultimately save his life.

After I left Prague, I kept in touch with Paul Eckstein through a regular exchange of letters, but this correspondence abruptly broke off for the most tragic of reasons. As history has shown, the gloomy prediction Dr. Eger had made when I was trying to decide whether or not to accept the Hamburg engagement came true shortly after I left the city. In September 1938, in my hometown of Munich, at a "peace conference" that made the name of the city synonymous with cowardly appeasement for decades, the British prime minister, Neville Chamberlain, and his allies signed an agreement allowing Hitler to annex the Sudetenland. Hitler's troops wasted no time marching into that unfortunate province on October 1, ultimately taking over the whole of Bohemia and Moravia the following March.

Fortunately Dr. Eger, being a Swiss citizen, was able to take refuge in his native country. Paul Eckstein wasn't so lucky. For a while, he was able to remain in Prague and continue his postdoctoral studies, but in 1941 he and his wife were rounded up by the Gestapo along with many other Jewish citizens of the city and carted off to the Warsaw ghetto. It would be several years before I would find out about his fate. My last letter to him was intercepted by the "authorities" and returned to me along with the "urgent advice" that it was inappropriate for me to be corresponding with a Jew. As I had no hope of further letters being delivered to the recipient, I sadly discontinued the correspondence, but my thoughts for the next several years were very much with this friend from my earliest days as a professional singer. While I had little reason to expect he would make it through the terrible persecution that followed, I hoped against hope that he might be one of the lucky few to come through it safely.

On a happier note, it was a unique experience for me the first time I heard—and even more thrillingly *saw*—the great Fyodor Chaliapin in the Prague theater. The reader should bear in mind that, at that time, audiences placed very modest demands on a singer's acting ability. One of the reasons why opera didn't mean much to me in my younger years was this neglect of dramatic expression when singing.

Of course, during my student years in Munich, I had seen a goodly number of fine singing actors on the stage: Hildegard Ranczak, Luise Willer, Heinrich Rehkemper, Paul Bender, and Wilhelm Rode. But they were the exceptions. Now suddenly I saw a singing personality whom I found boundlessly captivating. And the remarkable thing was I couldn't really say what impressed me more, the voice or the dramatic performance. I believe this was the first time that I had a presentiment of how much these two elements belonged together. You have to act with more than the voice and the use of language. This physicality is essential to acting. The way you hold your body, your head, the way you walk, move, use your eyes—all these elements must come together to form a unit. Chaliapin was the one who first sparked something that would ultimately occupy my thoughts for years to come.

In the Prague years, at any event, "acting" the "delineation" of an operatic interpretation was harder for me than the singing part, probably because I was not yet able to combine the two. I loved heroic-dramatic roles, but I had my problems with natural, normal characters drawn, so to speak, from everyday life. How I admired the actors who moved about the stage easily and normally when they played some drawing room comedy set in the present day. Elegant roles, such as Scarpia in *Tosca,* the Count in *Figaro* or Escamillo in *Carmen* were hard work for me. In those days I was still singing

Moralès in *Carmen,* but sometimes, in a matinée performance, I was allowed to sing Escamillo—a task that always left me somehow dissatisfied.

Once a Russian baritone made a guest appearance in our theatre singing
Escamillo. He had a reputation for being a dazzling singing actor. As usual
I sang Moralès, who is on stage during Escamillo's entrance. Full of curi-
ousity and expectations, I looked forward to the first appearance of our distinguished guest artist. Although sixty years have since passed, I can still see
in my mind's eye: a solidly built man of medium height, who instantly
riveted all of us to the spot with his natural, masculine appearance—far less
through his voice or its expression than through his attitude. He didn't
seem to be playing the role, he *was* Escamillo. And then came something
that left us all dumbfounded. During the well-known entrance aria "Auf in
den Kampf" (in those days everyone sang in German, even the Russian!)
he hardly moved at all, especially not with his arms and hands. He just
stood there. But how he stood! That's *it,* I thought to myself: don't do anything, just stand there and sing. Shortly thereafter I was again Escamillo
myself. On that occasion, I swore to myself, I would do it just like my great
colleague: just stand there and sing with the clearest of articulation and
without moving a muscle. The effect was singular: not one hand met another to give me the usual applause. Deeply embarrassed and disappointed
beyond the telling of it I slunk off the stage. On the way to the dressing
room I ran across two adorable Jewish gentlemen from the chorus. One of
them put a fatherly hand on my shoulder and asked, "Nu, so vot heppened
vid you? Vydja stop ecting?"

Then it dawned on me: *absolutely nothing* is too little. What a good lesson this event was for me on the way to what would surely be a twenty-year
development: on the stage, you mustn't stop *being* the character you are
playing—especially when, from the vantage point of the spectator, you
aren't *doing anything.*

There was a magnificent "singing actor" on the Prague roster, a so-
called *Charakterbariton* by the name of Theodor Scheidl. He stood six foot
eight so that I, with my mere six foot four stature, had to look up to him.
At the time he was well past the zenith of his career; I would guess he was
in his late fifties, but the impression that he gave on the stage was incredibly forceful. With amazing skill, he knew just exactly how to conceal the
age-related wear and tear on his voice. He was really made to measure for
a role like Boris Godunov. In this production I sang the Jesuit monk Ran-
goni and never tired of watching him. Many of the things I saw then were
later incorporated into my own interpretation of the role some four years
later when, with only twenty-seven summers behind me, I sang Boris at
the Hamburg Opera.

I can also remember his brutal Sebastiano in d'Albert's *Tiefland,* an opera today's audiences know virtually nothing about. Back then I sang the little role of the miller's apprentice Moruccio, who has a short, very effective scene with his master Sebastiano. During the rehearsal period, we became good friends. Theo was one of those colleagues who harbored no envy whatsoever toward me—a quality that is anything but the rule between a distinguished older artist and an up-and-coming youngster. There were days when we would sit together, and he would tell me all about his past triumphs, happy in the memory but without that self-glorification so often typical of older artists. "The two of us long drinks of water," he would say, laughing, "have a lot in common. But being tall isn't always advantageous. It carries with it problems you have to recognize and stay away from. We have to avoid making sweeping gestures."

After the war, around 1947, I visited the founder of the Glyndebourne Festival, John Christie, at his English estate. Of course he showed me the then rather small theater. "I'm afraid," he said with a sly grin, "you could never perform here, because the audience wants to see your hands when you stretch out your arms!" As a kind of confirmation, I was reminded of something Theodor Scheidl had said: "If we stretch out our arms all the way, it looks far too overpowering, as compared with a shorter performer. I've been watching you act. Kind fate has given you a whole collection of talents apart from your voice, ones you've already learned to make good use of: there is your tall stature, your posture, the way you hold your head and change the position while you play a part, your expressive hands, your eyes, the many nuances in your voice, the articulation of the words—you see, those are now no less than seven ways of expressing something. Now you have to learn to use those means more economically and not blow all your powder on a single shot, not use everything at once. Do you have any idea how much a good audience enjoys a bit of silence!?" Later on I began to realize how valuable my educative years in Prague had been, if only for the good advice I got from Theodor Scheidl.

One day during my second Prague season, Dr. Eger sent for me and inquired eagerly, "How are you getting along with our Italian guest conductor Antonino Votto?" I'd never heard of the man before I came here. Somebody said he had been Toscanini's assistant for a few years. They had very similar conducting styles.

"Well, how are you getting along with him?"

"Oh, magnificently—I really like him."

"He likes you, too. But he did recently say: 'Hotter—bene. Ma il urla.'" (Hotter's good, but he bellows.)

Before I could react, with some annoyance, he added, smiling: "Don't take it so tragically! He also said: 'All young singers do that.' And I have a feeling he may not be so far from wrong." Then without breaking stride in his conversation, he inquired, "How did you like Bockelmann recently as Wotan in *Rheingold*? You were standing next to him singing Donner."

"Oh," I exclaimed, happy with the change of subject, "he was terrific. What an interpreter! Just the way he handles Wagner's use of language!"

To which Eger replied, "What would you say if I were to send you to him in Berlin for two weeks? He said he'd like to work with you, for example, on diction. He's also a master of vocal economy, he could give you some good tips on that. Making the most effective use of your voice, you still haven't got that down pat."

"My teacher in Munich says so, too. By the way, my teacher: what do you suppose he would think of that?"

"You don't have to tell him, not right away, later perhaps. First get in touch with Bockelmann. Meanwhile I'll try to mobilize my reserves to finance your stay in Berlin. But heaven help you if you come back still bellowing!"

I was overjoyed. The thing I had secretly wished for was about to happen, thanks to the generosity and vision of my director. And then I suddenly remembered that my teacher Matthäus Römer had once said it would be a good idea for me to take a couple of lessons from a baritone, he being a tenor. So I started to Berlin with a clear conscience. The two weeks there were pure bliss. Every day I worked with the master and tried to absorb everything I could. I was enjoying a fantastic brushup course in interpretation. And for the first time I had a baritone teaching me the great art of using language and singing in equal quantities and simultaneously—just as I had seen Chaliapin demonstrate it so impressively. Bockelmann was kind and friendly toward me, so full of understanding that I, who was a rather diffident fellow, gradually opened my heart to him completely and talked openly of all my problems, large and small. That did me a world of good.

It's really amazing: today, so many years later, I know for certain that after Bockelmann there was a long line of important personalities, actively and passively involved in honing and developing my career—a few of them even more extensively than Bockelmann. But there were very few I trusted so completely. He probably had just the right way to work with a young, inexperienced fellow like me.

I also had the opportunity to attend performances at the Lindenoper. I heard a first-class *Meistersinger* there in which Bockelmann as Hans Sachs provided a prime example of an intelligent interpretation of this difficult, long role. I can't remember the rest of the cast; I only had ears for this honored, great expert.

Of course I heard other operas as well, but I can't remember all of them. For a listener from the provinces in Prague many left permanent impressions. One special experience was a *Rosenkavalier* under Erich Kleiber, whom

I saw and admired for the first time. Fourteen years later I sang under his direction at the Teatro Colón in Buenos Aires, but I'll report on that later.

Before returning to the initial scene of these remembrances in Dr. Eger's Prague office, however, I'd like to impart a few more memories of my life in Prague. Between the autumn of 1933 and the spring of 1934 there were two encounters without which my subsequent career would have been unthinkable. These were my first meetings with the conductors Bruno Walter and Clemens Krauss.

For the high school boy and music student Hans Hotter, Bruno Walter was, of course, a household name in the concert life of my hometown Munich. He also remained in my memory as the accompanist of song recitals with Maria Ivogün and Karl Erb. My teacher Matthäus Römer, who was more a recitalist than an opera singer, had sung under his baton several times and always spoke in the most respectful tones of his human and artistic greatness. In addition to their professional collaboration, Römer also enjoyed a close personal friendship with Bruno Walter that went back to the time when Römer was teaching French and English to the royal children at the court of the Bavaria's Wittelsbach monarchs. In the course of this activity, he made the acquaintance of the elderly Prince Regent Luitpold, who was an avid hunter, as was Römer. As their friendship grew, the prince regent, who did most of his hunting in the South Tyrol, offered Römer an opportunity to take over a hunting lodge he hardly ever used near the village of Kreuth on Tegernsee Lake, not far from Bruno Walter's country home. In time, the two men began meeting frequently to talk about music, the arts, and all the many other topics that occupied their keen minds.

I had another link to Walter in the form of Willi Wirk, a retired stage director from the Munich State Opera with whom I took acting lessons during the time I was studying singing with Dr. Römer—not something young singers frequently did in those days, but of inordinate help to me in my future stage work. Willi Wirk had been head of the staging department at the theater at the same time Dr. Walter was in charge of music there.

Now, in Prague's Lucerna Hall, Bruno Walter conducted Verdi's *Requiem*. A friend took me along to the green room and introduced me to the famous guest conductor. He remembered my teacher with great affection and invited me to join him and the solo singers for dinner. I happened to find myself sitting next to the illustrious Maria Németh from the Vienna Opera and gazed admiringly at the Hungarian prima donna, not suspecting that we would be facing off only six years later as Tosca and Scarpia on the Vienna State Opera stage. It was even harder to imagine that only three years later Bruno Walter would invite me, on a recommendation from Hans Pfitzner, to sing Borromeo in a new production of the composer's *Palestrina* at the Vienna State Opera.

This guest performance, however, did not take place until 1941, so unfortunately no longer with Walter. But he did send for me, even before the war, when I was already engaged in Hamburg, to sing concerts with the Concertgebouw Orchestra in Amsterdam. I was able to take advantage of this opportunity to share the concert stage with the "Gran Maestro" only because something unexpected had happened. During the Nazi era, German artists were not allowed to practice their profession outside the country without a special permit from Berlin. So I wired an application to take part in a concert of the Concertgebouw Orchestra in Amsterdam and expressly added "under the direction of Bruno Walter," who had been forbidden to appear in Germany because of the Nazis' "Jewish laws." I couldn't believe my eyes when the very same day—only two hours later, in fact—I received a telegram from Berlin reading "permission granted." This all happened in 1937, when government officials were still very much interested in the propaganda value of having German artists perform outside the country, and they even turned a blind eye to the fact that the concerts I was to sing would be under the direction of a conductor who was regarded as something akin to a "nonperson" in Germany.

I will never forget the radiance from an extraordinary artistic personality at the rehearsals in Amsterdam. The first concert was devoted to the works of Richard Wagner, and my part of the program included the *Holländer* aria and "Wotan's Farewell." I had just added the Dutchman to the list of my Wagner roles at the Hamburg Opera, but I would not make my debut as Wotan in *Die Walküre* until the spring of 1940 at the Munich State Opera. I sang "Wotan's Farewell" for the first time in public on the concert platform in Amsterdam and had the great fortune of Walter's expert guidance throughout this premiere. He took the time for a one-on-one rehearsal and concentrated completely on this scene. With youthful élan and obvious enthusiasm this man in his sixties exerted his every effort to teaching me that Wotan in his paternal affection uninhibitedly gives vent to the full range of his human emotions here. "Throughout these twenty minutes, you should be constantly close to tears—not in reality but in your artistic imagination. Otherwise you'll lose control. Try to imagine the face of your beloved daughter directly before you, and don't ever stop trying to express an abundance of emotion. It's not your own genuine sensation at the moment but rather the feeling you conjure up artistically that moves the audience."

Walter's words formed the foundation of my gradual shaping of this role. However many instructions, critiques, and opposing views from conductors I had to put up with in the course of a forty-year *Walküre* career; however many discussions I conducted with friends, opera lovers, critics, Wagnerians, including well-meaning and constructive ones; in however many often breathtaking *Walküres* I was transported to the heights of stirring artistic experiences by Hans Knappertsbusch, Clemens Krauss, Wilhelm Furtwängler, and Herbert von Karajan, when I got to the words "*Der Augen leuchtendes Paar*" (Those two glowing eyes), everything else faded into the background. Then it was only the glowing eyes of Bruno Walter and the echo of his words in Amsterdam in 1937. This man, so unjustly ostracized in the years between 1933 and 1945, had given me a gift for life in his foreign exile.

On one of my several trips to the Netherlands, I had an opportunity to enjoy a most unusual artistic pleasure. At a Concertgebouw event, Bruno Walter gave a lecture to a group of invited guests on Gustav Mahler, with whom we knew he had been very closely associated. In the course of his remarks he sat down at the piano several times to sing and play some of the composer's songs. It was a onetime, unforgettable experience, especially under the prevailing, repugnant political circumstances, which were clear in the minds of everyone in the hall. This evening as well he invited me to join him for a little snack, just the two of us, in his hotel.

We were both in unusually high spirits, conversed about art, and I tried to retain every word he spoke in my memory. Naturally, we touched on the subject of political developments in Germany. I told him that at first many people, not only the Germans, had been brilliantly misled by one of history's most ingenious propaganda machines into underestimating the danger of the situation. In the midthirties, a British delegation led by Foreign Minister Sir John Simon and his second in command, Anthony Eden, had been effusive in their praise of developments in Germany, and we were told that President Franklin D. Roosevelt had sent Christmas greetings to "the great man across the sea." A recent inquiry to the Roosevelt Library in Hyde Park revealed that this quote had no basis in fact; perhaps it was taken out of context by the Nazi Propaganda Ministry from a condolence message the president had sent Hitler on the death of Hindenburg, but at the time it was all over Germany. Soon, however, it became all too clear what was happening in our homeland, which was why I had been so reluctant to return to the country from Prague until my Jewish theater director, Dr. Eger, convinced me there was no escaping the tide sweeping over Central Europe.

After listening to my description of the brown shadow that had fallen on our country, Dr. Walter fell silent for a moment. I was virtually shattered when he then told me that, were it not for the grim conditions prevailing there, he would like nothing better than to return to Germany, rather today than tomorrow, if necessary on foot, if only he could conduct in his homeland again. Then he looked directly at me and asked, "How can you stand it there?"

I replied that I somehow had the luck of the draw in Hamburg, an international trading hub, where the cosmopolitan population had simply not

allowed National Socialism to seep into the whole fabric of society as per-
niciously as it had in many other German cities. Certainly nobody there
ever tried to force me to join the Nazi Party or engage in political activities
of any kind. Even the top Nazis there, I told him, were mostly businessmen
with more of an eye toward their foreign trading profits than on any kind
of solidarity with the rulers of the country in Berlin. All of this was to my
advantage, but of course I was anything but unaware of the terrible things
the Nazis were doing, both "officially" and "unofficially" through their
brown-shirted mobs, all over the country.

After listening carefully to what I had to say, Dr. Walter then said, "I
could certainly use an artist like you, and I could see to it that you got plenty
of work outside of Germany, especially in the United States." The offer was
more than tempting, but, of course, no man is an island, and I had to reply
that I could not consider resettling elsewhere. I had recently married, I had
a one-year-old son, and I also had to consider my aging mother with deep
roots in the Bavarian soil and my older brother, who had become a Catholic priest and was then teaching in a secondary school. The whole situation
would be a kind of Scylla and Charybdis one for me: as there was no way
any of us would be allowed to emigrate from Germany legally, I would have
to find some way to escape from the country. Were I to succeed, the Nazis
would promptly invoke their law of *Sippenhaft* (family liability), in which
family members would be called to account for anyone who turned his back
on the country, and there was no predicting how severe this "calling to account" might be. Even in the unlikely event that I might somehow be able
to get the entire family out of Germany, I would have to find some way of
supporting them.

Dr. Walter thought this over for a moment, then sadly admitted, "There
is no way I could possibly provide guarantees for so many people. Then the
best advice I can give you is to make your career back in Germany." I was
immediately reminded of my conversation back in the spring of 1934 with
my fatherly friend Dr. Eger, who also told me there would be no way of cir-
cumventing a return to Germany: sooner or later, the scourge was certain to
cover the whole of Central Europe and beyond; there would be no escaping
it, certainly not in Prague or Vienna. Of course, back in 1934 Dr. Eger and
I had no way of foreseeing how bad things would ultimately become. I
often wonder, if he were alive today, what he would think of the way things
have developed and that it was he, of all people, who first told me to overcome my disinclination toward returning to Germany. And so these two
influential Jewish artists had both advised me, despite my revulsion toward
the malignant regime that had taken over my country, to continue my artistic career there and hope that things might somehow develop for the better. As they finally did—but at what a terrible cost for all parties concerned!

Years later, in September 1949, I ran into Bruno Walter again in a practice room backstage at the Royal Albert Hall in London. In the course of conversation, he said spontaneously, "Remember our discussion back in Amsterdam before the war? I had to think about it quite often during the war, and to this day I am convinced I gave you the right advice back then."

It was an odd coincidence that brought me together with Clemens Krauss. A young tenor colleague in the Prague ensemble told me he had an opportunity to audition for the director of the Vienna Opera, Clemens Krauss, who just happened to be in Prague. "Have you got an accompanist? No?" I was hatching a plan. "Well, do you suppose I might accompany you? Perhaps you might tell him that I sing, too?" The colleague was agreeable to my suggestion, and the audition took place in the large Lucerna concert hall—completely empty.

In the first row sat the famous Viennese conductor, somewhat casually attired with a jaunty, pointed cap on his head—I can still see him in my mind's eye—and he gave the impression of being somewhat bored (he probably *was* bored). The tenor sang, I played, the listener made a couple of inconsequential remarks and was about to rise to his feet and take his leave of us, when my tenor friend interrupted him and actually said: "My accompanist sings too, and he'd like to audition for you." To which Krauss replied in his inimitable Viennese twang, "Aha! A singing *Korrepetitor!*" My heart was already on the express elevator heading for the sub-basement, but Krauss seemed amused by the situation. Swiftly dropping the air of boredom, he said in his typically charming manner: "Well now, looks like I'll have to play."

I clutched my heart, which had meanwhile returned to its usual position, and sang for him with everything I had. I can still remember what I performed: Wotan's short aria at the end of *Rheingold,* "Abendlich strahlt der Sonne Auge" (The sun's eye gleams in the light of evening). After I finished he looked straight at me pleasantly and made a remark I've repeated a million times shoptalking with fellow singers or giving interviews: "I like you. I like you so much that I'd like nothing better than to take you right back to Vienna with me. But that would be pointless. How old are you?"

"Twenty-five."

"And how long have you been singing opera?"

"Almost four years."

"Aha. Look, well, here's the story: you're too young for big parts, and you're too tall for small parts. Let me make you a suggestion: sing small roles for another couple of years, meanwhile a bigger one every now and then, and make sure you get plenty of stage experience. You needn't contact me again; you'll hear from me when the time comes."

To encapsulate that time somewhat, it took exactly three years before I again heard from Krauss. Now I'd like to dwell on Prague just a little longer.

Something happened there in the spring of 1934, that is to say toward the end of my time there, which still provokes gales of laughter from the people who were involved at the time. The main reason it has remained anchored in my memory is because my darling Mamma had a part in it.

With the departure of Jewish and politically dissident artists from Nazi Germany, the great Wagner singer, and Bockelmann's predecessor in the heroic baritone category, the unforgettable Friedrich Schorr, passed through on his final visit to Europe before going back to the United States to sing a few guest performances in our house. He had been one of the few artists from this part of the world to establish a firm foothold at the Metropolitan Opera (or anywhere else in the United States for that matter), and with the coming of the Nazis in Europe, that country would be his sole base of operations for the remainder of his illustrious career. As he had never sung in Munich before 1934, I only knew of him by name and I was now quite eager to meet him and see him on stage. At the time I was singing Donner in *Rheingold,* and stood beside him full of admiration; I then attended the *Walküre* rehearsals and was completely spellbound by his personality in the performances. Although he was only of medium height, he exuded so much authority that I wondered, as I had with Chaliapin, how he did it. Was it his voice or his use of language or his acting posture that allowed him to command the stage as he did? Or was it all of those things taken together in an ideal admixture?

I couldn't help thinking of the great role model back in my Munich student years, Wilhelm Rode, who competed with the bel canto artist Hans Hermann Nissen at the Munich Opera, especially in the Wagner roles, during the late twenties and early thirties. At the time, especially when he sang Sachs and Wotan, Rode seemed to be the non plus ultra on the operatic stage. And now there was suddenly someone who, just like Bockelmann, created the same strong impression. albeit a totally different one. Today I am convinced that all three of them served as the inspiration on which I laid the foundation for my own career.

But back to Prague. In that spring of 1934 my mother came to Prague for the first time. Although I had already been at home on the operatic stage for four years, she had so far never seen me in action. Trips to my earlier theaters in Troppau and Breslau would have been too long and strenuous for her. Besides, the travel costs were a bit steeper than I could afford! But now she was here in Prague for the first time in her life as a guest of her son—and what a welcome source of pride that was for him! Full of anticipation, she sat down in the auditorium. We were playing *Rheingold,* and I was Donner. She seemed to like it very much. She appeared somewhat surprised that I had developed some acting ability, although there isn't all that much you can show anyone in the role of Donner, but she said I moved around very nicely. Schorr sang a most impressive Wotan. The next day I sat beside her for *Walküre,* and we both found Schorr absolutely spectacular!

Two days later, on the morning of the *Siegfried* performance I received a call from the director's office at the opera house! "Mr. Schorr is indisposed and can't possibly sing this evening. You've already done the Wanderer—where was that, and when?"

"Yes, yes, two years ago at the Municipal Theatre in Troppau."

"Do you trust yourself to step in for Mr. Schorr this evening?"

"Me? This evening? The Wanderer? Well, I suppose I could."

So, that evening I sang my first Wanderer in Prague. The audience pampered me up and down and seemed to accept the change of cast. And my dear Dr. Eger was pleased as punch. After that, my friends roundly celebrated the event with me. And my mother? She told us all, "I was trembling from head to toe before you came on. I was sitting in a box in the front row, and there was this elderly married couple next to me. Shortly before the beginning of the third act the lady said to her husband: 'Well, I must say I like Schorr better tonight than I did in *Walküre.*'" Here I must repeat that he was a good head shorter than myself. The effect at the table was indescribable, not least on me.

My mother joined right in with the jolly mood at the table, sat there quietly and laughed in her familiar way to herself. It didn't take long before my mother had not only become used to her son's profession, but actually began enjoying it. When the successes came, she was even a little proud. But it seemed to me that the evening at the end of her visit to Prague represented a sizable progression in her attitude; I knew that the prospect of her son in a freelance, artistic profession had initially made her far from happy.

And how did I feel after that evening? The incident as such was funny. But, I did say to myself, what does the opinion of a couple of people in the audience mean in the long run? A few years previously, while I was still doing my training, doubting my choice of occupation was quite normal. It always amazed me that my teacher Matthäus Römer, otherwise a man of sober judgment, was always firmly convinced of my calling and spoke of the future in words like "when you start singing in Bayreuth" or "when you're famous" as if he were simply making a statement of fact—albeit with the qualification "provided you do everything that is necessary on your part."

Well, after the first four years of fairly successful activity I was still not sure whether I would manage more than an average career, despite someone's having confused me with one of the "greats." During my training period I didn't have only my own doubts to contend with. My mother was also extremely wary of too much optimism, even when it came from my teacher. And her judgment, especially hers, meant a great deal to me, because there had not been a father in our family for a long time. He had left this earth all too early, in the thirty-ninth year of his life, when my mother was a young woman of thirty-five, my brother ten, and I only a child of seven.

❧ Chapter 2 ❧

Looking back at my childhood, I always divide it into two periods: the time before and the time after my father's death.

When I think of the early years, I immediately recall a sense of blissful security, an uninterrupted succession of happy days. In the evenings I see and hear jolly times with friends of the family and my father's colleagues. People would sing to my father's accompaniment at the piano keyboard or with a lute in his lap. Far back in my memory there was also my "fatherly" grandfather, who played the zither, and I can recall he had a pretty good baritone voice.

As a young man, my father Karl Hotter was basically undecided as to which of his talents he wanted to exploit professionally, his musical ability or his gift of drawing. In many ways the decision was made for him, at least in the first instance, by his parents, whose lives were governed by the bourgeois values of craftsmen: Music-making for the fun of it was a virtue, but exploiting music to earn a living was quite another matter—the sort of thing gypsies do, but not respectable middle-class citizens of a major Central European regional capital.

Many generations of Hotters had been blacksmiths in Haidhausen, at the time a Munich suburb, and today one of the districts not far from the downtown area, directly to the east of the Isar River, which bifurcates the city. There in the Hotter blacksmith's shop on Wiener Platz the horses were shod up to the end of the nineteenth century, and that grandfather was the last member of the family who, in his younger years, actually plied that trade. The family chronicle tells us that music had always been important in the Hotter household, a heritage that has been a source of pride all my life. Nevertheless, when young Karl expressed an interest in perhaps becoming a professional musician, all understanding for this most perilous of callings stopped. He was reminded of a distant cousin, who emigrated to the United States at an early age, where he actually did become a professional musician, but had no success worth reporting back to the family. This was not a path Karl's parents wanted him to follow.

2.1. Grandfather Karl Hotter was the last in a long line of village blacksmiths in Munich's Haidhausen district. While he loved playing music himself, he thought making music for a living was the sort of thing gypsies do, not respectable craftspeople.

While Karl was still seriously toying with the idea of perhaps defying his parents and becoming a music student anyway, his family went on a summer vacation where they made the acquaintance of another married couple. Karl took an immediate liking to the daughter of the wife's first marriage, a young lady with the very Bavarian name of Kreszentia Winklmayr. Over the next ten years, Karl and Kreszentia's friendship developed into something more; nonetheless, although they essentially lived in the same city, they hardly saw one another. That is why it took a good ten years from that first meeting before they could say their relationship was solid enough to warrant serious thoughts of marriage.

2.2. My father, the second Karl Hotter, actually considered defying his parents and going to music school, but then he met my mother.

2.3. Kreszentia Winklmayr met my father when both were on vacation with their parents. Their courtship lasted a full ten years.

Kreszentia's father had been an artisan like grandfather Hotter, but he died while his daughter was just a small child; her mother then remarried into a family of civil servants, as respectable and middle-class in their outlook on life as the Hotters. In short, Kreszentia's mother and stepfather saw no impediment to the two young people becoming man and wife: like the Hotters, they were quite fond of music—as long as it remained avocational, a view with which Karl's fiancée completely agreed. As a matter of fact it was she who made it a condition of their marriage that Karl complete his studies in architecture to guarantee the family that was to come some kind of a secure income. Her new husband, she said, was welcome to make all the music he wanted in his spare time.

On the day of their wedding in 1906, when Karl was twenty-eight and his bride twenty-four, even before they departed on their short honeymoon, Karl made a detour to a piano dealer's shop, where he purchased a second-hand piano as his contribution to the new household they were setting up, and it was this piano that I remember him playing in the first years of my life. As a matter of fact, when I think back on my father, memory reveals him to me far more often at the keyboard than at the drawing board. But architecture was his trade and, once he had completed the studies that had been a condition of his bride joining matrimonial forces with him, he was employed as an instructor by the Hessian School of Building Trades in Offenbach, the city where I first saw the light of day. Even then, music remained his favorite pastime. Nevertheless, I can still see him before me working in his carpentry shop, making the furniture for our vacation home in the Spessart Mountains himself, even in his final years when he was forced into early retirement because of the lung condition that ultimately claimed his life.

Years later I often suffered from not having known more about my father as a person, no more than what a child of five to seven can take in. I see him, naturally, as a young man, and only as that: tall, very slender, always with a well-groomed beard, and with an almost delicate quality about him—if one can say that about a man. He had well-formed, incredibly dextrous hands, whether he was holding a carpentry tool, plying his drafting pencil, or sending his fingers gliding over the piano keys. He looked at me with calm, kind eyes, which often flashed with a humorous glint. His voice had a soft, masculine quality. They say that, like his father, he had a handsome singing voice as a boy, but lost it when his voice changed.

I can't remember ever hearing him speak in a loud or uncontrolled voice. My mother spoke more decisively, energetically. When I recall those days, I don't think my parents ever exchanged a harsh word, let alone argued—certainly not within earshot of us children. The image of my father, sitting at the piano, modulating from key to key, with a cigar in his mouth, his eyes

2.4.   In 1905, a year before they married, my parents had their picture taken together. Shortly before the wedding, my father went out and bought a secondhand piano to make sure our home would always have music in it.

sparkling, his face reflecting the spirit of a man content with himself and the world, has remained a vivid memory to this day. I often asked my mother to tell me more about his human qualities. At those times she was the least talkative, as if wanting to retain the memory of him for herself. She would only say it was a great source of pleasure to him when I, as a small child, clearly reacted to music and the sound of his singing. She said he often stood at my crib with his lute, playing and singing, and rejoicing over the tiniest reaction. And so, in the most literal sense of the world, I had music "placed in my cradle." My mother once said, "I think your Papa was responsible for the fact that you preferred singing to speaking." Later, long after his death, I was often reminded that she had to promise our father on his deathbed that she would send both sons to the Gymnasium (humanistic secondary school); that's how convinced he was of the importance of an academic education. If only he had foreseen under what difficult circumstances she then kept that promise! After all, the few years he had worked

2.5. Mother said I must have had music placed in my cradle, because I always grinned from ear to ear when there was some music being played at home. I guess someone was making music when this picture was taken.

2.6. My older brother, the third Karl in the Hotter family, and I were only children when we lost our father, but our mother resolutely kept the promise she made to him on his deathbed: that we would receive a thoroughgoing education.

2.7. Years later, my brother Karl became a Catholic priest and also achieved an excellent reputation as a religious educator.

did not produce much in the way of a widow's pension for my mother, especially as the remainder of her holdings simply melted away during the 1923 inflation. I never ceased to regard her with admiration and grateful adoration. How she managed with less than sparse means to support me through all those years and even get me through nine years of Gymnasium will always remain a mystery.

Chapter 3

The second half of my youth was not easy for me, because I had been used to an easy life and knew no other. Nevertheless, I believe I would have had more trouble adjusting to difficulties and setbacks in my professional training if I had enjoyed a more comfortable life in my younger years.

The hardest thing for me was having to grow up without a father. I know, however, that our mother, by dint of her powerful personality and unwavering strength of character, came close to replacing our father in most aspects of our lives. A quite different but equally important influence came from my maternal grandmother, also a woman with plenty of personality, a marked sense of family, and a fundamental artistic inclination.

I gave no thought whatsoever to my subsequent occupational choices during the earlier years of secondary school. My mother had a stepsister, the daughter of my grandmother's second husband, who gave piano lessons, and so I became one of my "aunt's" pupils, and actually enjoyed playing the instrument, even though enthusiasm for practicing was only sporadically present. Playing soccer, or sports in general, was far more interesting. When I was eleven years old, I was accepted into the school chorus, as were many other classmates. Shortly before puberty, I had to make an solo appearance at a school celebration. I still had a high soprano voice at the age of thirteen. My music professor, Mr. Weinzierl, entrusted me with the performance of the aria "Mein gläubiges Herze" from Bach's Pentecost Cantata. I didn't regard this as a particularly daunting task. I wasn't nervous even though I had to ascend all the way to a high A. My class teacher asked me kindly and with deep interest whether I came from a musical family. He said I should take great care to retain my vocal ability through my voice change. I didn't have a clue what he was so concerned about. He was really the first person who gave any thought to my voice.

When I was about seventeen, I decided, to the horror of my Gymnasium professors and with the hesitant agreement of my mother, that I would study music when I finished high school. As a matter of fact, my mother's reluctance might have prevailed had my grandmother not mellowed toward the idea of having a musician in the family—even though, being a highly

3.1. My mother, Karl, and myself visiting my paternal grandparents in the country.

pragmatic individual, she had her misgivings about a subsequent career in music for me because of my innate shyness and diffidence, which she felt might prove a serious impediment to making music in public. Yet it was her approval of the initial impulse that resulted in my mother's finally relenting and allowing me to enroll at the music academy.

The decision was made somewhat easier for her by the fact that my older brother, Karl, had decided on a career as a Catholic priest, which, while it didn't promise to make him very rich, still guaranteed a secure, steady income in addition to the respectability of that clerical position. This security made it easier for her to accept what she still feared might be a very uncertain future in my case. Yet even as I began my musical studies, I still wasn't quite sure where I wanted to go from there. At the time I was wavering between possibly becoming either a conductor or a high school music teacher. Fortunately, I continued my piano studies, which came in very handy when I finally did decide that singing would be my destiny, because I was always able to accompany myself and others both in learning my own music and then later in teaching my students.

My young music professor at the Gymnasium was very well disposed toward me. He conducted as a side job, so to speak, a church choir in northern Munich and offered me a job singing the bass solos at Sunday High Mass. The fee: five to ten marks. In addition, I had to help out at the organ, an instrument that had always fascinated me and one I was beginning to love more and more. In fact, I decided, once I had graduated from secondary school, that I would major in the "king of instruments," the organ, partly because of my sincere love of the instrument, and partly because an organist usually holds down a steady job throughout his professional life, plus earning a reasonable side income as a teacher; this sense of future security proved very comforting to my mother. As fate would have it, my subsequent voice teacher, Matthäus Römer, heard me sing in that church. When he approached me—I was eighteen and in my last year of school— and offered to train my voice, I was hesitant, in fact almost disinclined. I just didn't have the necessary capital. Besides, I wanted to study music. "Singing" as a profession was simply not to my taste.

Instead of doing an about-face and leaving me standing there, Römer invited me, along with my music professor, a gentleman by the name of Josef Saam, to the nearest café. There he tried to make it clear to me in a couple of sentences that there were more than enough music teachers and conductors, but people with promising vocal material were few and far between. He added that I needn't worry about paying for the lessons. I could take care of that at some later point in time. "When you're earning more than a thousand marks a month," he added with a chuckle. This was beyond my imagination. My music professor urged me to give it a try. When I told my mother about this at home, she initially thought it was a bad joke.

But fate took its course. My grandmother was again consulted and was, needless to say, immediately over the moon, but the possibility of my singing for a living was still far in the future. These lessons were seen only as a supplement to my musical studies and nothing more. For a couple of days the matter was ardently discussed, then Dr. Saam managed to convince Matthäus Römer to call on Mama Hotter. The visit took place behind my back. Römer made his deal with my mother; and, as I was still a minor, I had nothing to say in the matter.

And I? Meanwhile I had come to the conclusion that it wouldn't be such a bad idea for a music student to know a little something about singing.

And so, a couple of months before graduation, I began embarking on a bi-weekly pilgrimage to Dr. Römer's studio. In a short time, after only a few lessons, I was absolutely enraptured with my teacher—and not just because of the voice lessons. As unlikely as this may sound, he imbued in me an enthusiasm for singing, explaining that a musical person must sing as if he were learning to play an instrument. I have never wavered from this approach.

Not until much later—meanwhile my music professor had become a real friend—was the sequence of events made clear to me. My dear Römer had not just coincidentally happened into church that morning. The whole thing had been prepared long in advance by my music teacher at school. My visits to the choir loft continued. Meanwhile, with my final school examinations behind me, fate again took a hand. Dr. Saam was transferred to Passau and arranged to have me appointed his successor at the church. For a monthly salary of initially 90 and then 120 marks I became choir director (or, as they called it there, choirmaster) at Saint George's in Milbertshofen, and I remained in that position until my first operatic engagement. During the almost two intervening years I garnered my first practical professional experience as a musician.

I was particularly eager to develop greater skill on the organ I so loved playing. I tried to pick up as many tips as I could watching how my boss in the organ loft, Josef Saam, did things. Little by little, the decision to continue majoring in organ at the Music Academy took shape. I still couldn't muster much enthusiasm for a career as a singer and was contemplating a profession as an instrumental musician with a teaching position perhaps somewhere in my future. Secretly I continued to harbor a desire to conduct; this was in keeping with my idea of joining together with others to make music a reality. Saam supported this intention, allowing me to direct the choir more and more often and initiating me into the basics of conducting. This directing was a great source of pleasure for me, but meanwhile there was also a necessity to sing solos and play the organ.

Saam taught me the ground rules of free modulation and intonation on the organ for the *responsoria* in the liturgy of Roman Catholic sacred music and instructed me in adjusting to the often quite bold digressions from intonation on the part of the worthy clerics at the altar. In time I managed to establish excellent musical relations with the reverend vicar and his curate. The latter was my special friend: he came from a Lower Bavarian farm family, was a huge man, and had the soul of a child. His clerical duties included the care of the little parish garden.

I almost forgot to mention that in addition to my services on Sundays and holy days, I was also called upon occasionally to provide music for weddings, christenings, and funerals. Extra compensation was paid for these services both to the gentlemen at the altar and the musicians in the loft. I was usually the only participant, singing and accompanying myself on the organ. I still recall these early musical deeds with great delight.

My activities in the choir loft also involved frequent long rides on the streetcar. In the course of these travels I became acquainted with a phenomenon that no longer exists: the romantic doings in the Munich trolley car milieu back in the 1920s, when there were still power cars up front with one or two auxiliary cars trailing behind, each served by its own conductor, who sold the tickets, pulled a rope that rang a bell at each stop and called out the names of the various stations with a style all his own. While I was still going to school, I made daily use of these vehicles; even then, I made my own psychological observations, because the transport conducting staff included a goodly number of genuine originals. My route to school was the number 6 line between Goetheplatz and what is today known as Münchner Freiheit in commemoration of the Munich freedom fighters, urban rebels who rose up against the Nazis at the end of World War II. At the time it was still called Danziger Freiheit, resolutely mispronounced in Munich Trolley patois as "Danzinger Freiheit."

To acquire a greater understanding of my story the reader should know that Munich's power cars were not equipped with the usual arc-shaped power line contacts but simply had a rod with a little wheel on the top. The disadvantage of this version was that the little rolling wheels in the power contact often jumped the line at specific points, especially when turning corners. The trolley caravan would grind to a halt, and the conductor of the power car would have to try to juggle the pole with its wheel back into position before the journey could continue. One such hazard point for the number 6 line was at the Rindermarkt, shortly before the train reached Saint Peter's Church, the oldest house of worship in the city, and directly adjacent to the municipal focal point at Marienplatz, where City Hall stands. In those days, the streetcar went up Sendlinger Strasse to the aforementioned Marienplatz, then past the elegant shops on Weinstrasse and Theatinerstrasse to Ludwigstrasse, continuing on through the university district and the artists' colony of Schwabing. Every morning, the passengers of the 7:30 car (back then usually the same cast of characters, including the conductor) would wait for the familiar interruption by Saint Peter's, where the conductor would get out, maneuver the rod back in place, and return to his position of supreme authority in the car. Then he'd pull the bell rope and, as the crowning glory of this ritual, intone his proclamation, beginning in highfalutin', ever so proper German, "Ge-rade an die-ser Stelle," and then segueing with an irate accelerando into his local dialect, to wit, "hauts uns doch jedsmoi des Stangerl raus" (which well-meaning English subtitles might render more or less as "at this self-same po-si-tion, that consarned rod gits knocked smack-dab off the wire").

Somewhat farther north, on the way to Schwabing, one of these conducting originals would raise his voice and call out a station in a highly compressed description that would have even semanticists with advanced academic degrees blinking in confusion: "Nexstopadalsiesunifarestage!" This contraction, when broken down into its myriad component parts told the more initiated passengers that at the next stop, we would reach the junction of Adalbertstrasse, site of the Siegestor (a "Victory Gate" then commemorating the German victory in the 1870–71 war with France, partially destroyed in World War II, rebuilt with the war damage deliberately left in clear evidence, and now rededicated to peace), where the university had its main buildings, and then the trolley would pass the border to the next fare stage where the price of rides from certain earlier stops went up.

In my second period of "choirmaster" years in Munich I became a regular user of the number 7 line to Milbertshofen, a less than upmarket district north of Schwabing. In December, at the time of the Angelus services, which began at six o'clock in the morning, the weather was often so cold that in the then unheated cars, the trip resembled nothing so much as a polar exploration. Probably no one would have been surprised to find the trolley drawn by a team of straining Alaskan huskies with the conductor in a fuzzy sealskin parka cracking his whip over their heads and urging them on with salty Munich dialect imprecations.

In the winter of 1929, temperatures plummeted to record lows of around 30° below zero Celsius, about 22° below Fahrenheit. At 5:30 A.M. a mailman and myself were the only passengers on the route from Sendlinger Tor past the Main Railroad Station and on up Augustenstrasse and Schleissheimerstrasse. The conductor, the mailman, and I, three heavily clad figures, stomped our feet uninterruptedly to combat the cold. Of course the temperature was conversation topic number one. The moderator of this symposium and its distinguished guest speaker both rolled into one was the conductor. Treading from one foot to the other, he declaimed: "Now then, them scientists and researchers done did a whole mess of studies and come up with the conclusion . . ." A short walk to the other end of the car, a tug on the bell rope: "Next stop Gabelsbergerstrasse!" Then back to us: "They done figgered out that we're headed plumb into a new Ice Age, just like the one they had thousands of years ago, where there warn't nothin' but snow an' ice all over the place. How d'you like them apples?" Another saunter to the other end of the car: "Next stop Schellingstrasse." Ding-dong. "And one o' them Ice Ages is zeroin' in on us agin. Picture it, the whole dang shebang, all o' Bavaria up to its armpits in ice, no trees, no trails no more—all them mountains slam-bang iced and snowed up." Back to the rear of the car: "Next stop Josefsplatz!" Ding-dong. Back to us: "You come gallavantin' back to Munich and walk down Kaufingerstrasse, but don't expect to see no trolley tracks, 'cause they ain't gonna be none there, so there ain't gonna be no streetcars on 'em neither, nothin' but heaps o' snow right up the ying-yang! From Maximilianstrasse down to the Platzl, you won't even know where in tarnation you is at." Segue. "Next stop Hohenzollern-strasse." Ding-dong. "Ye'll have to dig yer way through to the Hofbräu-haus and then burrow through to them stacks of beer mugs, but you ain't never gonna get diddly-squat out o' them barrels o' brew, coz they'll all be frozen solid inside likes as how you're gonna have to chip off yer beer with a dad-blamed ice axe . . ." And so continued this bleak peroration right down to the Milbertshofener Kanal. Nobody got on the tram anywhere all along the route, and nobody got off, but every stop was duly announced in stentorian tones, and the bell rope was regularly jerked on. At the end of Schleissheimer Strasse, at the canal, the postman, who had not uttered a single word up to that point, made a move to get off the trolley. As he opened the door, we got the feeling he wanted to grace us with a parting re-mark, add just one point of summation to the gloom-ridden prediction we had just heard. Then he turned slowly in parting, his eyes gazing into nowhere, and from his lips emerged a resigned "Yes, indeedy dog, our days sure is numbered!"

For somebody with my wide array of interests and a fair degree of inde-cision as to which to pursue, there could have been no better person for a mentor at this stage of my life than Matthäus Römer, who had come to singing, as I would eventually do, by a fairly circuitous route. A true intel-lectual, Römer began his adult life by taking a doctorate in comparative lin-guistics and was so proficient in the field that he was appointed by the Royal House of Wittelsbach, the reigning Bavarian dynasty, to serve as language teacher to the princes and princesses in the palace in addition to his duties as a professional educator. He then met and married a rather well-to-do lady, who was so impressed by his singing (a pastime he was pursuing purely for the fun of it at the time) that she subsidized a move to Paris, where he would be able to study with the paramount vocal teacher of that era, the eminent Polish tenor Jean De Reszke.

De Reszke was the scion of a musical family, initially trained in singing along with his younger brother and sister, basso Édouard and soprano Joséphine, by their mother, who obviously knew her craft so well that her three children were all propelled via further studies with eminent Italian maestri into major international careers. One of those maestri, Antonio Co-togni in Rome, formed a significant link in the apostolic succession of vocal art. A major baritone in his home country, with a repertoire that ranged from Enrico in *Lucia di Lammermoor* to Telramund in *Lohengrin,* he went on to teach such sterling vocalists of the next generation as Beniamino Gigli, Mariano Stabile and the De Reszkes. Jean had one of those dream

careers: starting as a baritone in 1874, then moving on, at his brother's urging, to a tenor repertoire encompassing just about every role imaginable
from bel canto parts and the leads in the Meyerbeer blockbusters all the way
to principal Wagnerian roles in the largest and most prestigious opera
houses in the world, where he was renowned for his good looks, his majestic bearing, his equally impressive acting ability and musicianship, and his
incredibly versatile, rock-solid vocal technique. He then retired at the
height of his fame after only twenty-eight years on stage to continue his
musical activity as a vocal teacher in Paris and Nice, where he died in 1925.
Several of his many pupils went on to prestigious careers of their own, including such luminaries as the great Moravian tenor Leo Slezak, American
soprano Alma Gluck, English soprano Dame Maggie Teyte, the popular
American baritone Richard Bonelli, and, toward the end of his teaching
career, a Brazilian lyric-coloratura soprano who starred at the Metropolitan
Opera for fifteen years: Bidú Sayão. Another one of De Reszke's American
pupils, a contralto from Nashville, Tennessee, by the name of Sarah Jane
Walker, had not only a distinguished career of her own, but also wielded
a seminal influence on two other careers. Married to a Swede by the name
of Charles Cahier and performing, as she did throughout her career, as
Madame Charles Cahier, she appeared in Copenhagen as Azucena in *Il
trovatore* with a young local baritone named Lauritz Melchior, whom she
encouraged to become a heroic tenor, helping launch what was arguably
the most significant career in that voice category ever. In later years, teaching in Philadelphia, she was impressed by a young contralto in that city and
provided one of the first helping hands that led to the legendary career of
Marian Anderson—just as Matthäus Römer had offered me my initial vocal
inspiration.

It was this impressive background of an advanced academic education
plus the solid underpinning of his work with De Reszke that Matthäus
Römer brought to his training of a young Munich beginner who wasn't all
that enthusiastic about singing in the first place. Ultimately Römer would
have a job convincing me to follow the path that—as subsequent years have
proven beyond doubt—must have been foreordained.

Dr. Römer initially accepted, without much comment, my zeal to keep
making progress on the organ; he knew that I wanted to hang on to my
church job, not least because of the couple of marks it produced. My attendance at the music academy also found his silent concurrence, probably because he thought the expansion of my basic musical knowledge and ability
(along with my organ studies, I was also continuing my piano lessons)
would be useful for my future singing career, indeed, perhaps essential. One
day, however, he made it unmistakably clear that I couldn't go on like this.
"Keep your church job for the time being, in heaven's name, but stop

studying the organ. You're going to have to make up your mind what you want to be: a singer or a musician." And I let him talk me into it. With a rather heavy heart, "I hung my dream of making music," as I always put it, "on the nearest hook and became a singer instead." Only a seeming contradiction: of course I knew that a singer also has to be a musician! Römer was also the one who taught me that a singer must first regard his voice as an instrument with which he is making music. I've always been grateful to him for not holding my initial, slight reluctance toward the singing profession against me. He himself was the essence of a musician: primarily a recital and oratorio singer, he devoted far less of his career to singing opera.

A significant development for Römer had been his engagement at Bayreuth, where he sang Parsifal in the 1909 Festival under the musical direction of Karl Muck. My teacher's lifelong artistic friendship with Siegfried Wagner dated back to this time, a connection from which I would eventually profit. Through Römer's intercession I was allowed to audition for Siegfried Wagner in 1930, shortly before his death. He listened to me with great interest and mentioned the Herald in *Lohengrin* as one possibility for me in Bayreuth in the near future. (The "near future," however, took more than twenty years to come, due not so much to Siegfried's passing but to political developments.) And so it was quite natural that Römer guided my interest right from the beginning more toward oratorio and recital singing. I continued to retain this approach for a long time in my early years. Because opera didn't mean much to me, I displayed very little ambition to learn as many new roles as possible, especially as I had my problems with acting. Perhaps it wasn't just sheer clumsiness; it was the attitude of the time toward everything that happened on the stage.

Today's audiences would have a hard time even imagining the hammy goings-on that took place on the operatic stage in those days. There are any number of learned essays discussing the revolution in taste that took place after the end of World War II, and the radical change this development brought about on the operatic stage. Especially from the point of view of the operatic actor, a major readjustment was called for. Progressive stage directors—the foremost of the ones I experienced was Wieland Wagner—gave the impetus for opera singers finally to begin comporting themselves like human beings on the stage and not like hyperactive marionettes. Of course, even in those days there were some theatrical personalities amongst the singers. I've already mentioned a few, but they were more the exception than the rule. Today I am more certain than ever that my disinclination toward opera had its origins in this trend. And my initial insecurity in acting was largely anchored in my dissatisfaction with this traditional style.

Yet my rejection of the way opera was being presented in those days in no way impeded my love of the other performing arts. This love had been sparked back in my school days, when one of my classmates took me home to meet his parents. My friend's family, the Oldenburgs, owned a renowned publishing company and maintained a kind of cultural salon, where many people in the arts would get together, discuss artistic matters, and frequently perform little concerts in the Oldenburg living room, often accompanied by the lady of the house, my friend's mother, who was quite an accomplished pianist. She was the one who first introduced me to the art of the song recital and the classical lieder repertoire, as exemplified by the great works composed for this genre by Schubert, Brahms, Schumann, and the rest. Richard Strauss was a family friend and frequent guest, as Johannes Brahms and Robert Schumann, they told me, had been when earlier generations of the family welcomed them to their home.

With these early impressions of classical music fixed in my heart and mind, I began taking advantage of the vast cultural life the city of Munich had to offer—and still does. I loved every kind of concert, orchestral, instrumental, solo recital, especially art song concerts, and I was an enthusiastic theater lover. There, too, my teacher had pointed me in the right direction, saying, "Don't go to the opera too often. Look at the actors, how they walk, how they move, not just in the classics, in the modern plays, where they portray characters drawn from everyday life. That way you can learn whatever you need to know."

His ardent intercession and demand that I concentrate fully on studying singing were followed by an entire year of the most intensive work. We filed away at technical vocal problems, but his greatest effort was to teach me that technique must never be allowed to be an end in itself. Rather, for all its importance, it remains a means to an end. "What you have to learn is the realization that the alpha and omega of singing are founded on breathing, in the command of this most important element of a vocalist's craft. Whoever breathes properly is well on the right way." How often, even today, do I find myself thinking of his golden words: "The phonetic command of speaking is a significant part of vocal technique. Singing and speaking, harmonically unified, are like the prerequisites for a good marriage."

Actually, I didn't work with my teacher more than two and a half years before I went off to start my first engagement, but this relatively short training period was followed by twenty-two years of work together during the summer months, between engagements.

Now, how did this contract offer come about? In the spring of 1930 I was hired to sing in a small chorus in a performance of Hindemith's *Lehrstück*. The baritone soloist cast as the chorus leader fell ill, and I was offered an opportunity to take over for him. I learned the small part in two days and made my first public appearance in Munich on the stage of the famous Tonhalle (later destroyed in the Second World War). Fortune smiled on this debut by vouchsafing me a highly renowned conductor in the person of Hermann Scherchen, who guided me through the concert with great care and affection, as if carrying me in his hands. Afterward he asked me what I was planning to do with my voice. Before I could answer, he interrupted me, "Don't let people mislead you into bellowing opera. You'll only become an artist on the concert stage." Yet another one poking at my open wounds! When I told Römer about this, he really got annoyed: "He's a fine one to talk! A singer can only make a name for himself and earn a living with opera. Don't let anyone drive you crazy. Stay right on the path you've started on."

So my first appearance was a success, and there was even a positive write-up in a Viennese newspaper, which the director of the Stadttheater in Troppau just happened to read. He came to Munich, and I sang for him, whereupon he offered me a contract. The monthly salary was the princely sum of two hundred marks, but by way of compensation, the contract proudly described my function in the theater as "First Heroic Baritone"—as if the Troppau theater had a second or third heroic baritone.

My teacher was the first one who immediately advised me to sign. "You've got to put what you've learned into practice. You can't go on living at your poor mother's expense. You know enough to get you started, and the rest you can learn from experience over the next twenty years." And so I signed. A couple of weeks previously, I had turned twenty-one, thus becoming "of age." My signature under that contract was the first legal use of my adult status.

To this day I don't know where the self-assurance and confidence in my abilities came from. How many objections and warnings I had to listen to back then (and indeed later on). "It's a crime against such a youngster; he'll see where that'll take him." These and similar ones resounded among the Cassandra cries.

Of course, it might all have gone awry, as I clearly realized later on, but the way things developed justified my teacher's attitude. Fortunately, that so many of these early developments took place despite my justifiable reluctance to get involved in a stage career was to hold me in good stead for years to come. I never developed the kind of unrealistic ambition that has led so many other singers to take on assignments they are not ready for, or perhaps never will be ready to face. In my case, I never pushed my career beyond my own assessment of my abilities, which doubtless kept me out of many a dead end that might have put a premature quietus on my career.

With the die cast and the contract with Troppau signed, I took advantage of the interim period to learn the new roles I had been assigned and then work on them with Römer. It was then that it really became clear to me what a great help Römer was. There is no way anyone can stress strongly enough what an important part in the training of a singer the selection of

Original-Aufnahme aus dem Festspielhaus-Atelier R. Papenhoff

Dr. Römer
als „Parsifal".

3.2. In 1909, the year I was born, Matthäus Römer sang the title role in *Parsifal* at the Bayreuth Festival with Karl Muck on the podium. Years later, he would become my teacher, my friend, and the most significant influence in my life.

the right teacher is. You can hardly expect a young, inexperienced person to pass judgment on the suitability of a vocal teacher. He has to rely totally on the judgment and advice of more experienced individuals.

Experience teaches us that it is often the second or third teacher who can really show us the way to success in our training. It is and remains a question of luck. As in so many other important phases in my artistic life, fate was especially kind to me in the selection of my teacher. In previous comments, I gave plenty of space to the person of Dr. Matthäus Römer because it is gratitude and admiration that prompt my memory of that gentleman to this day.

My beloved grandmother lived to witness my first years as a professional singer, and there was only one point in time where she felt perhaps her early

enthusiasm for my musical ambitions might have been a mistake. This came
about during a break between my first season in Troppau and my second in
Breslau, when I visited home and enthusiastically related all the adventures
I had experienced to my family, using a hint of a Silesian dialect I had picked
up on the streets of Breslau. When I stepped out of the room for a moment,
as one of my aunts later related, Grandmother suddenly put on a skeptical
frown, and muttered, more to herself than anyone else: "A Preiss is er
gwordn!" In her eyes, I had abandoned my Bavarian heritage with my
newly acquired Breslau dialect and become the ultimate anathema in the
eyes of any true Southern German: a Prussian!

Before I traveled to the site of my first engagement I was invited to participate in a *Siegfried* performance on the occasion of the seven-hundredth
anniversary of the city of Lindau, to be held in that municipality's Nibel-
ungenhalle, to sing the role of Fafner. This was actually my first appearance
on an operatic stage, although we can hardly refer to it as an "appearance"
as this particular role is sung backstage. Fafner is a part for a low bass and
doesn't belong in my "Fach" at all, which is why this was a onetime event.
I am just mentioning this guest performance because I made the acquain-

3.3.   As a young singer from Prague visiting home in 1933. My maternal grandmother and
mother are on the left, and Bertl Rüttenauer, the aunt who gave me my first piano lessons,
is on the other side of the table. My maternal grandmother was a stolid lady who helped
pave the way for my career, then recoiled in horror when I briefly traded in my native
Bavarian dialect for a Silesian twang: "A Preiss is er gwordn!" (He's become a Prussian!)
she grumbled.

3.4. In later years, if anyone asked my mother if she was proud of her two sons, the reverend father and the musical artist, her lapidary reply was always: "Well, nobody ever asked me."

tance of a distinguished predecessor in the dramatic baritone category: Emil Schipper. He sang the role of the Wanderer in this performance.

This name meant quite a bit to the Munich music student. I knew that he was one of the best interpreters of Cardinal Borromeo in Hans Pfitzner's *Palestrina*. When, some ten years later, I assumed this role myself at the Vienna State Opera, and it became one of my favorite parts, we met again. Until his death in 1957 there was hardly one *Palestrina* performance in which he didn't come see me in my dressing room, and he always had words of praise for me—a rare case of generous recognition from a former colleague in the same voice category!

During my student years I met two other well-known Wagnerian baritones. One of them was the legendary Dutch singer Anton von Rooy; the other, the celebrated Wagner baritone at the Munich Court Opera at the beginning of the century, Fritz Feinhals. He had created the role of Borromeo at the world premiere of Pfitzner's *Palestrina*. Both of them heard me in a Munich student concert, and both came to the green room and had kind words for me. Feinhals said, "If you become an opera singer, make sure you always sing lieder in between opera performances." Right from the outset, this was the good advice I have followed all my life.

☙ Chapter 4 ❧

Troppau (in Czech, Oppava) was a small town with about forty thousand residents in what was Czechoslovakia back in 1930. Before the First World War, at the time of the Austro-Hungarian monarchy, it was part of Austrian Silesia. Troppau was one of those Sudeten German theaters that had served as springboards to success for a long line of actors and singers during their early years on stage. The theater, with its scant one thousand seats, lived on the enthusiasm of a small but loyal municipality, for which activities onstage and backstage, as well as outside this temple of the muses, ranked as one of the high points of social life, providing endless fodder for conversation all over town. I quickly felt completely at home there. The few actors and singers along with the members of the orchestra and chorus were a real family. Nothing could happen inside or outside the theater without its immediately being talked about everywhere.

My first role was the "Sprecher" in Mozart's *Die Zauberflöte*. I have no idea how much of the authority and dignity of this character I had been able to communicate. I just know that I was highly piqued when a local reviewer wrote that I lacked the wisdom for this role. In any event, I was motivated into writing a letter to this gentleman—the first and last letter I ever wrote to a critic. This severe adjudicator had exposed himself by writing that the lady singing the Queen of the Night had transposed her aria a whole tone down, which, of course, did not happen to be the case. How clever I thought I was when I wrote that I may perhaps have had insuffiicient wisdom for the Sprecher, but I was certainly wise enough not to make claims without having perfect pitch. I never received an answer from him, which may have been normal procedure, but later proved embarrassing to me.

On the whole, over the many years of my career, I can hardly complain about unfriendly reviews let alone out-and-out pans. Most artists claim they couldn't care less about bad reviews. I, however, find that dishonest; there is hardly anyone who isn't pleased with a good review or who doesn't get annoyed over a bad one. On the subject of write-ups, there is an anecdote that really should be inserted here, although the event actually occurred many years later: in 1948 and 1949 the great Erich Kleiber invited

4.1.   The very first operatic role I ever sang was the
Sprecher in Mozart's *Zauberflöte* during the 1930 season
in Troppau. It accompanied me throughout my career,
and I sang it one last time in 1990 to mark the sixtieth
anniversary of that debut.

me to take part in the Temporadas, the opera season in Buenos Aires. The
season there lasted six to eight weeks and took place in August and September. Being invited there shortly after the Second World War meant
quite a lot to many European artists; after years of doing without and the
horrors of the war, the mere fact of being able to eat one's fill was tanta-
mount to a celebration. Even among themselves, the artists developed a
close relationship to one another, and this feeling was reinforced by Erich
Kleiber's fatherly, amiable manner. We had lots of fun together, and often
sat together laughing and joking.

The morning after the *Don Giovanni* premiere we all got together, and
some of us complained about what they referred to as the unfriendly
write-ups. Erich Kleiber commented with a chuckle, "How can anyone
be so stupid as to get upset over a couple of dumb reviews. Follow my ex-

ample: I haven't read a critique in years. They just ruin the joy of your success. Listen, let's all go out to eat at El Sol tonight and not talk about the
performance any more." When I called up the Kleibers that evening to find
out exactly when this dinner was to take place, Kleiber's daughter answered
the phone and said to me: "I don't know what time you're supposed to
meet. Papito just went down to get the papers with the latest reviews." I
made sure everybody heard this story, and actually "Papito" became even
dearer to our hearts because of this little human frailty.

Back to Troppau in 1930. As the eight-month season progressed, I followed up the "wise" Sprecher by singing Alfio in *Cavalleria rusticana* and
Tonio in *Pagliacci*. I had a lot of fun "playacting," especially in *Pagliacci*,
even if I was still a pretty raw beginner. Nonetheless, it was an early effort.
After that there was a *Tannhäuser* with my first Wolfram and, bringing up
the end of the season, a *Siegfried* in which I was allowed to sing the Wanderer. A couple of weeks before the premiere I had just turned all of twenty-
two. Pure madness, said the experts before and afterward. They may have
been right. But it went well.

Much later, thirty years to be exact, Anja Silja sang Senta in *Der fliegende
Holländer*, and she wasn't much older than I had been in Troppau. And
whenever people got upset about her age, she used to say, "What about
Hotter? He was the same age when he sang the Wanderer. And he's still
singing, isn't he?" Well, there *is* a big difference between singing a heavy role
at the Municipal Theater in Troppau and singing one at the Festival Theater
in Bayreuth. Apart from that, there are no general rules for such things.

Alfred Jerger, the onetime *Charakterbariton* at the Vienna Opera and the
first Mandryka in the world premiere of Strauss's *Arabella* in 1933 in Dresden, once told me he sang Gurnemanz when he was a beginner of twenty.
And the American singer Regina Resnik was nineteen when she made her
debut at the New York City Opera as Santuzza in *Cavalleria rusticana*—not
to mention Astrid Varnay, who stepped in for an ailing Lotte Lehmann as
Sieglinde in *Die Walküre* with an all-star cast at the Metropolitan without
ever having sung on any stage in her life before; she was 23 at the time, and
her career, like Resnik's, lasted for decades! There are any number of similar
cases without any adverse consequences for the individuals involved, but I
am convinced there were, are, and always will be more than enough singers
who damage their vocal material irreparably with escapades of this kind.

Of course the level of artistry in the little Municipal Theater where I had
my first operatic engagement wasn't all that high, but the enthusiasm for
something new and the joy of my first experiences in the thrilling world of
the stage more than compensated for many of the drawbacks. Just before I
left Munich, my teacher told me, "You'll see, it will never be quite as wonderful as in your first year on stage." As the season then drew to a close (and

4.2.   One of my first assignments in Troppau was the daunting role of the Wanderer in Wagner's *Siegfried*— quite a challenge for a singer in his early twenties, but fortunately the theater was fairly small.

in moments of sober reflection I had to admit there had been plenty of mediocrity involved), it was hard for me to believe that prediction. Not until years later, when many of the events there became enshrined in my memory with a light golden tinge, did I begin to realize what Römer had been talking about. Nothing of what came afterward could be compared with the romantic glow of those first impressions.

And yet, on the grey days, when doubt dominated many other elements on the horizon, my old misgivings returned, and I began wondering if this really was the best choice of profession for me over the long run. Maybe I should go back to studying conducting while I still had a chance. After all, I was reluctant to believe in a big career, and I knew I wouldn't settle for a medium-sized or even a small one, not at all.

In my second year on stage, I let Georg Hartmann talk me into moving on to the Municipal Theater in Breslau, where he was the director. This was a larger ensemble in a larger house, which thus had higher expectations. Seventeen years later, Hartmann was again my boss, when for four years he ran the Munich State Opera, before turning over the reins in 1952 to another "Hartmann," Rudolf Hartmann, who headed the opera house in my hometown during a period of great success.

I never really felt happy or at home at the theater in the Silesian capital. That discontent may have had something to do with the fact that I found nobody there I could turn to, let alone lean on. While I may have picked up a couple of local expressions that upset my grandmother, Silesian dialect remained a closed book to a dyed-in-the-wool Bavarian like me. Beyond this, the roles I was cast in were mostly uninteresting for me. Nevertheless, there were a couple of fairly daunting challenges for this twenty-three-year-old singer, still a young cub in his second year on stage. My first assignment at the Breslau Opera was Jochanaan in Strauss's *Salome,* hardly a simple debut at a new house for an inexperienced singer: the role is vocally exposed and theatrically unusual in the static, almost motionless interpretation the composer saw as the right approach to the superhuman radiance of this young prophet, obsessed with his mission, just as Oscar Wilde had envisioned him. A characterization like this calls for appreciably more dramatic power than having to cram a lot of exaggerated pseudorealism into this character the way many a young stage director asks singers to do these days. The whole mystery of this ecstatically glowing zealot first became clear to me, when the composer was able to communicate his understanding of the character during a new production of his opera in Munich in 1937.

An additional enrichment of my repertoire that year was Amonasro in Verdi's *Aida,* a role I enjoyed singing and especially loved acting during the ensuing years, to such a degree that it became one of my most frequently performed characterizations.

And then there was an unforeseen, but quite successful excursion into the land of operetta. In Paul Abraham's *Die Blume von Hawaii* I was cast as Captain Stone, a sprightly baritone role with a couple of good musical numbers. The work had just come out, having received its world premiere back in 1931 in Leipzig. I believe the only reason I took on the offer was because I was aware that the Vienna Opera baritone Alfred Jerger, whom I so honored and admired, had so successfully created the part of Stone in the original production. This Viennese colleague, born back in the imperial times in Brno, a man with whom I often shared the stage in Vienna during the 1950s and 1960s, and a theatrical polymath, who conducted, staged productions, wrote libretti, and subsequently became director of that prestigious institution in the Austrian capital, was a magnificently versatile artist,

4.3.   It was in Breslau, in 1932, that I also sang the first of
many performances of Amonasro in Verdi's *Aida*. For quite
a few years, the soprano who sang my "daughter" was
generally older than I was.

a *Charakterbariton* of great proportions, a brilliant actor, and a clever, extremely witty man in the bargain—no wonder I got along so well with him
and learned so much from him. I will never forget the first time I saw him
on stage: in 1928 in Munich in Ernst Křenek's jazz opera *Jonny spielt auf*
(Jonny Strikes Up the Band). I can still see him as Jonny, singing "Nun ist
die Geige mein!" (Now the fiddle is mine!), leaping with a single bound on
top of the grand piano. An overwhelming experience for a young high
school student! Ten years later, when we were preparing a new *Arabella* in
Munich, Richard Strauss animatedly told me how Jerger had taken over the
part of Mandryka on short notice during the prerehearsal phase of the *Arabella* world premiere and had made a major contribution to the success of
this new opera. Many of the instructions Strauss and Clemens Krauss then
gave me during the 1939 *Arabella* rehearsals went back to the way Jerger had
originally understood and portrayed the role.

As far as the Breslau performance of *Blume von Hawaii* was concerned (the piece ran successfully some twenty times at the theater there), I look back on those days with great happiness. Not until later did I realize how important this operetta infidelity had been for me, for quite practical reasons. The interaction of singing, speaking, and dancing was an edifying interlude for the performer in me, who was still determined to keep learning as much as he could and had to. How often did the stage director—he was a buffo tenor in the house—have to urge me to stand straight! Tall and lanky as I was, I was constantly going around a little stooped over. Then he shoved a broomstick behind my back through my bent elbows—a very long rehearsal morning!

The leading lady in the operetta was an attractive Norwegian soprano who moved about the stage as if she owned it. Her name was Erica Darbo, and despite the fact that she was no longer a spring chicken, she had a tremendous radiance in performance. She gave me plenty of good advice for this unfamiliar world of operetta. And, she once told me an interesting story: already a well-known theatrical personality back in her Nordic homeland in her younger years, one day Darbo received a visit from a young, gorgeous woman, who introduced herself as a Norwegian actress. She had been invited to go to Hollywood to do some screen tests for a motion picture. She said that she liked my Norwegian colleague's name so much that she asked her permission to adopt it as her own. As she was an actress and her colleague a singer, she thought the same name would not be all that important. My colleague made it clear to her that this was quite out of the question. When the actress then refused to let up, she finally relented, but to make sure the names would not be letter-for-letter identical, she insisted the actress make a slight change in her name, to which the actress replied, "How about calling myself *Garbo* instead of Darbo?" My colleague agreed, and the young actress went on her way rejoicing. That's the story my Breslau colleague told me. She claimed that's exactly how it happened, yet I can't help wondering if her Norwegian actress admirer might have had anything to do with a Swedish actress who changed her name from Gustafsson to Garbo and went to Hollywood by way of Berlin—but then again, my colleague claimed it happened just as she said, and why should Madame Darbo have made the whole story up out of whole cloth?

At the Breslau Opera in 1931, there was one institution that no longer exists: the collection of oddballs and eccentrics who maintained a strange, off-the-wall existence in the atmosphere of a permanent ensemble. Everyone made fun of them behind their backs, yet they were not only accepted as coming with the territory, but actually regarded with great affection. There was, for example a basso buffo by the name of Wilhelmi, over sixty, and thus looked upon as downright ancient by us young whippersnappers. It was said that as the company Methuselah, he had a special clause in his decades-long contract allowing him, on account of an old bladder problem, to keep a veritable *pot de chambre* in his dressing room, available only to him, for use in between his appearances.

My dressing room was located directly next to his, and I can still hear the goings-on that took place in there when that bass-clef Orpheus had a performance. Immediately upon entering his dressing room, he would begin warming up with triad solfeggi, which took him from the lower depths up to the stratospheric heights of his range and then back again. While doing this he used a tuning fork, which he slapped with an audible metallic bang, then used the A that resounded as a tone to call in his dresser, a gentleman by the name of Beck. The acoustical result of this was then an extended "Böööööööööck," always resounding on that A—interspersed with some unrecognizable noises, which gave us the impression he was availing himself of the rights and privileges granted under the terms and conditions of his contract.

It once came to pass that another bass, housed with several other colleagues in a third dressing room, became annoyed with Wilhelmi's voluminous warming-up noises, and raised his bass voice in the familiar imprecation: "That Wilhelmi can kiss my . . . ," followed by the usual anatomical reference, a challenge that briefly hung in the air. For a brief moment, a pregnant silence dominated the scene. Then, however, the dressing room door of the imprecated one slowly opened, and he began striding at a stately pace, his held high, toward the room from which the fateful invitation had emitted. He stopped in the doorway to the other room, and uttered the self-controlled, yet theatrically wrathful reply: "I most certainly will not!" He then did an about-face and strode with the same dignity back to his own dressing room.

They had a baritone there, well past his prime, but still equipped with a healthy, serviceable voice, who would occasionally step in for an indisposed colleague, receiving a mere pittance for his efforts. One afternoon, he called me up and lamented, "I'm flat broke again. Look, you're scheduled for a Tonio in *Pagliacci* next week. How's about doing an old pal a favor and canceling? That would put a hundred in my pocket, and I'll split the take with you fifty-fifty." With a monthly take-home pay of 220 marks, I found the temptation almost irresistible. Today, almost seventy years later, I'm sure the expiration of the statute of limitations will allow me to clear my conscience and confess that I didn't even try to resist.

When Easter time rolled around, I was flabbergasted to discover that I would have to take over Amfortas in *Parsifal* on very short notice. In a single week, I learned this dream role by a kind of total immersion process, which marked my first collaboration with a musician from the United States, Weston S. Gales. His activity in Breslau actually marked the conclusion of a dis-

4.4.   After a year in Troppau, I moved on to the Silesian capital of Breslau. I hope the statute of limitations has passed on my peccadillo of dropping out of one performance of Tonio in *Pagliacci* so a semiretired colleague could earn a little money.

4.5.   During my first season in Breslau, I was given exactly one
week to learn the enormously difficult role of Amfortas in
Parsifal.

tinguished career, starting, as I had done, as an organist and a church choir
director, then moving on to a post as music director of the then newly established Detroit Symphony. After conducting assignments in American
and European capitals, he returned to the keyboard in his later years as an
opera coach, including a stint at the 1928 Bayreuth Festival, where he accompanied *Parsifal* rehearsals for no less an authority than Karl Muck. He
then took time off from a well-earned retirement to help out in the theater
in Breslau, where I was the beneficiary of his long years of experience. Mr.
Gales's tutelage helped me get the role memorized in the short time allot-
ted. Soon the music was wafting around my brain day and night, and I
began looking forward to the solemn event with keen anticipation and considerable inner reverence. There was no stage rehearsal, let alone an orchestra run-through, merely two hours on the rehearsal stage to provide me
with the bare essentials for my characterization of the afflicted monarch.

4.6.   In his younger years, he had been the first conductor of the Detroit Symphony Orchestra. Shortly before retiring, Weston S. Gales worked as a solo coach at the Breslau Opera, where he taught me the role of Amfortas in that fateful week. He was the first of many fine American musicians I would work with in my long career. Photo courtesy of Archives of the Detroit Symphony Orchestra.

Shortly before curtain time, I checked backstage for props. The Grail was an oversized metal goblet, which struck me as cumbersome and a far cry from celestial. I was then told that, at a given musical cue, I would have to flick a switch causing the interior of this mega-mug to glow with something short of divine light. I found the whole exercise unutterably profane. I gulped a couple of times, trying to force myself into the decorum I deemed appropriate to my solemn task and attempted to hoist the chalice with some vague semblance of devotional exhilaration. While I was engaged in this exercise, one of the electricians ambled over and, with the directness that has endeared stage crews to the artistic community from time immemorial, delivered the Silesian equivalent of "Damn shame that baby ain't full o' beer, ain't it?" With that, my beatific demeanor promptly evaporated, and it was all I could do to keep from cracking up.

The spring of 1932 had entered the land, and all and sundry began thinking about the end of the season and making plans for the one to follow. To everyone's surprise, young Hotter had developed somewhat more successfully than the people in the executive suite had expected: in short, Intendant Georg Hartmann saw himself called upon to cast this twenty-three-year-old tyro, in all seriousness, as Telramund in *Lohengrin* and even Hans Sachs in *Meistersinger.*

It was my good fortune that two older and wiser colleagues intervened and warned me most emphatically of the perils of taking on such demanding assignments at my more than tender age. The colleagues convinced me, and I turned both roles down. Hartmann blew his top and demanded the names of the people who had advised me to decline an offer the theater director deemed correct. Now I was accused of ingratitude and sent into exile. In practical terms this meant that all my interesting roles were expunged from the list. They tried to humiliate me by giving me only the very smallest of parts to sing, and even a couple in which I didn't utter a sound: pure extra parts, such as King Duncan in *Macbeth* and the Indian, Muff, in *The Bartered Bride.* My spirits hit rock bottom, and it seemed to be only a matter of time before I bade farewell to singing.

Then, again just at the right moment, fate took a hand.

The man cast as the father in *Hänsel und Gretel* fell ill a couple of days before the premiere. Somebody remembered that I was still around; I had all of two days to learn the part, and I was pushed out on stage after only a single rehearsal. The press and public pampered me and vouchsafed me a grand success. Quite unexpectedly a guest from Berlin named Richard Lert, a conductor at the State Opera "unter den Linden" in Berlin (and in private life the husband of author Vicky Baum), came to the performance and paid a visit to me in my dressing room afterward. He seemed quite impressed with my voice and suggested he might be able to arrange an audition for me at the Berlin Opera. I was pleased with this turn of events, without being particularly impressed. I still had no inkling of what would happen on that trip to Berlin.

Let me briefly remind you of the story I told at the beginning of this book: my remembrances of Paul Eger and his intervention into the progress of my Berlin visit. Instead of the Berlin Opera, a lucky star guided my path directly into the helpful arms of my Prague director and the two edifying apprentice years at the German Theater in that city.

In the spring of 1934, shortly before my Prague engagement came to an end, my esteemed fellow baritone and mentor, Rudolf Bockelmann, without knowing it, played the role of destiny; still under the impression of his successful work with me, he recommended me to the State Opera in Hamburg, the city where he himself had developed to star status. The result was the invitation for me to come to Hamburg and audition for the theater near the banks of the Elbe.

On March 20, 1934, then, I was sitting in the train from Prague to Hamburg. During the long journey I had enough time to think everything over in full detail and let the events of the previous years pass in review. Now it again occurred to me that Eger had only given me a two-year contract back in Berlin. Although I had established a good foothold in his theater, and the audience there clearly liked me, he had not expended a single syllable to talk me into staying in Prague. On the contrary: he urged me to move on. What an unusual attitude for a theater director to take toward a young beginner! Could he have been in cahoots with Bockelmann right from the beginning? Might the two of them have cooked all this up together? I wouldn't have put it past them.

In any event I was happy not to have concealed anything from him. Should Hamburg not pan out, I would still have been able to stay another year or two in Prague. My expectations with regard to Hamburg were thus not very high; I was more curious than enthusiastic. I also had my misgivings on account of the political situation.

The following day I sang on the rehearsal stage of the Hamburg Opera. Two gentlemen listened to me, then briefly conferred and asked me to come back around noon so they could hear my voice on the main stage. When I returned, I was told the main stage was not yet available, and so we went back to the rehearsal stage. By this time some eight gentleman had assembled, among them the intendant and the general music director. I recognized the latter by sight: Eugen Jochum. The gentlemen put their heads together, then one of them asked, "Have you already sung Alfio (*Cavalleria rusticana*) and Tonio (*Pagliacci*)?"

"Yes."

"Do you think you could sing those two roles at this evening's performance? We have these operas in the repertoire, and we'd like to hear you onstage."

I thought it over briefly. I had sung these parts some fifteen times. I agreed, and we took our leave of each other until that evening.

This was a development I truly had not expected. That afternoon I traveled down the Elbchaussee to Klein-Flottbek, as a Prague colleague had suggested. It was a glorious spring day. I sat in the sun, looking down at the

Elbe and the ships sailing by. I was overcome by an incredible sensation: If they want you here, that would really be something!

In the evening, as I sat already made up in the dressing room, the theater director came in and offered me a five-year contract. "We thought, with a contract backing you up you'd sing even better." My eye fell on the monthly salary for the first year. Without even trying to restrain myself, I said: "I'm afraid I can't sign for this amount."

"Why not?"

"I promised my director in Prague I wouldn't accept anything less than eight hundred marks a month."

Wordlessly, the director left the dressing room. In the intermission he returned and presented the rewritten contract. "Please send our kind regards to Mr. Eger, although we have yet to meet him. He certainly was quite a surprise to us."

It was also a great artistic success for me. I used the modest performance fee to treat myself to a sleeping car berth back to Prague and fell asleep in the best of moods. Previously I had called my mother in Munich and given her the news. She congratulated me; her voice sounded hoarse, but I could hear something like emotion in her words.

The engagement at the Hamburg State Opera marked a milestone in my career. As if spontaneously, a new chapter began. Here, at a renowned operatic institution, I had suddenly acquired a higher rank. The era of small roles and walk-ons was over. At the age of twenty-five I had moved up to what they call "a leading singer." Without noticing it, a change had taken place in my position vis-à-vis the other singers. All at once, I was no longer a beginner. And so my four-year period as an apprentice and journeyman drew to a close.

The decision to remain in Prague for two years proved wise. Unfortunately the political situation shut me off from any future contact with my so highly esteemed Paul Eger. He left Prague a year after I did. A deeply felt thanks from the distance of a few years would have been my heart's desire. I am happy at least to have erected a monument to him on these pages.

From an artistic point of view I had taken the only sensible advice. What about the political climate and its influence on personal and professional conditions? I still didn't have a clue to what degree my original misgivings were justified, and I looked forward to my first contacts in Hamburg with no small degree of distrust. Right up until the end of my time in Prague, everyone there was talking about the terrible situation in Germany. Throughout the entire year of 1933, a veritable cascade of fleeing immigrants had arrived in the Czech capital. And the things they had to report sounded anything but encouraging.

4.7. I sang my first Kurwenal in Wagner's *Tristan und Isolde* during the 1935 season in Hamburg; for many years thereafter this stalwart warrior held a special place in my heart.

4.8. Nowadays, baroque opera is all the rage, but back in the 1930s, we were already performing classics of the early eighteenth century. In this 1935 production of Handel's *Julius Caesar,* I sang the title role.

When, one week after starting work at the city on the Elbe, I was chatting with one of the other singers in the company, I played dumb and asked
innocuously how much the altered political situation had affected theatrical
life. My opposite number at first expressed himself in fairly vague, evasive
terms. He said this sort of thing played a subordinate role in a city like
Hamburg with all its international trade relations. Then he moved in closer,
looked fleetingly to the left and right—a gesture I would see more and
more and, indeed, learned to use myself—looked me right in the eye and
said in a somewhat muted tone: "We had some reconnaissance done on you
in Prague and found out you can be absolutely relied on. At our theater, you
just have to watch out for a few people: two bureaucrats in the administra-
tive office, one of the soloists, two members of the chorus, a gentleman on
the technical crew and one or two men in the orchestra. So watch your step
with them; you can talk freely and openly with everyone else."

That's what it was like in those days in Germany. It took me a little time
to get the full impact of how bitter earnest the whole political situation was.
Meanwhile, after more than seventy years, hardly anybody still remembers—
or wants to.

Through my many contacts with young people, I keep hearing how
earnestly the younger generation wants to know what was really going on
during the early years of the Nazi regime. This is why I'd like to report a bit
about what was happening in the theater sector. To do this, I have to repeat
what I already mentioned and what new friends soon confirmed. The whole
attitude toward political developments was in fact somewhat more moder-
ate and freethinking in Hamburg than it was elsewhere. Of course, many
members of the top Nazi echelons were constantly trying to convince me to
join the party. Remarkably enough, my blunt refusal to do so was not held
against me. Even in later years nobody put any pressure on me in this regard. I presume my elevated position at one of the country's major operatic
institutions helped me there; the privilege was *not* accorded artists at
smaller theaters or in subordinate positions. In the eleven years, from 1934
to 1945, during which I worked as a singer under the Nazi regime, I never
had any problems with political authorities in the practice of my profession.

Moving on, I will not recount the progress of my life chronologically.
Too many thoughts go through my mind and often too intensely as I move
from phase to phase. I hope some digressions will be permitted, because my
life was also interrupted time and again by unexpected, new developments;
I'd like to report on these as close as I can to the way I lived them.

Like my period in Prague, the time in Hamburg was marked by encounters with great and often highly influential personalities. I'd like to
begin with Wilhelm Furtwängler. During my student days in Munich I still
hadn't had a chance to see him on the podium. But in Breslau I did see and

hear him once, and was fascinated beyond measure. It may perhaps baffle the reader that the individuals who take pride of place in my memory are largely conductors. The answer is simple: for a musician, the influence of conductors and—yet another stroke of good fortune for me—composers makes the most difference.

Of course, there were many theater directors, stage directors, and singing colleagues without whom my development and the progress of my professional and personal destiny would have been unimaginable. But Furt-wängler was one of the greatest individuals whose acquaintance I made relatively early in my life and career. Much has been written about Furt-wängler both as an artist and a human being—and much of it does not do him justice. I experienced him as one of those impressive musical interpreters, whose fascination does not come across half so much in mechanical sound reproduction as it did in person.

His conducting technique was something all its own. At any event, I was aware of very few people for whom the expression "radiate" was as appropriate as it was for him. At the end of the day, it's the results that count. Only a very few have the gift of bringing the spiritual quality of music into the foreground so well as he.

The first time I sang under Furtwängler was in a *Siegfried* performance at the Paris Opéra, a few years before the war. Because of a number of unfortunate circumstances—a precipitously revoked release from Hamburg, canceled flights—I was unable to get to Paris until just one hour before the beginning of the performance. Under duress, Furtwängler declared his readiness to allow me to perform without having rehearsed with me. Shortly before the beginning of the performance he came into my dressing room, cordially shook my hand and remarked with charming gruffness: "Don't look down at me too often. I'll keep up with you."

Several boulders were lifted from my heart at that moment. I had silently prepared myself to face an irate maestro, and now such a decent gesture!

It was a thrilling, electrifying performance. Siegfried was sung by one of my favorite colleagues: Max Lorenz! And as Brünnhilde I saw and heard the famous French soprano Germaine Lubin. What an artist!

During the second act there was an unusual, very amusing incident: granted, the appearance of Fafner, provoked by Siegfried's horn call, is generally a fairly comical interruption of the story. The horn here was blown by a musician backstage. The entire solo, generally feared because of its exposed register, ends on a high note, which in the Paris performance turned into a derailment—a phenomenon musicians refer to as a "crack." At that moment I was listening in the wings. Then I heard somebody call out from the audience: *"Mais Monsieur Rochet, c'est scandaleux!"* Monsieur Rochet was the opera director and was seated in the proscenium box, visible to one and all. I found it indescribably funny to call down shame on the director of a theater because an unfortunate musician had blown a clinker.

This Paris performance was now followed by a number of other appearances on the concert or opera stage. In 1941, Furtwängler was the musical director of a new production of *Fidelio* at the Vienna State Opera. I was Pizarro. During the fourteen-day rehearsal period we were both staying in the same hotel, where he often invited me to join him for a meal. Once something quite unexpected occurred: after an orchestra rehearsal of the first act, he walked across the stage, saw me standing there and came over to me. "Were you out in the house just now?"

"Yes."

"Tell me, in the Leonore-Rocco duet, Leonore twice sings the phrase '*Ich bin es jetzt nur nicht gewohnt.*' [I'm just not used to it yet.] There's this *ritardando* in the repeat—was that too much?" I could hardly believe my ears: the famous Furtwängler was asking me, a young, still not very well known singer whether he had taken a *ritardando* properly. (In fact, he sometimes did take that passage pretty slowly.) He interrupted my silence impatiently, "Well, tell me, yes or no?"

"My goodness, maybe it *was* a bit too much . . ."

He abruptly turned aside and was gone. The next day he came shooting past me on the stage, suddenly stopped, and asked with a smirk, "Well, was it better this time?" And disappeared toward the pit.

I was impressed by the way he handled direct personal relationships: he could laugh heartily and take enormous delight in unexpected developments in the theater or on the concert stage. Once he invited me to a concert with the Berlin Philharmonic. It must have been in 1939, shortly before the start of the war. That evening they were giving Pfitzner's Little Symphony, (which sounds a bit like Haydn) its world premiere. I sang Pfitzner songs and the baritone narration from *Der arme Heinrich.* Shortly before the beginning of the concert I saw him standing in front of a full-length mirror in the artists' dressing room. He tossed a critical glance at his dress suit and the grooming of his already somewhat thinning hair. Then he raised his right hand with the baton and let it slide down with that famous zigzag motion of his. After that, he nodded amusedly at me in the mirror and said: "Conducting always does involve just a tad of histrionics, too, don't you think?"

How pleasant he seemed with his bright blue eyes—which could change their expression spontaneously if an attractive female happened into his line of vision! He could sometimes come up with the most masterly turn of phrase when the issue was musical interpretation. Some of those illustrious phrases are engraved on my memory. My students or master class participants know them already and always chuckle when an oldster like me repeats them. Furtwängler used to say, for example: "*Forte* in music does not mean noise, just as *piano* does not mean weak." Or: "A strong, loud tone must not be like a hammer stroke, it must always *vibrate* like the clapper in a bell." His statement about "continuing to make music," "not stopping," or "not interrupting" a melodic line was also famous: "Don't let yourselves be tempted to interrupt the music at the bar line. Bar lines are there to remind you of the rhythm, the beat. If you've got rhythm in your blood, just imagine the bar lines are just written in pencil; you can erase them any time you want them, when you don't need them any more."

Furtwängler could also be fickle. He was inclined to heed insinuations from people who didn't know what they were talking about. Especially toward the end of his life, many people he had once trusted had to suffer the consequences of this attitude. I, too, lost all contact with him in his later years.

Years later Walter Legge, one of the most experienced masters in the art of perfection in recording, played some of my records for Furtwängler shortly before his death, and he said he was clearly impressed.

At the Hamburg Opera, right from the outset, there was a whole series of new roles, which greatly enriched my repertoire. Pizarro, which I had just sung to replace other singers in Prague, was now given to me in a new production with a goodly number of rehearsals. I still had problems with the dialogue, especially because this *Fidelio* production was in a very conventional style.

One great source of pleasure was my collaboration with the "general" of the house, Eugen Jochum. I also soon adjusted to the mentality of the average Hamburg citizens. I didn't find the difference between southern and northern lifestyles as extreme as so often claimed. On the contrary, there seem to be many parallels. As in Bavaria, people there tend to be close-mouthed and reserved and do not instantly seek to make contact with others. Nevertheless my relationship with the south German Jochum rapidly became very good, and in the circle of my singing colleagues I was soon accepted as a friend and partner.

There was something there that belongs in every good ensemble theater: we had real so-called house stage directors, people who belonged to the house, as the name implies. Especially for the younger, not so experienced singers, it was important to work with people who were constantly available. Here it was Rudolf Zindler and Oskar Fritz Schuh. Both of them also directed new productions. Of these two men, it was Zindler to whom I owe a great deal; over time he was able to help me get over my inhibitions about acting. It is no secret that very few singers are born actors. Setting aside the fundamentally hopeless cases, there are many who are quite well suited for "acting," but who first have to learn that singing opera means, right from the beginning, never separating singing and acting. So many of today's stage directors know absolutely nothing of the physical act of singing. And members of today's generation of young singers are often forced into assignments they are simply not mature enough to tackle; their vocal technique is still only semideveloped.

How many people with above-average talent and equipped with suitable and valuable vocal material are condemned to failure just because during their training very little emphasis, or none at all, is placed on the fact that technically correct singing is predicated on good speaking technique?

After a half-year in Hamburg, fortune smiled down on me with special warmth. It sent me what Friedrich Rückert once called "my good spirit." As I write these lines, nearly seventy years have passed since I met my wife. Once again I had the luck to encounter a human being who, at just the right time, gave my life a push in the right direction. My future wife put in her appearance just at the point in time when I was about to conclude my years of training and finally resolve all doubts about my choice of profession.

Helga Fischer, the woman with the classically beautiful countenance, was an acting student. Her esteemed teacher was then director of the Drama Theater in Hamburg, Ernst Leudesdorff. She was just taking her first steps on the boards of the Thalia Theater. When after a couple of months we decided to turn our budding relationship into one for life, she made it unmistakably clear that she was only prepared to take this step if I were agreeable to her continuing to train as an actress. An actress by my side was just what the doctor ordered for me, especially as I realized with joy that she had a heart for music.

She shared the rehearsal period of a couple of new productions with all the tensions thereunto appertaining, where joyful expectations regularly came crashing down into bitter disappointments. She suffered along with me when a new character failed to develop as the stage director had envisioned it, and shared with me the joy and satisfaction when things came off successfully.

In my few years of professional experience I had already acquired considerable insight into the life of my colleagues and had begun to learn what an important role the people in an artist's inner circle play. The actual work isn't done only in the rehearsals. Outside the theater, during our leisure hours, often until late at night, when the things we've worked on in rehearsal begin to take form in the imagination that comes with solitude, doubt is banished, and determinations and decisions come to fruition. A suitable conversational partner, who inspires discussions, influences new solutions, and thus participates in the emergence of a new character makes a viable contribution to artistic creativity. And so it was something like an organic development when my future companion one day surprised me

4.9.   Fortune really smiled on me in Hamburg when I met and married a local beauty by the name of Helga Fischer. The wedding took place on July 7, 1936, at the Blutenburg Chapel on the outskirts of Munich, with my brother Karl celebrating the Nuptial Mass and extending the blessings of the Church on the happy couple.

with the decision that she had decided to give up her own theatrical plans. As she said with gallows humor, *one* maniac in the family was quite enough.

The "maniac" in question appreciated this decision, very much as a matter of fact, and still does. How understandable it was, when my wife over the course of the years—especially in times when it becomes all too obvious that not "all the budding dreams of a young heart ripen into maturity," as Goethe's Prometheus puts it—had her doubts as to whether this greathearted decision had been worth the sacrifice. Now, after some seventy years, with Helga no longer present on this earth, there is no doubt in my mind that a very benevolent star must have shone down on my life with her advent. Perhaps it was this deep mutual respect that helped us avoid those pitfalls that can so often lead to disaster. From the point of view of the artist and the often nerve-killing existence of a singer, I know that I owe much of what I managed to accomplish to my wife. It really is a heroic challenge for a woman to spend her life by the side of a singer. When I think of the worries the war and postwar years brought with them, my wife has certainly earned the place she surely now holds in paradise.

4.10. And we remained a devoted, happy couple for sixty-two years until Helga passed away in 1988. Among her myriad qualities, Helga possesed the sublime faculty of expressing criticism straightforwardly without ever being hurtful or demeaning.

Once, soon after the end of the war, she was able to enjoy a look back into the land of her youthful dreams of happiness as an actress, when the two of us mounted the concert podium together to collaborate in a performance of the fairy tale "Die schöne Magelone." She recited Ludwig Tieck's tales, and I sang the Brahms romances based on them. Bavarian Radio also recorded the event. When we later asked for a copy of the recording we were told: oh, sorry, that tape was unfortunately erased. Oh, the miracle of technology!

The Hamburg years were marked by those ongoing experiences I was able to gather in the warm nest of an ensemble family. I know that the benign effects of such a good atmosphere cannot be weighed against the profitable opportunities a modern singer has on the international jet-set route. It also leads nowhere to discuss the relative merits of the two systems: ensemble theater and permanent guest appearance activity. The up-and-coming, successful singing star has no choice; he is offered no alternative to today's international operatic life.

How often have I railed against the fate that vouchsafed me a singer's life that, before reaching its apex and the prospect of an international career, was painfully interrupted—perhaps brutally thwarted—by the horror of five years of war and ten difficult postwar years (not to mention missing out on the blessings of the recording industry). The long-playing record was not introduced until the mid-1950s, at a point in time when I already had twenty-five years of professional experience behind me. Despite all of this, I am happy to have lived and worked in the era of the ensemble opera. And the Hamburg period is certainly a significant part of that time.

When I look back on the artistic impressions connected with my work in the Hanseatic city, my mind's eye automatically focuses on the image of a man it was a pleasure to have known and worked with. I am speaking of the composer Hans Pfitzner. He came to Hamburg in early 1935 to look after a new production of his first opera, *Der arme Heinrich,* and to conduct it himself. It isn't easy to describe Pfitzner in a way that will justly bring together the proportions of his artistic significance and the impression he made as a human being.

Right from the beginning I was struck by the scope of his education and by his unusual intellectual approach to all those elements that come together to form what music is—not only his own but the whole classical world of music, insofar as he accepted it with his extremely critical taste. He expected the highest standards from his artistic collaborators, and yet was equally ready and willing to subject himself to the same stringent demands. Pliability and tolerance were not his long suit; no wonder he often had trouble coming to an agreement with other people. He was regarded as overcritical and—because he was anything but willing to make conces-

4.11. The 1935 Hamburg production of *Der arme Heinrich,* Hans Pfitzner's first opera, was also my first encounter with the composer whose work and personality would be indelibly imprinted on my memory.

sions—also as stiff-necked. His belief in the ideal in art was boundless and unshakable, almost unworldly. That was why he had one problem after another in relations with others, especially when the subject was music. Oddly enough I never had any problems in my own collaboration with him. He seemed to like me. I accepted his peculiarities, not to mention his quirkiness, and always tried to find some kind of access to his extraordinary approach to artistic matters.

After a longish collaboration I began to understand why he had a reputation for being such a difficult individual in operatic and concert circles. It was even rumored that the relationship between the two great contemporary composers, Strauss and Pfitzner, was not exactly unmuddied. In fact, Pfitzner was alleged to have snarled, "If Richard, then Wagner, if Strauss, then Johann."

For someone who knew them as well as I did, both professionally and personally, this animosity was thoroughly understandable. Vis-à-vis the worldly, easy-to-get-along-with, invariably charming creator of the *Rosenkavalier,* the Moscow-born, perpetually mistrusting, somewhat distant, great, mystic-lyrical German composer was at a disadvantage right from the start. Of course there had always been a whole series of stories people in musical circles uninhibitedly told about them with great delight and amusement. Meanwhile, several decades have come and gone, and many of those tales are forgotten. But why shouldn't today's musical generation have a chance to laugh or at least smile at some of the things that totally convulsed their forebears some eighty years ago?

In 1917, Pfitzner's opera *Palestrina* was given its highly successful world premiere at Munich's Prinzregententheater. Somebody mentioned to Richard Strauss that the composer had self-critically confessed in a private conversation that his work on the second act had been particularly difficult for him. Strauss's smug comment on this: "If composing is so hard for him, why doesn't he just give it up?" But the target of this irony was able to rise valiantly to the fray. In a discussion of Richard Strauss's compositions, the conversation turned to the *Alpine Symphony,* and Pfitzner remarked mockingly, "He must have picked up a hernia climbing one of those mountains." The reference is a pun: the German word for "hernia" is "Bruch," and there is a theme in the mountain climbing sequence of Strauss's symphony that is more than vaguely reminiscent of a theme in Max Bruch's famous violin concerto. Strauss, for his part, didn't take this at all amiss. In one orchestral rehearsal under the direction of the composer himself, he said to the musicians: "Gentlemen, we'll begin at the break" (in German, Bruchstelle).

The discussion on Pfitzner's attitude toward the Nazi regime has also not fallen silent after all these years. I am only in a position to pass judgment on those things that took place in my presence, and these were unambiguous. Is there a clearer language than the one uttered in the following anecdote?

When a couple of Nazis approached Pfitzner trying to convince him to write something for German young people, he replied sarcastically: "How about a pimpfony in bal major?" Another interesting play on words in German: "Pimpf" was the rank given to the youngest members of the Hitler Youth Movement, and Baldur (bal dur = bal major) was the given name of Baldur von Schirach, the Nazi bigwig who headed that movement.

During the rehearsal period for *Der arme Heinrich* he once asked in passing whether I knew any of his songs. When I replied in the affirmative, he invited me to sing some Pfitzner lieder along with some ballads by Carl Loewe in a radio broadcast, proposing that he accompany me himself at the piano. I was deeply touched by this high honor and readily agreed. He left the selection of the ballads to me. As I knew that he had orchestrated some of the Loewe ballads, I selected one of these orchestrated compositions, namely "Odins Meeresritt," presuming that he would find this work particularly pleasing. Well-prepared, I then looked forward to our first rehearsal, which was scheduled for Hamburg's Broadcasting House on Rothenbaumchaussee.

The previous evening I was sitting with some guests in my Hamburg apartment on Isestrasse, when the telephone rang around ten. I picked up the receiver, and without any greeting whatsoever I heard a well-known voice in the highest dudgeon ask me, "Have you taken leave of your senses? I'm not Backhaus.[1] No human being can play those difficult passages in 'Odins Meeresritt'! . . ."

"But, Maestro," I interrupted in great consternation, "we can do another ballad. Please forgive my selection. Perhaps 'Der Wirtin Töchterlein' . . . ?"

"No, no," he interrupted brusquely, "the program is already out. I just have to bite the bullet. Very well, then, tomorrow morning at nine on the dot!"—and without further comment he slammed down the receiver. This was shaping up to be quite a broadcast!

The next morning I was already in Broadcasting House promptly at nine. I knew Pfitzner was a study in punctuality. When I reached the floor manager's desk, I asked if the maestro had arrived: "Is that an old guy with glasses and a little goatee? He's already been in room 45 for an hour playing like a nut."

I scurried over there. From a distance I could hear the well-known difficult passage with the sixteenth triplets. Fearing the worst, I walked into the room, but, miracle of miracles! Pfitzner sprang to his feet in the best of moods. "You see, my young friend," he said putting his arm around my waist on our way back to the grand piano, almost placatingly, as if he had something to atone for. I said nothing, deeply embarrassed, and picked up my copy of the Pfitzner songs. "No, no," he said, "we'll go right to those ballads with the Chopin étude bars. Did you know that Loewe wasn't just a good composer, but also a crackerjack piano virtuoso, who used to sing and accompany himself at the same time?"

I hadn't known that. He sat down on the piano stool. "Now we'll move right to the end, and I'll show you what I was practicing this morning." He looked somewhat reproachfully up at me and played for me like a school-

1. Wilhelm Backhaus was a pianist who, among other things, was renowned for his outstanding digital dexterity.

boy who had done his homework assiduously, flawlessly playing the difficult passage with great gusto. "Fabulous!" I found myself saying with total honesty. And he, who so often squinted myopically and glared distrustingly through the thick lenses of his spectacles, slapped me on the knee as I sat beside him and cried out with a beatific glow on his face: "It is, isn't it?" Much more of this, and I might have given him a hug; that's how amiable I found him all of a sudden. Anyway, this brought me considerably closer to this so frequently misunderstood individual.

At about the same time something else happened that had the great Pfitzner appearing in quite a different light. My wife and I invited the maestro to lunch at our apartment in the Harvestehude district of Hamburg and were very proud when he accepted the invitation. I escorted our distinguished guest into the dining room, where my wife waited to greet him. At this point, the reader should know that women, especially attractive ones, always exercised a highly invigorating effect on Pfitzner. So he walked over to her with his arms extended to give vent to his delight without so much as a modicum of shyness. Standing directly in front of her, he noticed with his nearsighted eyes that she would soon be giving birth. The change in his attitude was indescribable. Like a little scamp caught with his hand in the cookie jar he precipitously bowed slightly to her, took her hand in both of his own, and kissed it as if it had been festooned with the pontiff's ring. With great care, the seventy-two-year-old guided the incipient mother to the table, pulled out her chair, and gallantly helped her into it. Then he turned to me and said in hushed tones: "Motherhood—the greatest miracle of nature!" And during the entire luncheon he never took his eyes off of her. He was the most charming and attentive table companion, told witty stories, and was otherwise almost downright unrecognizable. How I wished that a couple of people who had nary a good word for this often cranky individual might have been present!

We singers working on the new production of *Der arme Heinrich,* not to mention the musicians in the orchestra, were all very curious as to what kind of conductor Hans Pfitzner would turn out to be. Of course, he had a full command of his music right down to the last little detail. With widespread arm movements he led us in his emotionally dictated joy of music-making through the obstacles of the sometimes acerbic and not always direct tonal language of his *Armer Heinrich.* He was earnestly committed to the task and held the aforementioned highest expectations of our abilities. There was hardly any of his occasionally sarcastic, oftentimes biting humor to be made out.

During the preparation and performance phase something happened in direct correlation to his activity as a conductor of his own work. In a dramatically significant moment in the plot, the composer had inserted a cymbal crash: the slamming together of two metal discs to create a shrill tone that heightened the climax of a dramatic intensification even more. Pfitzner placed great importance on this effect in his work and told the percussionist who was to execute the cymbal crash several times that this was the most important moment in the entire opera. As this moment comes about at the end of an act, the musician always arrived just a few minutes before it was due at rehearsals. Every time, Pfitzner would worry long before the moment as to whether the musician would show up on time. When he finally did put in his appearance, Pfitzner tried to convince him that he should have been there much sooner to follow the plot and then carry out that crash with a full understanding for the dramatic sequence.

The musician seemed unmoved, and the rest of the orchestra began finding Pfitzner's worry amusing. An evil spirit must have gloated over the premiere performance: exactly one hour before the cymbal crash was due, the Hamburg Transit System broke down, the musician was unable to arrive on time, and the cymbals did not crash. The curtain fell, and Pfitzner seemed all but ready to faint dead away. After that he went into a fury and spoke of sabotage and other evil deeds. It took a long time before he calmed down and could be talked into conducting his work to its conclusion.

A few days later, during a week of contemporary music, in conjunction with which *Der arme Heinrich* was also being given, there was a symphony concert. Among the distinguished guests in the audience was Maestro Pfitzner.

Meanwhile the cymbal crash affair had somewhat faded from memory. Everyone assiduously avoided mentioning it in Pfitzner's presence. The evening's program also included Franz Liszt's blood-and-thunder orchestral work *Mazeppa*. I just happened to be standing within earshot of Pfitzner during the intermission and was an ear witness to his livid condemnation: "That atrocious, caterwaul of a work. Did they really have to play it? All those cymbal crashes! Terrible! I counted them precisely. There were thirty-two of them, and he played every single one. In my *Armer Heinrich,* there's just one—and he *missed* it!"

There are all kinds of anecdotes about Hans Pfitzner, most of which reflect his sharp wit and the quirky way this tone poet's mind worked. I've only told a few of the events I witnessed personally.

When I sang my first Borromeo in a new Hamburg production of *Palestrina* in 1937, I had no clue how close to my heart this role would become over the course of my career. Oscar Fritz Schuh was our stage director, and Hans Pfitzner had been invited to stand by us as we prepared this difficult work. At the first stage rehearsal, he greeted me pleasantly and said with a smile, "Are you aware of the fact that, as far as I know, you are the first person to be typecast in this role?"

I looked at him in incredulity.

"How old are you now?"

"Twenty-eight," I said.

"You see! At the time of the Council of Trent, Cardinal Borromeo was all of twenty-five years old."

I was completely dumfounded.

"Now make sure," he continued, "that you get the right maturity combined with the right age!"

On May 5, 1944, Hans Pfitzner celebrated his seventy-fifth birthday. On this occasion I dedicated an entire recital in the aula of Munich University to his songs, and personally invited him to attend. He thanked me most cordially in a letter and apologized for his absence. He added, he was annoyed that the Munich Opera would not be giving *Palestrina* for his birthday. (The Bavarian State Opera in Munich had already been reduced to rubble in an Allied bombing raid on October 2, 1943.)

I saw Pfitzner for the last time in February 1949 in Vienna, when he was attending the final new production he would witness of his *Palestrina* at the Theater an der Wien two months before his death and shortly before what would have been his eightieth birthday. When he left us forever on April 23, we mourned a great master and a remarkable human being.

I am often asked by operagoers what city has the best audience. I always found this question hard to answer, because I'm never sure what criteria to apply in making this kind of judgment? Of course, we artists love a hearty round of applause from the auditorium. Besides this voluble reaction, there is another element I greatly treasure: the ongoing allegiance, the loyalty of an audience.

Of course this was at a time when there was no such thing as an international opera business, and in all the operatic institutions large and small, there were permanent resident companies. It went without saying that the opera fans were more strongly attached to their local favorites, preferring them to the few international luminaries on the circuit at that time.

If I had to decide today where the most loyal opera fans were or are, I would immediately think of Hamburg. I myself was able to witness how constant they were, and, beyond this, how deliciously original the operagoers in the Hanseatic city could be. My singing colleagues had an inexhaustible repertoire of such stories, with which we "newcomers" were generously supplied.

Around the turn of the twentieth century, for example, there was a legendary tenor among the singers there, a native-born Hamburg lad by the name of Heinrich Bötel, who must have been enormously popular. I can remember how the whole city turned out in heartfelt sympathy when the eighty-four-year-old man was borne to his grave in 1938.

In the early years of the century, the great Enrico Caruso made a guest appearance in the theater on Dammtorstrasse and ignited a veritable conflagration of applause with his appearance there. A couple of days later two opera fans were discussing that sensational evening. One of them said: "You heard Caruso sing. Was his voice really that fantastic?"

Answer: "Perhaps, but Bötel sings louder."[2]

Another famous reaction was provided by a lady at a performance of *Tristan und Isolde*. During the third act, when Tristan is ranting and raving in ever wilder delirium, she commented: "If he keeps that up, you just watch, he's sure to snap out of it."

Or the comment of a member of the audience on the two protagonists: "I can't figure out what Tristan sees in Isolde. That woman hasn't got one jolly bone in her whole body."[3]

During the intermissions, my wife became involved in one unusual conversation after another with some of the patrons in the lobby. Once, when *Fidelio* was on the menu, somebody said her: "Now then, Mrs. Hotter, your husband cuts quite a villainous figure as Pizarro. Delightful! He often has those scurvy creatures to play, and he does it quite splendidly, really, Jago, Scarpia, that sort of thing." Then she inquired conspiratorially, "Do you mind if we ask you a personal question? Doesn't some of that villainy rub off at home?"[4]

Somebody came up with the following observation in a *Parsifal* performance: "It's a very moving show, isn't it? There's just one thing I can't quite figure out: what kind of a wound has that Amfortas got, 'the wound that refuses to heal'?" The gentleman next to him: "Probably an ulcerated leg."[5] This is just a small selection from the repertoire of the loyal and original Hamburg public.

Before I had sung the role of the Dutchman myself, I once attended a performance in which my friend and colleague Rudolf Bockelmann was appearing in his former home base as a guest artist in this role. In the third act, Daland's sailors and the local village girls try to get the Dutchman's crew to say something, calling out to them: "Seamen! Come on, wake up!" After a long pause, they repeat these words, louder and a halftone higher. The second attempt also proves fruitless, and there is another long interruption. When the second long rest came about in the aforementioned performance,

2. "Vielleicht. Aber Bötel singt ss-tärker"
3. "Ich weiß gar nicht, was der Tristan an der Isolde findet. Die hat doch gor nich so 'n büschen was Munteres."
4. "Durfen wir Sie wohl was ganz Intimes fragen? Bleibt da privat nich' 'n büschen was von nach"
5. "Wahrscheinlich ein offener Bein."

4.12.   Playing the many villainous characters that happened to fall into my voice category—such as Puccini's Scarpia—had some of the ladies in the audience asking my wife if the villainy didn't occasionally rub off at home. Photo, © Photo Fayer, Vienna.

a clearly audible voice emerged from the row behind me penetrating the stillness with the observation, "Again no answer!"[6]

Pfitzner's Hamburg activity and the experience I gained from this interaction extended into the year 1937, but 1936 was also a year rich in experience, which guided my development virtually by leaps and bounds to new levels. Right at the beginning of the season I had been entrusted with an assignment many people thought had come about a bit too early for me. My

6. "Wieder nix!"

zealous henchman and patron in dramatic matters, Rudolf Zindler, got them to cast a twenty-seven-year-old baritone in the title role of Mussorgsky's *Boris Godunov*. In this effort he was heartily supported by the musical director of the house, Eugen Jochum, who would also be conducting this work. In my first few months in Hamburg, I had managed to establish a human and artistic understanding with him. His natural way of making music appealed to me greatly. He was invaluable to me in interpreting Mussorgsky's music. Ignoring the objections of all those who found me much too young for this task, the two men worked unflaggingly with me on this fascinating role.

I found the slow development, the gradual growing into a character, which had been an unfamiliar experience for me heretofore, both motivating and challenging. I recalled the rehearsals of the same opera in Prague; the interpretation of my experienced colleague Theo Seidl appeared before me and helped me propel my own efforts forward. Chaliapin's unique dramatic radiance also returned to life and released new elements in my own imagination. It was in these weeks that I sensed a profound fulfillment and satisfaction in my profession: I was learning how to combine a number of elements simultaneously and with equal value effectively into a single interpretation.

Unfortunately I had not seen Chaliapin on stage as Boris during my Prague period, but I did have some of his old recordings with selections from this opera. Just by listening to his vocal performance, into which the words were firmly anchored, I felt as if I were actually watching him act.

There was never a specific favorite role over the course of my operatic career, but Boris was certainly one. Although I only sang the part in Hamburg between 1936 and 1940 (exactly twenty-two times, although I did do it once more in a Munich radio performance several years later, again under Jochum's direction), it remained a pride and joy throughout my professional life. Perhaps the time this character was coming into being enjoys a special place in my memory because it stood right at the outset of my relationship with my wife as a good omen for a life together abundantly rich with artistic experiences.

The general management of the Hamburg theater honored this work and the success I had with my new role by immediately rounding off my salary upward and proposing that the Hamburg Senate award me the title of Kammersänger.[7] Two days after the premiere, I traveled with my future wife to the south, parting company in Stuttgart: my fiancée went on to

---

7. A title once conferred by royalty, and still given by the various German and Austrian Federal States to performing artists, somewhat equivalent to a knighthood in the British Commonwealth.

4.13.   The 1936 Hamburg production of Werner Egk's *Zauber-geige* brought together two dyed-in-the-wool Bavarians on the banks of the distant Elbe: the composer and the baritone who sang the role of Kasper in authentic South German lederhosen.

Munich to be initiated into the mysteries of Bavarian cuisine by my mother. Plagued by a mean case of the sniffles, I boarded a plane to Barcelona to begin my first extended foreign engagement at the Gran Teatre del Liceu in that city. It was also my first long-distance flight, undertaken back then in Lufthansa's good old "Auntie Ju 52."[8] My stay on board, in those days

8. The Junkers 52 aircraft had a certain "hand-knitted" quality, which prompted many a wag in those days to call the plane "Tante" ("Auntie").

without pressure compensation, had the effect that, on arrival, my sniffles were gone with the wind, but my ears were so stopped up I needed a couple of days before I could hear properly again.

My contract required me to bring some of my own costumes along. My roles there were the Wanderer (*Siegfried*), Gunther (*Götterdämmerung*) along with the speaking role of Pasha Selim in Mozart's *Die Entführung aus dem Serail*. For this part, I had packed a Near Eastern robe with a Turkish curved saber plus a turban with a peacock feather and a huge glass ruby in my luggage. The airport building was a Quonset hut, and passport and customs control took place outdoors at a table on which I had to set down my luggage. Needless to say, the Spanish customs officer wanted to have a look at the one with the costumes. So I opened it. Right on the top of the case was the Turkish costume complete with sword and turban. The officials gaped in bewilderment, and before I could open my mouth to explain what this was all about, the nearby Lufthansa flight attendant instantly grasped the situation and reacted accordingly. Behind his hand he muttered something about "his majesty" and "incognito" and escorted me with a look of proud solemnity to the exit. This whole story sounds incredible, but it really happened. Ah, the good old days!

The blocked ears provided yet another amusing epilogue. In the first musical rehearsal the following afternoon, my ears were still completely shut, and I had problems hearing the piano, which led to some insecurity in my singing. The musical director, Karl Elmendorff, whom I still remembered well from my days sitting in the Munich audience, took me discreetly to one side and said with a smirk, "Be honest. Of course you haven't sung the Wanderer yet!" I denied this ineffectually and assured him the problem was with my blocked ears. Elmendorff again responded with the same knowing smirk.

A week later we had rehearsals for *Götterdämmerung,* and I actually never had sung Gunther before. My Hamburg tenor colleague Hans Grahl helped me and guided me with a firm hand through the rigors of this completely unfamiliar opera. Meanwhile, my ears had reopened, my voice was in good shape. Elmendorff was satisfied and said happily to me after the rehearsal: "Well, I can see you've sung *this* role plenty of times."

The days in Barcelona in the circle of many new colleagues were interesting and jolly. This was my first long-term foreign guest appearance away from Hamburg. Being able to walk around without a coat in January, the different restaurants with the unfamiliar Spanish food, the comical intermezzi with the new language—all of these factors led to considerable confusion. Then every day new experiences in the rehearsals in the Spanish environment on the stage. We didn't have many rehearsals, but we did have plenty of free time, as compared with Hamburg where rehearsals were our daily, not always very flavorful, bread.

At the end of January I received a group telegram from good friends in Hamburg congratulating me on my Kammersänger appointment. Before my departure from Hamburg, these same friends had mentioned that the famous, former star tenor at the Vienna State Opera, Leo Slezak (not only one of the greatest vocal artists of the century but also a tremendous wit, who wrote a delightful collection of humorous books), had once played a prank on a fellow tenor by having him informed that he had been given a phony Kammersänger title. What would be more obvious than to conclude that these same friends were pulling my leg, especially when no confirmation of this award arrived, either from the opera house or from the city of Hamburg? And so I held my tongue, afraid I might make a complete fool of myself.

Among the members of our guest ensemble was also a young baritone colleague from Dresden, Arno Schellenberg, years later a renowned member of that opera company, who proudly told us the Kammersänger title he had just received made him the youngest holder of that honor in Germany. When I discovered he was four years older than myself, I had a powerful itch: if this really wasn't a prank, and I had truly received this honor, then I with my twenty-seven summers would be Germany's youngest Kammersänger! The temptation was enormous, but my suspicion even greater. Not until eight days later did I finally receive the official confirmation from Hamburg.

That summer, in the circle of our families, we celebrated our wedding. We called a couple of days off in the mountains our honeymoon. We proudly turned down free tickets to the Berlin Olympics. Our new apartment in Hamburg's Isestrasse was simply more tempting.

A few months before I had appeared in a concert in Amsterdam with Bruno Walter. But I've already related that story. In April, Eugen Jochum entrusted me with the role of Christ in the *Saint Matthew Passion*. After our enjoyable experience making music together in *Boris Godunov* three months previously, we grew even closer in musical sensitivity during our excursion into the world of Johann Sebastian Bach. This unique experience of being able to take part in this work for the first time took place in the dignified setting of Saint Michael's Church. The performance, in the middle of a period of extended operatic activity, was a welcome interruption. The silence and the retreat to within ourselves were highly salubrious. The performance also brought me together with a singer I had admired for as long as I could remember listening to music: Karl Erb, even then a legendary Evangelist.

It was he, along with baritone Heinrich Rehkemper, contralto Luise Willer, and bass Paul Bender, who had laid the groundwork for my understanding and love of recital singing. He made a few flattering remarks on my interpretation of Christ. When I mentioned these to the Dutch soprano

Jo Vincent, who was also taking part, she said: "You can take that as a major compliment. Erb is famous for his hypercritical tongue!" So I was appropriately proud. But I also came in for my share of the other side of that artist. After Jesus's last words, "Eli, Eli, lama sabachthani!" he turned to me and said: "You're singing it differently from the way I feel it, but the Evangelist repeats Jesus' words, so I'll repeat them the way you sing them." That impressed a much younger man like myself considerably.

For the opening of the 1936–37 season the Hamburg Opera offered its audience a production of *Otello* that was highly regarded throughout Germany, and with it a new, incredibly interesting role in the form of the villain Jago. Once again, as with *Boris Godunov,* the tried-and-true team of Jochum/Zindler was at work. A good personal relationship with my tenor colleague Joachim Sattler, who impressively portrayed Otello, further enhanced the first-class working atmosphere on stage.

Only later did I become aware that from the development of Boris to Jago, I had reached the point where, right from the outset, I was totally concentrated on the dramatic creation of a new character. As much as the vocal command of the part continued to be the supreme rule of interpretation, I constantly caught myself pouring the full measure of my ambition into the formation of the dramatic constituent. Whatever motivations came from Zindler, everything contributed to bringing across the diabolical quality in this snakelike creature, without playing the villain in an obvious way—all of which was welcome. There were hardly any vocal problems. Everything seemed to resound and function on its own. I recalled to mind my friend Theo Scheidl from Prague and his good advice. Suddenly it was sufficient just to play with the words now and then without overindulging in too many gestures. A certain head position, an altered expression in the eyes said everything the director wanted. And because, while doing this, I forgot to pay attention to vocal matters, everything worked automatically. If my colleagues had asked me how I did it, I wouldn't have known what to answer.

By the time Christmas rolled around, and I had a few *Otello* performances under my belt, one evening, at the end of the performance, I found Herbert von Karajan standing in my dressing room wanting to know if I would like to sing the baritone solos in the Brahms *Requiem* with him the following spring in Aachen and Brussels. I had never seen him before up close, and I was surprised at how short and almost delicate he was. I knew he would have hated me if he had been able to read my thoughts. Although, as always, he seemed a bit shy, right from the first he exuded a resolute and orderly nature.

I must have looked at him with some surprise, because he immediately said, "Yes, I got the idea during your performance of Jago." Anyway, I found the idea of coming up with the Brahms *Requiem* while listening to someone sing Jago quite original.

In fact, I did come to Aachen, where Karajan was still musical director, and then to Brussels in March 1937. It was our first collaboration, and we would continue to make music together in unique harmony. The soprano solo was sung by the unforgettable Ria Ginster with the same celestial quality as the inimitable Elisabeth Schwarzkopf years later. I spent the whole concert almost hypnotized by this great artist, and I was fascinated by his radiance. What impressed me the most was his indescribable command of everything and the calm he exuded. For me, this Brahms work, along with the biblical words, has always been so thrilling and stirring, I had a hard time reining in my inner emotion.

And there stood a musician, an almost delicate individual, who with his twenty-nine years seemed almost totally unmoved by what was stirring me so deeply, in full command of himself, who with short but precise motions stood seemingly above it all and was able to transfer the full measure of his artistic concept to the participants in the performance. When we got together afterward, I simply couldn't control myself and, despite the fact that we hardly knew one another, asked him, "Please tell me how you do it. You seem to be almost untouched by this music, which palpably gets under any sensitive musician's skin, without ever losing your self-control." Then he did something I very seldom experienced with him in all the many long years we worked together. He looked me straight in the eye and said, "How much time and effort do you think that cost me!?"

As with many other prominent artists, I am unable to come up with any unambiguous answers to the question of his real relationship with the Nazis. He certainly needed no protection and would have had his extraordinary career under any regime without any help from political quarters. Without a doubt, he, like many others, preferred to place the practice of his artistic profession at the service of the audience that was unable or unwilling to leave the country, instead of documenting his rejection of the political climate by emigrating somewhere else. Anyone who feels a need to condemn that attitude will have to ask his conscience, How would I have acted in the same situation?

In the course of the year 1937, the Hamburg Opera entrusted me with four more important new roles, two of them dramatic: Wagner's *Der fliegende Holländer* and Cardinal Borromeo in Pfitzner's *Palestrina,* parts that I sang with special dedication and joy in many opera houses throughout the following years. In complete contrast to these were two character roles, actually more suitable to the buffo repertoire, which was why nobody expected me to be able to handle them: the title role in Puccini's *Gianni Schicchi* and Don Basilio in Rossini's *Il barbiere di Siviglia*. Often it is dis-

4.14.   After all the solemn gods and heroes in Wagner's operas,
a character like Puccini's *Gianni Schicchi* came as a pleasant
comic relief—and the opera is so wonderfully short!

advantageous to be particularly successful in a certain specific role, as was
my case with the father of the gods. People felt I was just "predestined" for
that part, and I was on my way down a single track to the heroic baritone
category. No wonder nobody was willing to accept me in a buffo role—
just as I had my problems as a Wagner singer being taken seriously as a
song recitalist.

I'll never forget a collegial conversation I had back in Prague with the famous character actor Max Pallenberg. How he lamented that people are so
unwilling to accept an actor they usually see in comic parts when he takes
on a serious characterization! Of course my knowledge of the audience's
bias doubly spurred me to prove that I could also be funny on the stage. The
role of Schicchi, in fact the whole opera of *Gianni Schicchi,* had really cap-

tured my heart. I was always sad that this Puccini work never became a real
audience-pleaser.

I was able to craft Don Basilio in great detail, again with Rudolf Zindler's guidance, during a long rehearsal period. Here I had the immeasurable
benefit of a unique role model for this grotesque character part in the person of the highly regarded basso of the twenties, Paul Bender. Munich
audiences spent many a delightful evening witnessing his portrayal of this
character.

This jolly excursion into the buffo category was also regarded by Zindler
as a welcome opportunity to get me in the mood for another venture into
the merry world of Shakespeare's comic genius: a projected *Falstaff* production. In the spice kitchen of comical characterizations I also received the
necessary inspiration for the interpretation of funny lieder—a branch of
recital singing that most inexperienced concert singers wisely avoid.

Eighteen years came and went before I again put on Basilio's long hat
to subject it to the usual rainwater gag. This was in Herbert List's Munich
Barbiere production, which has remained legendary to this day. It was first
presented at that city's Cuvilliéstheater in 1955 with my unforgettable co-
conspirators Erika Köth, Hermann Preg, Fritz Wunderlich, and Max Proebstl, in German, of course, and in the dialogue version. "Thank goodness
they do it in Italian now!" says the one faction. "Pity!" says the other—
and among those others are, not least, the German singers who know that
comic effects always come over better in the local language. But nothing
would be farther from my intention than conjuring up the "original lan-
guage/local language" issue, especially as I myself am a defender and advocate of opera in the original language.

One thing is certain: so many delicious things happened during those
Barbiere performances in the "Cuvy," as we used to call it, so many unforgotten slight fluffs in the dialogue, so many crack-ups on- and offstage—I
wouldn't have missed that experience for the world.

⊰ Chapter 5 ⊱

The most outstanding event of the year 1937 was the much-longed-for contact with the State Opera in my home town of Munich. My first attempts at establishing that contact went back to 1929. Barely twenty years old, a music student and church choir director, I had become friends with a young tenor from the elite ranks of soloists in the house on Maximilianstrasse by the name of Josef Janko, whom I coached on his new roles. This was still back in the era of Clemens von Franckenstein.

My friend Seppl,[1] later a beloved member of the Graz Opera for many years, actually managed to organize an audition for me in the Residenztheater. A couple of days after the audition, I found out from my tenor friend that even the great Hans Knappertsbusch had been present. He gave Janko the message, "Tell the young man to learn to sing properly, and then he can get in touch with us again."

The second contact came about in December 1934, just as I had begun feeling at home in Hamburg. I received a letter from the management of the Munich Opera advising me they were interested in a guest performance so they could take a closer look at me. We agreed that I would appear as the Wanderer in *Siegfried* on December 16. On the evening of December 15, shortly before my planned departure from Hamburg, I received a telegram reading: "GUEST PERFORMANCE CURRENTLY NOT FEASIBLE."

What had happened?

Hans Knappertsbusch, the conductor of the *Siegfried* production had fallen into disfavor with the regime because of some anti-Nazi sentiments he had expressed in public. To give him a kind of slap on the wrist, a horde of brown-shirted troublemakers had been ordered to attend just this *Siegfried* performance, so they could riot against Knappertsbusch during the intermissions. The demonstrations actually took place, with the result that Knappertsbusch did not appear on the podium for the third act, and the end of opera was conducted by Karl Tutein. The general manager at the

---

1. Seppl is a southern German diminutive form of the name "Josef," a little like "Joey" in English.

time, Oskar Wallek, must clearly have known about the planned distur-
bances and wanted to spare me a guest performance under such hideous
circumstances.

Some thirty years later, I found myself sitting with Knappertsbusch after
a Bayreuth performance. The conversation happened to turn to that *Siegfried* performance in December 1934, and I told him how sorry I was that I
hadn't been able to sing that evening. "How so?" asked Knappertsbusch in
astonishment, "That's news to me. I always thought you were a Nazi yourself, and that you were the one who canceled because you were making
common cause with that rabble."

That's why it took until March 1937 before Clemens Krauss contacted
me (I had been told he would be back in Prague in 1934) and invited me to
meet him in Berlin. When I arrived there in the best of spirits, he told me
that he had just been appointed general manager of the Munich Opera and
would like to engage me for that house. When, at the very earliest, would I
be able to present myself to the local audience in a guest performance?

On April 12, Munich presented *Siegfried,* and I was overjoyed to find
myself on the stage of my secret longings singing my heart out. The performance was successful beyond my wildest imaginings. The whole family
and all my friends were sitting trembling in the orchestra seats; my revered
Matthäus Römer, who had never heard or seen me onstage before, wrote
me a letter overflowing with congratulations, and the entire Munich press
composed anthems that were so rapturous they almost made me blush. A
contract was signed, and an agreement was reached with Hamburg allowing me to spend part of the year performing in the Bavarian capital. A goal
I had yearned after for so many years had finally been reached: all of a sudden I was standing on the stage beside the singers I had idolized in my
youth. Many of them accepted me on the spot, but some of the old guard
were not immediately all that pleased with the greenhorn and were maintaining a "wait-and-see" attitude. One of the artists I most admired, Ludwig Weber, didn't like me at all and made no secret of it. With many of the
others, the acceptance process was long and arduous, but by dint of considerable patience and endurance, I managed to win most of my colleagues over.

I had my first opportunity to "practice" this a couple of weeks later
during the rehearsal period for my first new Munich production, Strauss's
Salome, in which I had been cast as Jochanaan. This brought me, apart from
the collaboration with the new colleagues, also the sensational experience
of meeting Richard Strauss. All of this needed a fair bit of digesting on my
part: the unfamiliar atmosphere of one of the world's top opera houses and
its renowned tradition, a magnificent auditorium with which I was more
than familiar, an elite orchestra and a theater administration organized right

5.1. Back in the 1930s, Wotan was clad as the traditional audience expected him to be, in armor with a winged helmet.

down to the minutest detail—all of this visibly animated by the atmosphere of the new artistic direction under Clemens Krauss.

Let me try to describe the effect of all these impressions by going into a little more detail on the various decisive personalities in the theater. Once again, these are largely musicians, conductors. Without long reflection, my first thought goes to the man who probably had the greatest influence on my entire development: Clemens Krauss. He was, after all, the one to whom I owed the contact with the opera of my native city. Because there were so many who helped guide me along the right way on my upward path, it seems almost ungrateful to try to differentiate among them. Perhaps I am a bit partial when I speak of this great theater man, but discussing Clemens Krauss can only be pleasant. You have the choice of reporting on the theater director, the conductor, or the mentor and pedagogue. And then you have to add the way he used all the skill he had acquired from his solid professional experience, his instinct for suitability and talent, and his impressive background and education, to combine these many functions. He was the ultimate authority, to whom we all subjected ourselves, and—only occasionally with inner resistance—deferred to. But we respected him because he also respected *our* contribution to artistic success and gave his artists freedoms that often came about so unexpectedly that we neglected to take full advantage of them. All of these fortunate circumstances made for an extremely lively collaboration.

None of us could complain about boring rehearsals. On the contrary: sometimes things could get pretty rough. I can remember days when tears flowed, and yet we also laughed a lot and had plenty of fun. Krauss was not at all fond of discussions in front of the whole gang, not even on artistic matters. Besides, it was unwise to lock verbal horns with him, because the man's wit was so surgically honed we usually wound up on the short end of the stick. Away from work, however, in a small private conversation or one-on-one, we could talk to him about anything—well, almost anything. He trained us to form our own opinions.

The general manager's superior ability was every bit as convincing as was the general music director's. Here, too, it was his instinct that helped him assign the right people to the right positions. His accomplishments in planning, assembling, and ultimately running an operatic organization, not just in Munich, but also in other places, are well known and their uniqueness is lauded by the cognoscenti. I often wondered what it was that fascinated both the young singer as much as, sixty years later, the author of these lines. What was so awe-inspiring about him?

He was a gentleman, the likes of which one seldom finds—and hardly ever in the theater.

He had an orderly way of going about his work.

He was the master of his craft in all its many facets. Especially impressive was the understanding, almost fatherly way he looked after us singers, his professional expertise and his thoroughgoing knowledge of anything related to voices.

I liked the aura of his somewhat unapproachable authority at work, this aura that combined with a charming cordiality in personal relations.

5.2.   On the podium or (anywhere else in the theater he served as general director),
Clemens Krauss was always master of all he surveyed. Photo, courtesy of the Salzburg Festival.

I appreciated his perspicacity in artistic matters, the reliability of his views, and his eloquent use of language, especially his precision in telling his employees what he wanted from them.

He had an incredible diplomatic adeptness in his relations with the various members of the operatic organization, which was often enough comparable to an operatic menagerie.

He had a delectable sense of humor and what is especially remarkable, despite his vanity, he was nevertheless capable of laughing at himself.

And what special things could we younger members of his ensemble learn from him? Here are three of his most impressive principles, which I have stored in my mind for life:

- Don't ever forget to pay respect to the work, its creator, and his intentions.

- An artist must realize early in his development that the very first thing he must do is learn and master the craft of his trade.

- An artist must be able honestly to recognize and take to heart the limitations of a talent, especially his own. Talent is simply the pre-requisite for ongoing artistic success—and success can only be acquired through orderliness and hard work.

The following anecdotes are intended simply as highlights; they describe situations in which I was personally involved. This one came to pass during the rehearsal period at the Salzburg Festival during the war. The scene was the rehearsal stage in the festival theater. For weeks and months, day in and day out, we had been rehearsing *The Marriage of Figaro*. Our stage director was Walter Felsenstein, the great, brilliant Felsenstein. Anyone who knew him knows what that means: we were all suffering. Not just from the torrid summer heat, but also from the countless, endless repetition of tiny scenes and even tinier ones. We were still acting like marionettes in a trance, wax in the fingers of the great, obsessed sorcerer. (May he look down from his aerie on Olympus and forgive me!) In the middle of the rehearsal, Clemens Krauss, the musical director of the production, appeared. Nobody had seen him walk in. Up until then, he hadn't attended any rehearsals, and hardly anyone noticed him. For a couple of minutes he attentively, yet silently, observed what was going on. Then a mumble escaped his lips. I could just barely make it out, as he was standing only a few feet away from me, "I just love Strindberg!"

At the end of one of the repeat performances of my first *Walküre* in the spring of 1940 in Munich, the audience accorded us some enthusiastic ovations. Krauss was conducting; his wife Viorica Ursuleac sang Sieglinde. We had just gratefully taken our bows before the curtain and were on our way back when a couple of enthusiasts called my name. Something like that is always a little embarrassing for the recipient of these calls. Generally Krauss would say, "Whoever paid can take a solo bow," and we all laughed, of course. My eye fell on Krauss, but this time he didn't say it. He rather walked toward me and said very quietly, with an ironical look in his eye, "Bohnen? Who's Bohnen?" (The reader will have to realize that Michael Bohnen had been a famous Wotan in his day some ten to twelve years previously.) The little dig at me for the benefit of his wife was obvious.

Remarkably I was not hurt by the little affront, but rather somewhat amused. Nevertheless I couldn't resist the temptation to reply, "He must be a conductor." The same moment I regretted that quick rejoinder; after all, he was my boss. Somewhat shocked at myself, I stepped out for another curtain call with the others, and on the way back, I avoided making eye contact with Krauss. He seemed not to take anything amiss. At least, he displayed no reaction. Suddenly I heard, just loud enough for my ears, Krauss grumbling to himself, "Very good! Ask a stupid question, get a stupid answer."

Five years later, shortly after the end of the war, there was a story in the American military newspaper *Stars and Stripes* to the effect that a new *Otello* had come out in the Charlottenburg Opera in Berlin, conducted by Michael Bohnen. The reporter had obviously gotten it wrong; what he certainly meant to write was that Bohnen had been the stage director. About a year later, Krauss, who at the time was residing in Leopoldskron Palace in Salzburg, sent me a message through a friend asking me to stop by and visit him and his wife on one of my trips between Munich and Vienna, which I then did. During an extremely pleasant coffee hour I was pleased to note that Krauss had lost none of his charm and delicious humor. He suddenly rose, walked over to the desk, and took out a newspaper clipping, which he set down in front of me. It was that ominous report of the *Otello* production in Berlin. With that he said in a dry-as-dust voice, "You were right back in Munich. He *was* a conductor."

At the end of 1937, in my second new production after *Salome,* I sang my first Grand Inquisitor in Verdi's *Don Carlo,* a role I would later portray more than four hundred times. In one of those Munich performances I had the misfortune of making my entrance in the dungeon scene too late. In those days, guest singers received their pay for the evening in cash. I had just collected my fee, some one thousand marks after the usual deductions, all in small bills and coins, and I was on my way to the dressing room when somebody yelled over the loudspeaker, "Hotter, where in blazes are you? You're on!"

I raced to the stage area and could already hear my entrance music, but I still had to cross over at the back of the set to the other side of the stage taking long steps in my clerical robe—my fee still clutched in my fist—while already singing my first bars. As I finally landed successfully in the door, eight measures had already come and gone, and my heart was pounding all the way up to my esophagus. Sweating profusely, I concluded my first phrase. In the pit, Krauss sat shaking his head annoyedly back and forth. King Philip, as portrayed by Hans Hermann Nissen, was kneeling before me on the stage with his back to the audience, waiting in accordance with the plot for my blessing. Trembling, I raised my left arm, whereupon Hans Hermann hissed between his teeth, "You give blessings with the right hand, you numbskull!" But I had my right hand behind my back clutching the money! So I gave him a left-handed blessing. After that I slunk as quickly as I could back into the dressing room, without a thought of a curtain call. Afterward I asked colleague Nissen, who shared the dressing room with me, "What happened afterward? Did Krauss say anything?" Nissen replied laconically, "Matinee performance!" A judgment like that is downright shattering. The picture of contrition, I sneaked out the back door of the theater, and finally managed to calm down somewhat as I lay down in the sleeping car from Munich to Hamburg.

5.3.   A 1937 Munich production of Verdi's *Don Carlo*. Hans-Hermann
Nissen as King Philip looks as if he's still annoyed with me for giving
the Grand Inquisitor's blessing with the wrong hand.

The funniest reaction to the whole story was the comment of a member
of the audience at the aforementioned performance: "Who had the brilliant
inspiration of having the blind inquisitor unable to find the door and making a late entrance? Incredibly effective, that!"

That was back in 1937. Over the following years, we had several *Carlo*
performances, always under Krauss's musical direction. Neither in any of
the subsequent performances nor in the numerous other operas in the various interim periods did Krauss utter so much as a syllable over that embarrassing late entrance because of the money.

Five years later, we had a rehearsal for a lady guesting at the theater in *Don Carlo*. I was also summoned to this rehearsal. Sorely plagued by the grim premonition that this story of the late entrance might still rate a negative mention, I went through my role as precisely as possible. My entrance in the dungeon scene arrived. Krauss sat in the pit with a deep freeze in both eyes without so much as a passing glance at me. The scene slowly approached its conclusion. Would he really not say anything to recall that unfortunate event? That wouldn't have been like him at all, even after so long a time. He really did say nothing, and hope began to spring up in my heart. Then suddenly he interrupted, turned with the most amiable expression on his face to the ladies of the chorus and said: "Ladies, please take a step forward just in case Mr. Hotter has another entrance . . ." By this time, I had already disappeared from the stage. Whenever I hear the theater director's speech in Strauss's *Capriccio*,[2] I think of how Krauss had behaved toward me like a true La Roche.

A new *Siegfried* production in Munich was in the offing. The role of the Wanderer was sung by the tried and true Hans Hermann Nissen. I was cast in later performances. The rehearsal period was just winding up, and the premiere was about to take place. At this point, Krauss summoned me to his office one morning and said a few words about team spirit and our duty to subordinate ourselves to him. I was already wondering what he was getting at, but whatever it was, it didn't sound good. Then he found words of highest praise for our colleague Nissen, how actively he had participated in rehearsals, and how he deserved a great success in the premiere. As one must always cover one's bets, he asked me not to make any other plans for that evening just in case I might be needed to step in.

"Yes, but," I began, protesting, suspecting disaster, "but that evening I have a leave of absence to sing a concert in Cologne."

"You know, my dear friend, that the management, if necessary, can revoke any leave of absence, and I consider it necessary that you be available to substitute for your colleague in case of emergency."

He saw the disappointed look on my face and asked sympathetically, "How much would you have earned in Cologne?"

"A thousand marks—that's a lot of money for me—apart from the experience of singing Christ in the *Saint Matthew Passion* under Pabst and . . ."

"Well, you can make that up some other time," he interrupted. "I can understand your disappointment, but I have to ask you just once to do without. All the best, my dear friend." And so saying, he extended his hand for a brusque farewell.

I rose to my feet and silently left his office, livid with rage. When I arrived

2. . . . to a libretto written by Krauss.

5.4. I was looking forward to a concert in Cologne, but
fate intervened, and I had to take over the Wanderer in a
Siegfried performance in Munich.

home, still fuming, my wife told me the Opera had called and said that the
stage doorman had a letter for me. Still in a foul mood, I picked up the en-
velope, and apathetically opened it. Out came a thousand-mark bill with a
little note on which was written, in Krauss's handwriting: "As a poultice for
an injured soul." I apologized to him, and his theater now had an ensemble
member with a greater feeling for the virtue of team spirit.

Of course, Clemens Krauss doubtless also had a few less attractive personality traits. He could occasionally sink into a foul mood, and when he
was feeling grouchy, he was anything but charming. Apart from this, he had
a tendency to show his brighter side only to the people he liked. I can remember one rehearsal at which nobody could do anything right for him.
He kept coming up with something else to complain about, obviously for
the pure joy of mischief. I was already getting ready to explode and walk off
the stage, when his wife, the famous Viorica Ursuleac (we used to call her

the "queen mother" behind her back) restrained me just in time, whispering, "Stick around; sometimes he treats me the same way!"

Only a short road leads from Clemens Krauss to Richard Strauss. At rehearsals for the new *Salome* in May 1937, I was of course a most attentive ob-
server in a completely different environment, full of unfamiliar new impressions. Right from the first rehearsal, the head of the house, Clemens
Krauss, sat there, directing the musical sequence of the plot without inter-
fering in any way with the stage director, Rudolf Hartmann, or his directions. And right beside him, Richard Strauss, the composer was seated. He,
too, was there right from the beginning of the rehearsal period. The impression he radiated was unexpected: without making anything whatsoever
of himself and his presence, the then already seventy-three-year-old maestro leaned back in his chair, inconspicuously clad in a light linen jacket, and
now and then exchanged a couple of words with Krauss. It was very excit-
ing to see how Krauss, despite his own, enormously powerful personality,
took careful note of every hint, of even the smallest suggestion from the
composer Strauss. I don't think I'm wrong when I claim that Richard
Strauss was the only person—at least in significant matters—to whom
Krauss always deferred. We could really sense the symbiotic relationship between the two men. And it seemed the most natural thing in the world
when Strauss sprang to his feet with youthful vigor, walked over to one of
the singers and, in his slight Munich dialect, gave him or her a bit of advice.

The climate on stage was relaxed, buoyant, and radiated calm and light-
ness. This working atmosphere continued over the coming years in all the
Strauss productions and is one of the most interesting and worthwhile experiences I had in my long working life.

Anyone who, like me, attended concerts or opera performances in Munich during the 1920s occasionally had the pleasure of hearing Richard
Strauss on the conductor's podium. Two such evenings are still clearly etched
on my memory. As my readers will remember, the then fifteen-year-old was
still not entertaining the slightest ambitions of becoming a singer, only the
vague idea of living in some way with music. And so it was a special experience to witness a conducting composer who had an incredible effect on
me. This tall man was able, with his few brief but striking motions, to exude
such a high level of calm and authority that I instinctively held my breath.

How could I have suspected back then that only thirteen years later I
would watch him conducting again at the same place and on the same
podium, only this time with the view from the other side of the pit, as a
member of the cast in his opera *Salome*. Once again I was bowled over by
the incredible mastery, the same economical motions of the beautiful hands
that I remembered from that earlier time. Added to this were the all-commanding eyes, firmly and calmly directed toward the participants, some-

5.5.   This picture has a certain symbolic value: despite their powerful personalities, Clemens Krauss and Richard Strauss always collaborated hand in hand. Photo courtesy of the Richard Strauss Institute, Garmisch.

times the only mediator among himself, the orchestra, and the stage as the baton briefly remained still in his hand. I had the great good fortune of witnessing him on three evenings as my musical director: in two performances of his *Salome* and in one performance of Wagner's *Flying Dutchman*.

"How was it with him conducting? Did he go with the singers? Did he give cues?" singer colleagues continue to ask me to this day. "How were his tempi? Did he make large, expansive motions or did he just beat time?" It was his calm superiority that impressed me the most. The brisk tempi he selected for the *Dutchman* were particularly striking. At work and in private conversation he never tired of pointing out that, as far as he was concerned, Richard Wagner was the only composer besides Mozart who could be taken seriously.

It should be noted here that Strauss was often very impulsive and in a momentary mood would say things that we couldn't take literally. When once (I'll deal with this in greater detail at a later stage) I had the good fortune to work with him on some of his lieder, he said, in characteristic fashion almost to himself, "Actually, of all the things I've written, my lieder are my favorites." I'm not sure if this was a final judgment, but he did sound very serious.

I am often asked what was the special quality, perhaps also the most surprising quality, of this "gran uomo," and how his genius revealed itself. Questions like these are answered with many variations by both qualified and unqualified individuals. I'd like to try to present the answer from my vantage point. It was his unique knowledge of practical matters in the practice of the musical profession, the high level of conducting experience that he conveyed to everyone, be they orchestra musicians, up-and-coming conductors, or—especially—singers in the early stages of their development. That he was able to offer so much useful assistance so energetically and vol-

5.6. At a Munich performance of *Der fliegende Holländer,* I had the pleasure of singing the title role with Wagner's lineal successor, Richard Strauss, on the conductor's podium.

untarily of course had a great deal to do with his always being present during the weeks of preparation for one of his works. The worthwhile hints he
would give a young singer as the neophyte grew into a new role, his un-
complicated way of addressing problems and finally mastering them—all
were drawn from this ageless seventy-five-year-old's inexhaustible wellspring
of experience. All of these attributes were a great, indelible experience for me.

And the thing that made the greatest impression on me: whatever he
said or did, it happened with the greatest simplicity. We never had the feeling of having someone before us who was aware of his significance or
flaunted it in his interpersonal relations. There was never the kind of pre-
tension one often experiences with individuals to whom destiny has been
especially kind. Here is another little indication of how much Strauss regarded himself as a practical working musician and not as the greatest composer of his time—which he certainly was. In the years before the Second
World War, before it became fashionable for celebrities to have unlisted
telephone numbers, I read to my astonishment the following entry in the
Garmisch telephone directory: *Dr. Strauss, Richard, Conductor.* Not, as one
might expect, "composer"!

On July 24, 1938, Strauss's opera *Friedenstag* was given its world premiere before an international audience at the Munich State Opera. The following year on the eve of the composer's seventy-fifth birthday, on June 10,
1939, the first Austrian performance of this work took place at the Vienna
Opera. During the entire first week of June the weather was oppressively
hot and humid. The pollen from the flowers was in high season—and so
was my annual hay fever. On the morning of June 9 we had our final rehearsal, and my nose was thickly swollen. My larynx, including the vocal
cords, was also severely affected. I couldn't even think about singing. Sad
and depressed, I slunk into the house on the Ring and told the gentlemen
in the managerial offices that I didn't think I was in any condition to sing
that day's rehearsal let alone the next day's performance.[3]

Strauss and Krauss tried to calm me down, and Krauss said, "By all
means do the rehearsal, keep acting as you have been doing, but don't sing,
not one note. And then we'll see how things develop tomorrow." And
that's what happened. I went on stage, acted, and remained mute for two
hours. At the end of the rehearsal I went back to my dressing room in ab-
ject misery, whereupon Strauss burst in and said, glowing, "Wonderful! My
congratulations! It sounded just terrific!"

"Dr. Strauss," I wailed, "are you making fun of me? I didn't sing a note."

"Yes, that's true," he interrupted. "But I heard how it will sound tomorrow."

3. The house on the Ring is the Vienna State Opera on the Ringstrasse.

5.7. The commandant in Richard Strauss's *Friedenstag* was a Strauss role I had the privilege of creating both in the Munich world premiere and at the first Vienna performance.

And he was right. The next day my hay fever was completely gone, and the performance was a huge success for all parties concerned.

On the morning of this glowing midsummer day, however, none of us could have foreseen what else would happen that evening. Around midday we received the news that Adolf Hitler had quite unexpectedly arrived in Vienna and would be attending the opera that evening. I had been so involved all day with my role and the disappearance of my hay fever that I completely forgot the unexpected visit from Berlin. Only during the performance did I think for a moment about the effect that this was likely to have on the cast party afterward.

The audience received the opera with cheers of jubilation. Afterward, without any further explanation, we were all transported in official cars to the famous Koblenzl restaurant. It was a wonderfully warm night, and the tables had been set outdoors in the courtyard. I hastily counted eight tables lined up together with about twelve chairs at each one. This was, in any case, more than we would need for the people in the performance and their guests. It turned out that just about every Viennese theatrical celebrity had been invited, intermingled with people from the higher echelons of the municipal and national government.

I also met among the guests the motion picture director Gustav Ucicky, who had just begun shooting a new film at the Viennese Rosenhügel, (*Mother Love*) starring Käthe Dorsch. I was offered a small acting role, playing Dorsch's young husband, an assignment that subsequently turned out to be a lot of fun for me. Ucicky congratulated me on my success in the opera and took me by the arm, "Do you happen to know Gustaf Gründgens? No? Then come along, I'll introduce you to him." This was an opportune encounter for me, because a new production of Mozart's *Don Giovanni* was scheduled for the following autumn at the Berlin State Opera with Herbert von Karajan on the podium, Gründgens as stage director, and myself as Giovanni, a singularly tempting opportunity for me. Unfortunately this plan never came to fruition because of the outbreak of World War II.

The great actor, who enjoyed my deepest admiration, was charming and laid-back as he shook my hand, and we both looked one another over curiously. Ucicky smiled at Gründgens, "This evening's opera star has joined the ranks of screen actors. He'll be acting with Käthe Dorsch in my new film *Mother Love* and . . ."

Gründgens, who had not taking his eyes off of me the whole time, interrupted the famous filmmaker and said to me in his characteristic twang, "What will you be playing? The mother?" Only he could get away with a remark like that.

Meanwhile the guests at the opening night party were asked to take their seats for dinner. My seat was at the outer end of the eight tables. During dinner I discovered that Hitler had meanwhile arrived, unnoticed and unannounced, and was sitting at the last of the tables on the opposite side of ours. The dinner continued conventionally and without any further surprises. As we were about to get up from the table, somebody who looked very official whispered to me, "Brace yourself. The Führer will be coming over any minute now. He wants to meet you."

"Aha," I thought, "here we go, now you're in for it." Before I had a chance to think about it, I saw everybody rise, and somebody shoved me over to the end of my table. All eyes turned to a group of men, with a man I had only seen from a distance at its head. Now he was only about ten yards away from me. The whole thing seemed like a scene from a play, a little unreal. Everything seemed to take forever. In those few seconds something that acquaintances had often warned me about went through my head: "Just wait until you meet him, you'll never escape him. When he starts sizing you up with those steel-blue eyes, your defenses will vanish."

Now there he stood before me looking me in the face, the hands, as we so often saw in pictures, folded over each other directly in front of the middle of his body. I too had folded my hands together. My right hand hesitantly began to rise, but everything within me protested. What can I say, I just did not want to raise my arm. Whereupon he took my hand in both of his and said with a friendly smile, "Grüss Gott, Mr. Hotter, hearty congratulations for your success this evening."[4]

The effect on me was unmistakable. That he had greeted a Bavarian with a Bavarian greeting was of course very clever; nobody would have expected it. I could imagine that he had zeroed in on my unwillingness to raise my hand in the usual "Heil Hitler!" greeting. To avoid an embarrassing situation, he met me halfway and achieved exactly what he wanted: I was dumbstruck.

He walked over to the table and invited me to sit down beside him. He remained a few minutes while coffee was being served and said a couple of insignificant things until I asked him how he had liked the opera.

Try and imagine the situation: we were a scant three months away from the outbreak of a war he had been assiduously planning for ages, and somebody actually asked him how he had liked the content of a drama in which, as if by a miracle, the Thirty Years' War comes to an end to the general jubilation of everyone concerned. Of course he gave no indication of what was going through his head at the time. On the other hand, an opera called *Friedenstag* (Day of peace) was not exactly the ideal drama for someone who was in the process of instigating a war. In any event he said the subject of the opera didn't particularly appeal to him. He asked a few questions about my singing career and then, to my amazement, he said quite abruptly, "On June 29, 1932, in the concert hall of the Bayerischer Hof hotel you sang the two Sachs monologues from *Meistersinger*." So saying, he quickly took his leave and went over to one of the other tables, leaving me behind, rather baffled.

While allowing these experiences from 1939 to pass in review before my mind's eye, I cannot help thinking how often nowadays when the talk turns

---

4. "Grüss Gott" is a form of greeting in southern Germany, especially in Bavaria, somewhat equivalent to "howdy" in the southern United States. During the Nazi period, the "Heil Hitler" greeting with the upraised arm was virtually mandated by law.

to artists who made big careers in Central Europe during the Nazi period, it is taken for granted that they were either Nazis themselves or owed their careers to the protection of some Nazi bigwigs. I have quite intentionally reported on my totally involuntary and peculiar encounter with Adolf Hitler, which had no effect whatsoever on me and certainly not on my career.

As a matter of fact, shortly after this event took place, I was again approached by some party official, as I had been before in Hamburg, and he said to me, now that I had made the personal acquaintance of the Führer, I would certainly want to join the party. I told him frankly that I had always kept my distance from party politics and saw no need to get involved at this time, which he seemed to accept, as the subject was never broached again, nor were there any repercussions against me for not choosing to become a party member. Today, when I read stories about my contemporaries who had basically the same professional status as myself at the time being "forced" to join the National Socialist Party in the interests of their careers, I can't help being skeptical about the veracity of these claims.

I mentioned Strauss's casual remark to which I owe my awareness of his tender relationship to his art songs. What I now have to report is perhaps the most significant experience that bonds me with that great musician. In 1944 I was accorded the great privilege of being invited by the Vienna Musikverein to sing a recital in commemoration of Richard Strauss's eightieth birthday. I contacted the guest of honor to ask his advice on how to put together the program. He suggested arranging the program in chronological order, starting with the early songs. Amiable individual that he was, he invited me to his Garmisch villa to make the final selection.

I can still recall that wondrous day: in the cozy atmosphere of his home in the Loisach Valley, at the foot of the Zugspitze, we, my wife and I, were pampered by Dr. and Mrs. Strauss with a delicious midday meal—not an everyday pleasure in that war year of 1944. After that, the maestro took me into his study, where something most extraordinary took place in the hours that followed. He sat down at the piano, where he had prepared a sizable stack of sheet music and song albums. For four hours the artist then guided me uninterruptedly, with the youthful élan and enthusiasm that marked his almost eighty years, through a seemingly endless series of songs of which I had almost no awareness, singing and playing them. While doing this he found a full palette of nuances and hues in the expression of the words and commented on the compositions in between the various performances with wise, occasionally refreshingly earthy, remarks. I sat there in total astonishment. I myself said as little as possible, in an effort to etch every word, every tone as well as I could into my memory. Slowly, not until hours later, did it dawn on me that I had unexpectedly become the lucky eye- and ear-witness of once-in-a-lifetime music-historical event.

5.8. I will never forget the sublime afternoon I spent with Strauss in his sanctum sanctorum listening to the composer sing and play his own songs to help me prepare for a recital of his music. Photo courtesy of the Richard Strauss Institute, Garmisch.

The recital took place on June 10, 1944, the eve of the eightieth birthday in the Vienna Musikvereinssaal. As Strauss took his seat in the box, the Viennese gave him a huge birthday ovation. After the concert he came to my dressing room, embraced me, visibly moved, and then left the room without a word. I myself was moved to tears and would have liked nothing better than to see nobody else, but that would have been unfair to the enthusiastic, loyal Viennese audience.

Let me mention a couple of significant remarks from the mouth of this great musical creator, some of them spoken on that momentous day in Garmisch and some I picked up over the course of the years during our collaboration. I cannot remember them all word for word, but I certainly do recall their meaning. One remarkable thing is that I read some of these thoughts in notes from his father, the principal hornist in Munich's Royal Bavarian Court Orchestra, Franz Strauss:

> Only sing a song if you both understand and like the music and the words equally. Otherwise you are in no position to give a valid interpretation.

> Try to speak directly to your audience when singing a song as if you were telling them a story.

Don't ever separate the words from the music, and learn to decide
when one of these factors should temporarily step into the foreground.

Use the alternation between *cantabile* and *parlando*. Or sometimes
bind these two elements.

Recite the words of the poem to yourself over and over again in the
rhythm of the composition.

Learn to recognize the difference between naturalness and artificiality
and set severe standards first for yourself and then for the others.

The cardinal rule for singing, especially in song recitals: *sing piano,
speak forte*.

In most of the Richard Strauss biographies we will inevitably find a chapter on the subject of "Richard Strauss and the Game of Skat." Yes, he really
had a wild passion for that card game. I can tell you a thing or two about it,
because I was one of the select group who were welcome at the maestro's
card table. So many evenings during the Salzburg Festival and in the
Garmisch villa I have witnessed the joy with which he played that game. All
of us admitted to the table learned something from his all-dominating passion, his clever moves, and his often daredevil strategy.

The question has been raised as to who would have dared to take on the
great master at his favorite game. Mostly we, his opponents, lay in waiting
for an opportunity to counter one of the great master's cunning tricks.
When he was in a good mood—and he always was as long as he was winning—he would constantly make witty side comments, such as when one
of my singer colleagues picked up the right card, "Good work, my friend,
you'll get a nice new role!" Or when someone didn't play too well, "You
can crack on all the high notes you want, but you mustn't discard the wrong
ace."

Once during our vacation period, my friend and tenor colleague Franz
Klarwein invited me to spend a couple of days in his house in Garmisch.
Hardly had Strauss found out about it when he invited us to his house for
a heavy-duty game of Skat. And then something unusual happened: the
maestro began getting carried away with his bold tactics, and noticed after
three moves that his impetuous playing style had backfired, and he didn't
have a chance of winning. Furiously he threw the rest of his cards on the
table and wrathfully began uttering an imprecation that probably only a few
initiated individuals can ever claim to have heard: "Now you can all kiss
my . . ." All in all, he had lost almost eight hundred marks in this round.
With savage energy and grim determination, along with a sizable portion

of luck, in the space of two hours he managed to bring down his losses to some three hundred marks. Then his wife Pauline walked into the room to ask how much longer this game was going to take today.

"Well then, gentlemen," said the head of the house resignedly, "let's call it a day, and," indicating the current accounts, continued in muted tones, "we can settle this score some other time. I'll see you out." We rose, Strauss walked us out to the road, shooting short, searching glances back at the house. Then he reached into his jacket pocket, took out three crumpled hundred-mark bills, pressed them into my right hand and grumbled, "Now

5.9.   Franz Klarwein and I had Pauline Strauss, the composer's wife, to thank for winning a card game with her cardshark husband. She decided enough was enough, and we happily headed home with our winnings. Photo courtesy of the Richard Strauss Institute, Garmisch.

hit the goddamn road, you miserable rapscallions!"[5] With that, he turned on his heels and strode back to his house. With our tails between our legs like schoolboys who had just been bawled out, yet nevertheless slightly triumphant, we cleared out of the battlefield. A propos "rapscallions": by this time both of us were established members of the solo ensemble and proud fathers of families.

At another skat game during the 1944 Salzburg Festival, I took advantage of a break for refreshments to approach Strauss and ask him directly about the origins of his passion for the game. He looked me, as was his style, right in the eye and smiled, "I'll explain that to you, my dear friend. Everything I see, the people, the animals, everything in nature in all its variety, makes sounds for me, it releases musical inspiration. Now that I'm growing older, however, the process of transferring the sounds I hear inside me to paper doesn't work so well as it used to. That's why that inner music has become somewhat of a burden. Fortunately there is one thing that makes no sound, and that's playing cards. That's why I abandon myself with more enthusiasm than ever before to card games. Anyway, I sometimes have a feeling that the people who write about me are more interested in my fondness for skat than they are in my music. So please do me a favor, and when you speak of me, don't just talk about skat." An injunction I shall hereafter follow.

5. "Und jetzt schaut's, daß weiterkommt's. Saubuam, elendige!"

ᡪᡪ Chapter 6 ᡪᡪ

Before returning to operatic life in Munich during my early years, I'd like to interrupt the flow of this narrative briefly and do a little general stock-taking on some of the things I learned in these early years and a few other maxims that have been added or amended since that time.

In the course of an extended career, I have picked up a number of pointers, both general and specific, that have served as guideposts along the way. Many of them may seem deceptively simple at the outset, but I would urge the reader, whether he or she is someone interested in an artistic career or simply an enthusiastic listener, to give them serious thought. I believe an awareness of these ideas can add considerably to the enjoyment and understanding of any musical performance, whether on the operatic stage or the concert platform.

First and foremost in any artistic endeavor: there is no point in trying to do anything you have not learned how to do. There are any number of parallels between a life in art and the old structure of the crafts trades dating back to the time of Hans Sachs. As in shoemaking, carpentry, and soap boiling, art, too, has its periods of apprenticeship, its journeyman years, and its era of mastery. Not every artist will pass through all these phases and become a master, but a good journeyman has a great deal to contribute to a musical production. Talent has a great deal to do with it, as does the character of the individual concerned, but without a solid apprenticeship at the outset and the concept of mastery as a goal for everyone, plus the investment in the learning time required for moving from one of these stages to another, there will always be something lacking in any artistic expression.

I would carry this concept further by suggesting that anyone who is not seriously committed to the learning process will never derive the joy from the art that more than compensates the artist for all the sacrifices involved. Those sacrifices can be considerable, both on a material and a spiritual level. Seeing our contemporaries move from one phase of success to another in what might seem a less demanding calling while we are still grappling with the basics of what we are trying to do can be fiendishly frustrating. And there is one frustration that will always be with us. Unlike the crafts trades, there is no moment in an artist's career when the training period comes to a complete end. When an operatic artist's academic training concludes, and the professional career begins, is when learning really starts in earnest. I can recall an interview several years ago with actor Charlton Heston in which he was asked the difference between art and craft. He replied that while there is no art without craft, a pure craftsperson can be satisfied with, say, a perfectly made chair or a totally symmetrical vase, while the artist is never completely satisfied. As I see it, this dissatisfaction can be an engine to propel the serious student—and we are all students—to more meaningful and fulfilling accomplishments.

When my career began, most singers, even on the upper echelons of the profession, were involved in the ensemble of a theater, which became a kind of artistic family. In this setting we youngsters were constantly picking up pointers from all sides, while many mature colleagues learned more about what they were doing from the challenge of having to explain the fundamentals of their work to others, turning impulse into intention, and making artistic moments repeatable. I regret the disappearance of so many of these ensemble family opportunities, which are especially nourishing to the most talented of the younger performers. These are the colleagues who may spend a year or so in a small provincial theater and then the remainder of their careers freelancing on the road without the "nest warmth" available to us in so many theaters, that served both as operatic homesteads and the bases of operations for all the barnstorming tours. This is why I would fervently urge any beginning artist to enter into an ensemble situation with a full awareness of the profits to be derived from this important developmental phase. Even a mediocre conductor or stage director faced with getting a production on the boards in the face of pitfalls that never confront companies at the higher levels of the profession can teach us some very basic things that will never be more graphically driven home anywhere else.

Regardless of who may be guiding their early steps, young artists are well advised to listen attentively to that guidance and hold their tongues, even when what they are hearing may seem poorly articulated, unwise, or just plain wrong. An ability to differentiate between the practical and the impractical can only come about by simply doing what one is asked to do and then seeing for oneself whether or not it really works. There is no point objecting to something you haven't tried, and it can lead to conflicts that will stymie further cooperation. What is called for here is a diplomatic approach, an honest attempt to get along with everyone. This advice applies not only to the early stages of the career. It is one of the prime prerequisites of functioning effectively in this profession, and it can pay invaluable rewards when the artist has the good fortune to be engaged in a company that provides a goodly portion of top-quality motivation and inspiration.

One indispensable attribute is a keen awareness of what we are capable of doing, and what we are still lacking, at any phase of the career. A dearth of self-awareness leading to our misjudging our own capabilities could greatly impede our artistic progress or even cost us our very careers just when we seem to be heading for higher ground. Performers often regard it as advantageous to be able to talk glibly about their own achievements, especially in the circle of their colleagues, but when we find ourselves in situations where fateful decisions have to be made, nothing less than total self-honesty is acceptable. That means constant reflection on those two essential issues: what can I do now, and what am I still lacking?

Artistic freedom is not something we can simply take for granted; it has to be earned. I believe Richard Strauss was the one who articulated that maxim. Whoever first said it, I believe it to be one of the most essential rules of the game. It comes to mind in so many situations, particularly when vocal music, some of it conceived for the stage, is being presented in concert, and artists use the absence of a guiding stage production to take liberties they might otherwise not be accorded.

In life as in art, we must be able to put in hard work on the achievement of any objective, and to maintain a constant scrutiny of what we are aspiring to and how effectively we are achieving it, just like the checks and balances implemented by professional athletes in their daily exercises. Of course, the essence of this, for all the emotional involvement in artistic expression, is the discipline of objectivity. It is all very well to be able to express something honestly, but that honest expression first takes fire when it is communicated to a receptive audience, and the only way we can gauge that crucial element is by putting ourselves in the position of the audience and asking ourselves to what degree we have sparked the communicative flame. We must learn that our job is not to feel every emotion we are expressing but to maintain the critical distance that comes from depicting these feelings without allowing them to cloud our awareness of getting them across to the audience. This is done by memorizing the emotions all of us have experienced at some point or other in our lives and duplicating them on the stage, not by getting tied up in an emotional state ourselves.

The great Russian basso, Fyodor Chaliapin explained the phenomenon this way: in rehearsal, he said, he went through all the ups and downs of the character's emotions. During that phase of development he could be a horror, a euphoric or a tortured individual. Then, having, so to speak, digested all of this emotional fare, he was able to step to one side of himself and begin thinking analytically about such questions as, What was he doing with his hands or his head? What posture had he assumed here? Here, again the element of self-control ties in, making certain sequences of emotionally motivated action so much a part of ourselves that we can express them no other way. One of Chaliapin's mentors in Russia and an artist and teacher who can be justly called the father of modern acting, including operatic acting, Konstantin Stanislavsky, stated the case even more succinctly when he described it as the "as if" sensation. I must evoke the impression "as if" I were happy or sad, but in the final analysis, it is not I who should laugh or cry. The real laughter or tears must come from the people out front. There are a thousand possibilities for evoking the illusion of any given emotion, and it is our job to join forces with our director and find the most suitable stratagem to convey the emotion of the character we are portraying. But getting lost in that emotion ourselves is most certainly not one of the viable alternatives.

Under the best of circumstances, we should be able to educate our audiences and train them to expect only honesty and directness from the stage. Too much artificiality and empty posing will blunt an audience's response to what makes real theatrical sense. If instead we can instill an understanding for authenticity on the stage, it will help us make the feelings in our musical scores come alive for our spectators and inspire them to plumb the feelings we are communicating.

Perhaps this explains why many members of an audience, who have shared in the emotional content of a particularly charged theatrical experience are surprised when, still somewhat unsettled by the emotional impact of what they have witnessed, they visit a member of the cast backstage, and find him or her in a fairly well balanced state and ready to celebrate the accomplishment of the evening's task with a well-earned glass of beer.

What does this all add up to? Primarily an appreciation of the very high calling our abilities have given us the right to look upon as our own. While this appreciation may give us just cause for pride, that pride must always be tempered with modesty. Anyone who has had the privilege of one-on-one contact with artists on the highest level of the profession is invariably struck by the remarkable modesty and downright humility all true artists possess. It is this characteristic that leads me to the conviction that art is essentially a kind of religion, one that can only be approached with profound respect and sincere humility: respect for the great masters who have given us our artistic challenges, and humility in the face of our ability or inability ever to meet those challenges fully.

Moving more specifically into the field of opera, the major challenge here is a German term that is not easy to translate into other languages: *Gestaltung,* essentially the craft of dramatic depiction, giving a character its form and personality. In this effort, there is one absolute and irrevocable point of departure, and that is the music. Whatever we may do on the stage must never be merely concurrent with the music or, in a worst-case scenario, apart from the musical impulse. The music drives all the action on stage and dominates every other consideration. Any attempt to work against the music will have the same effect as trying to sail against the wind: it is doomed to failure. By the same token, every move we make on stage must also be subservient to the exigencies of our vocal technique. With vocal expression as the prime communicative element, it makes no sense ever to impede our ability to produce the vocal sound in any way. Many singers may be agile creatures capable of producing the necessary vocal sound in tandem with a variety of stage actions, but this comes about because they have learned how to make effective compromises with the process of singing technique. Nonetheless, we may rest assured the vocal expression is always paramount in their consciousness. Singers who are learning a role and growing into its demands *must* incorporate the physical, theatrical element into their practicing as early as possible, so they know where those compromises will need to be made and thus develop a technique for keeping the vocal sound flowing under all circumstances.

As I mentioned before, when I first began my operatic career, after initially studying keyboard instruments and then singing as an end in itself, the dramatic element was still fairly alien to me. In that era of exaggerated histrionics, good examples for honest acting on the opera stage were few and far between. The legitimate theater gave me what I perceived to be greater honesty of expression, while I found operatic acting terribly artificial and stilted. Consequently, when I first started acting in opera myself, I believed that this evasive concept of *Gestaltung* mostly had to do with moving around the stage—if you will, moving in general. It was not until much later that I began to develop an awareness for that mystical bond between musical impulses and dramatic expression. In many cases, stage deportment, or simply maintaining a proper posture and using the face and the eyes concentratedly, can have far greater dramatic impact than an overabundance of stage action. Beyond this, I came to realize how important the use of language is in operatic expression: simply pronouncing the sung words with clarity and conviction is essential to any dramatic statement.

I fear the significance of language as a dramatic element in opera has been sadly neglected in today's approach to vocal music. Perhaps this neglect has something to do with the fact that most singers in earlier times always knew what they were singing about; they generally sang the operas in their own languages or in an acquired language they could comfortably handle in conversation. But the finest of today's singers still distinguish themselves by their grasp and understanding of whatever language they may be singing in. Simply parroting syllables you learned by heart will never have the same effect as a thoroughgoing understanding of the linguistic singularity of the text. While none of us can ever achieve so thorough an understanding and mastery of every language we sing as we have of our native tongue, it should remain one of those goals we never quite reach, but always strive for. Trying to sing in a language of which we have no knowledge impresses me as a road with more obstacles than destinations.

On another level, however, even watching television nowadays gives us a sad awareness of the disrespect many contemporary dramatic performers have for the element of language. In an effort to achieve "naturalness" (whatever that means), so many modern theatrical directors encourage actors to mumble and slur their dialogue to the point where it becomes virtually incomprehensible to the most attentive listener. They tell the actors not to speak in an affected manner but simply to talk as one would in real life. All of this makes sense as far as it goes, but we should, in all honesty, first define "real life" in this context. Does anyone in real life make a conscious attempt not to be understood? Add to this the necessity of seeming to be in a real-life situation, convincing the audience of what the ancients called "the illusion of the first time," while still projecting the voice to the back of a large hall with possibly thousands of seats, and you see where the real challenges lie. Here is another area where compromise is inevitable, and where the rewards continue to be significant: a real professional can speak or sing distinctly without seeming affected, be understood in the back of a large auditorium, and yet be appreciated as natural by the patrons in the front rows or audiences in front of the motion picture or television screen. This clarity is one of the essential elements of the craft. An inability to speak clearly can only lead to an inability to lend conviction and honesty to acting or singing. All the aforementioned factors convinced me of how far dramatic expression goes beyond the mere agitation of hands and feet or pacing up and down. Indeed, sometimes the honest depiction of a character benefits most greatly from an absence of physical action, letting the words and music unfold their full significance to the consciousness of the listening spectators. Physical posture is always important, but it is erroneous to believe that acting consists of the urge always to "do something." Indeed, nothing could be farther from the honest perception of "real life." Yet another phase of our activity we simply have to learn. It will not happen by osmosis!

In my own repertoire, there were some significant scenes, where this kind of physical stillness and allowing the words and music to be the message were the interpretation of choice. One of the most telling examples of this is Wotan's narration in the second act of *Die Walküre*. Many of today's stage directors ask baritones to wander all over the stage during that scene, flailing the air with their arms. All this extraneous action simply gets in the way of the dramatic thrust of this very important scene. The real art of portraying Wotan in that second act is simply to sit still and tell his story. Only one single time does he rise to his feet, but that one time can be a shattering moment, and it should not be overshadowed by any stage action before it.

Of course, I didn't invent that action, or shall we call it that conscious dispensing with action. Every time I think about that scene, it evokes learning moments in the relatively early stages of my career, such as the collaboration with Bruno Walter in Amsterdam I mentioned earlier. Before we rehearsed with the orchestra, we ran through the music with Dr. Walter accompanying me at the piano. Just before we began our practice session, the conductor wisely remarked that he found it very advantageous for a good operatic actor to sing music like this in a concert situation, because he is forced to express the entire dramatic scene exclusively using the word linked with the tonal element. This stricture graphically brings home the eternal truth that a complete command of both the text and the singing apparatus is the same thing, and it is the same vocal chords that articulate both the words and the music.

I later raised the subject with an otolaryngologist, and he told me that the physiological process of speaking and singing is the same with one significant exception: when we are speaking, only the edges of the chords vibrate. Singing, by contrast, not only brings the entire vocal chords into vibration, but also generates further vibration; the basic concept of resonance comes from the fact that the sound waves continue from the point of origin in the larynx and run throughout the entire body. This is why we have to learn how to use the full potential of our physical resonance through a conscious interaction of tension and relaxation at all the right points. It has nothing to do with vocal strength but rather focuses on the technique of singing, which means keeping the body sufficiently relaxed in the right places to make it possible for it to radiate the sympathetic vibrations from the vocal apparatus. I have observed this phenomenon in situations where I feel my voice is resonating well, and am amazed to discover that when I touch my arm, this part of my body is also resonating. We can also see this in animals whose whole bodies also go into action when they make a vocal sound, or watch a tiny baby and notice the remarkable volume level they are able to create by simply not getting in the way of the sound. For that matter, look at how small a canary is, and then notice the incredible amount of sound that tiny creature is capable of producing.

It is hard for us singers to combine that sense of controlled physical relaxation with the demands of a physical acting portrayal, but it can be done if we learn how to avoid forcing our physical motions to the degree where they impede the singing process. This was one of the important tenets I learned from Wieland Wagner, who taught us that the time for action is never concurrent with a powerful phrase, but rather as a preparatory gesture before that phrase or as an added emphasis after it has been sung, thus drawing the full potential from the dramatic and musical moment (quite apart from the artificiality of emphasizing a musical expression that is strong enough in and of itself by stomping a foot or raising a fist, to cite only the most frequent abuses). And on those occasions when a gesture is called for, we often discover that one hand says more than both, and a certain look more than a hand. It's all a question of discipline—what the poet William Ernest Henley called being the master of one's fate.

There were times, I must admit, when even Wieland Wagner seemed somewhat impeded in his control of the stage action by the demands made by his grandfather's score. Yet when I called his attention to that point once he looked at me somewhat baffled and inquired, "What ever gave you that idea?" By this time, I had done a bit of stage directing myself and I was keenly aware that it isn't always the easiest task to find a common denominator for the dramatic and the musical moment. But I had learned that when you subordinate the drama to the music, the music will always make the drama happen, whereas if you try to force the drama on top of the music, you will wind up with neither in the final analysis. This is why an opera director not only needs to know the elements of music, but also the basics of vocal technique. Without this knowledge there is no coordination of these diverse elements. This doesn't mean a director needs to be a singer any more than a conductor needs to be able to play every instrument in the orchestra. But just as the conductor must be aware of the musicians' options and limitations, based on their abilities and the possibilities of their instruments, so, too, the director must know what he can ask a singer to do, and when the exigencies of vocal production must take the dominant position in the staging. This awareness comes from years of cooperation with singers and a regular interchange between the collaborators leading to an automatic sensitivity to the singers' needs.

I discuss some of the best directors, and the things I learned from them, at various places in this narrative, but at this juncture I would like to point out that not all of them were the big names in the field. In many cases, these were the house directors I mentioned before, such as Rudolf Zindler in Hamburg, people with a thoroughgoing grasp of the craft and the ability to impart their knowledge to a fairly inexperienced young singer, as we all once were. These were the people who taught us that the process of singing does not take place outside the acting moment but rather interacts with that moment to propel it forward.

All these things the artist has learned must yet be subsumed to one cardinal lesson. No artist should ever practice his or her profession without bearing in mind that none of what we are able to do would have been possible without our having received a multitude of gifts: not just the talent of singing or making music but also the very ability to learn and absorb those disciplines without which the initial gift would merely be an undeveloped raw material. This ability is cause for profound gratitude.

Back in my early youth, I was sadly disappointed to witness the way the majority of people treated their professions with indifference if not downright distaste. As the years went by, this initial impression has been confirmed by a multitude of disillusionments. In my own case, although at the beginning I did not feel myself "called" to the profession of singing, I soon began to love this profession. Later on, when the first successes came my way, I was more than happy, and I began to understand what my teacher meant when, at the very beginning of our work together, he told me: you must never stop thanking your Creator for what He has given you. I have since passed this along to my own students: the greater your talent, the greater your obligation to work and make something of those talents. The older I get, the more grateful I am for being able to love this profession of mine, a profession in which we can and must make full and equal use of body, mind, and spirit.

Chapter 7

Now I'd like to return to the beginning of my activity at the Munich Opera, when, during preparatory rehearsals for the new *Salome* production, the persons Richard Strauss and Clemens Krauss began exerting a powerful influence on both my professional and human development. I've already mentioned that I had met a goodly number of singing colleagues, who, older in both years and experience, had received the "intruder" from Hamburg partly with skepticism if not out-and-out rejection. I found the atmosphere in Munich fairly stodgy and conventional, clearly dominated by a certain pecking order oriented toward vocal personalities who had ruled the roost here for years.

Two of them, however, Hildegard Ranczak and Julius Patzak, both of whom I had admired and greatly respected from my student days, and who shared the stage with me as Salome and Narraboth respectively, immediately offered to go on a "du" basis with me, the German equivalent of first names in the English-speaking countries, and still not so prevalent a custom as it is in that part of the world. At that time, this was anything but the order of the day in Germany. They treated me with such cordiality that they made it easy for me to feel well and at home in my new surroundings.

A third individual from the ranks of the great Munich singers, another artist I had admired and revered from my early operagoing days, and whom my teacher Matthäus Römer described as a paradigmatic vocal role model, was Viennese bass-baritone Georg Hann, whom everyone in the theater called "Schorschi," the equivalent of the English "Georgie" in southern Germany and Austria. In our *Salome* production he sang the First Nazarene, a small role, but one Strauss called "important."

Hann could be described as something of a natural talent. He had studied singing in his native Vienna with the intention of establishing a concert career. His prowess in this field can still be heard in a magnificent CD reissue of a recording of Franz Joseph Haydn's immortal *Die Schöpfung,* in which he sings the bass solos together with Trude Eipperle, Julius Patzak, and the Vienna Philharmonic under Krauss. His engagement in Munich in

7.1. Not everybody at the Munich Opera was happy with the greenhorn who arrived in 1937, but Hildegard Ranczak was a good friend right from the word go. Here we are together as Carmen and Escamillo.

1927 was virtually the first time he stepped on an operatic stage. His career was a remarkable consummation of his gifts as a singing actor.

Unlike Ranczak and Patzak, Hann maintained quite a reserved, almost unapproachable attitude toward me. I still made my home in Hamburg and only came to Munich sporadically for guest appearances. At one gathering of colleagues—referred to in the prevalent brown-shirted style of the day as "*Kameradschaftsabende*" (comradeship evenings)—this reserve suddenly melted. These were occasions for members of the chorus, the orchestra, and

7.2.   My first of many collaborations with Hildegard Ranczak was in *Salome,* and the composer found her interpretation of this complex character as forceful as I did.

the technical staff to get together with the soloists in a kind of community spirit, which found me sitting with a jolly group of new colleagues and friends. I had already spotted our "Schorschi" at an adjoining table in a jovial mood under the influence of several cruets of wine and was more than pleased when he amiably raised his glass to me and waved me over to his table. That came as a surprise; in all these months we had barely exchanged any more than a couple of courteous words with one another.

In all honesty, I must admit, I was not totally unprepared for this invitation, as I had been involved in making it happen, eager to patch up whatever resentments he might have harbored for some of the roles he had, in the ten years before I joined the company, regarded more or less as his private property, but in which I was now being cast either along with or instead of him. Of course, I had nothing to do with these casting decisions, and I wanted to make it known to him how much I admired his work and considered it a privilege to share the stage with him. But he was not the kind of person one could approach directly with such a statement; he would quite reasonably have thought I was trying to curry favor from some ulterior motive.

It so happened at the time that we had a conductor in Munich who was married to a journalist, needless to say, specializing in news of the musical and theatrical world. Although a brilliant and delightful person, the lady was so enamored of her profession that she practiced it outside of office hours by disseminating information anywhere and everywhere. In short, she was an incurable gossip, and the best way to get a bit of information into public circulation would be simply to tell the lady to keep it to herself. From the time I came to the Munich Opera, her husband and I became good friends and spent a great deal of time strolling around the downtown area, taking a meal together, and generally enjoying one another's company, frequently with his very intelligent wife in tow. On one of those occasions, I just "casually" happened to mention that my teacher had told me that many of the singers at the State Opera were not much worth listening to from the point of view of inspiration, but two significant exceptions to that rule were Heinrich Rehkemper and Georg Hann. The way they sang, I told the conductor and his wife, was something I could learn from, and certainly had since coming to the theater. This was neither a lie nor an exaggeration. Römer had really said that about Rehkemper and Hann, and my own experience had more than confirmed his high opinion of them both.

In the space of only a couple of days, this information was imparted to the two gentlemen in question. Rehkemper, a genuinely nice person who needed no flattery to win him over, told her he was touched by this commendation from a younger colleague, while Hann was admittedly a bit flattered but still stinging from some of the roles he had lost, considering himself "demoted" to buffo parts. Nevertheless he seemed pleasantly surprised that I considered him someone worthy of learning from, as was evidenced on that evening when he waved me over to his table.

So I walked over, not entirely unsurprised by the gesture, to where he was sitting, and in a gush of verbiage in his inimitable Viennese dialect he told me he heard from the conductor's wife that I had told her such nice things about him as a singer and human being, and that pleased him very much. Then he raised his wine glass and promptly declared, "Look here, you can call me *du!*" which he instantly followed up with the remark, "But I gotta tell you one thing. I didn't much like you when you came here. You snapped up all my good roles. Now I gotta sing all the old geezers. And lemme tell you one more thing, even if you don't believe me: I'm a really good baddie."

The evening ended buoyantly, in the best of moods. We had become two colleagues who admired one another and for many years worked together on stage. We shared a dressing room in the house on Maximilianstrasse and had lots of fun in everyday rehearsal and performance situations. In the course of our friendship, he made one or two delicious remarks about our colleagues that often made it easy to take their negative attitude toward me with a grain of salt.

One of those colleagues, as I mentioned before, was basso Ludwig Weber, another Viennese artist who should, in Hann's opinion, have been a bit more charming in the tradition of the sons of that city. He was, however, anything but. Weber had worked his way up from a position in the Volksoper chorus to a status as an international soloist in Munich. As such, he regarded himself as the king of the theater, where he often walked around backstage in the foulest of moods, prompting Hann to quip, in a sideswipe at his adopted home turf, where the natives are not exactly noted for the worldly charm and sophistication, "Look at him, Viennese, but as grumpy as a Bavarian." In fairness, I should report that, toward the end of his career, Weber did soften up a bit and even treated me with a bit more cordiality, but Hann's description at the time fit him to a T.

Krauss had the good sense to cast Hann in those roles where he was strongest and made the best impression: character roles and comic characters, where his inborn comedic skill, with the right guidance, came through hilariously. For me, he was *the* Faninal in *Rosenkavalier,* born to sing Waldner in *Arabella,* and was a Monsieur la Roche par excellence in *Capriccio,* a role that had been written for him, and which he sang at the world premiere. On top of that, there was the characteristic sound of his technically well focused voice. He was doubtless the kind of individual we like to call a true original, a rare breed in any theater, and one that bids fair to become extinct in the operatic world. Of course there are all kinds of delicious stories about him. Even if one or two of my readers already know some of these, I'd still love to pass along a couple. They all took place a half century or more in the past, but I witnessed them all, and I can vouch for their authenticity.

On the evenings when he conducted, Clemens Krauss liked to withdraw to a small room near the stage where he would carefully groom himself and then spend a few minutes quietly getting into the mood for whatever artistic activity lay ahead. From this room, located in the mezzanine slightly above the stage level, a narrow, old-fashioned winding staircase led down to the stage, which one had to reach by crossing a part of the corridor adjoining the gentlemen's solo dressing rooms. Krauss loved turning his first appearance in his dress suit into a real stage entrance, in which he would flaunt his evening cape, moving his arms ever so skillfully to reveal the scarlet lining inside, thus enhancing the general impression. One evening, shortly before the beginning of the performance, four major singer colleagues were standing exactly on that spot between the winding stairs and the stage access, conversing animatedly about something. Among them was our friend Schorschi, who, in stentorian tones, was clearly chairing this ad hoc session. At that moment a flunky appeared at the foot of the stairs, a preparer of the way, door opener, and general dogsbody for his director, inconsiderately and abruptly interrupting the Kammersänger's expostulations with the words, "Please, gentlemen, would you kindly step to one side. Any minute now, the *Herr Direktor* will be coming through." To which Hann annoyedly replied: "What? You mean the seven o'clock express is about to mow us all down?"

The scene of the next two episodes was the stage of the Nationaltheater on the day of the first stage rehearsals for the world premiere of Strauss's *Friedenstag* in the summer of 1938. Of course there was suspense in the air. On stage, the setting was marked by a couple of platforms, and to one side a staircase led to a peephole. The two characters who begin the drama are the captain and his commander, portrayed by Hann and myself. The curtain was up, and on the ramp down to the orchestra there were some twenty-five people sitting in close ranks with their backs to the auditorium: the composer, the conductor, the librettist, the publisher, the set designer, the chief *Korrepetitor* (vocal coach), the head of the costume department, and a few other potentates, each accompanied by a couple of assistants, plus a group of soloists waiting for subsequent entrances or simply curious to hear what the piece sounded like. The scene was still shrouded in total silence. Krauss exchanged a few words with Strauss, then Hann poked his elbow into my ribs and whispered, "Check that out! They're all behavior monitors!"

Then the rehearsal began. In the aforementioned work we all found ourselves in the period shortly before the end of the Thirty Years' War. The commander is in conversation with his captain, in the course of which he demands several reports as to whether or not the enemy forces are already approaching. To find this out, the captain must climb the stairs several times to view the scene and then make these reports to his commander. As this scene was repeated over and over, poor Schorschi had to keep running up and down the stairs. During a brief break in the rehearsal, he moaned softly, "Oh boy, I just love playing postmen."

The following story is one of the best known of that period, and has made a major contribution to the immortal reputation of that beloved Viennese basso. It took place during the orchestra rehearsal for Verdi's *Falstaff*. Krauss was conducting and seemed to be in less than the best of spirits that morning. They arrived at the scene in which Sir John is hidden in a laundry basket. Verdi wrote dream music for this sequence, but unfortunately the monkeyshines so many Falstaffs feel they have to perform in this scene seldom allow this music to reach its full effect. Our Schorschi also seemed to be laying it on with the traditional trowel; in any event, that's how it struck the already grumpy Krauss, who was generally quite fond of Hann. This time, however, he made no secret of his disapproval and groused, "That sounds hideous—as if Weiss Ferdl were singing in the basket." Weiss Ferdl was a local Bavarian backwoods comic, a kind of south German Gabby Hayes if you will, who used to sing funny little songs in a rather squeaky voice. When Krauss later interrupted the rehearsal to say something to the orchestra, the laundry basket lid was raised, Falstaff's face came into view, and Hann said, straight to the conductor, "I didn't know Weiss Ferdl had such a terrific voice!" Reliable witnesses report this remark sent Krauss into gales of raucous laughter.

The following anecdote is my personal favorite, which is why I saved it for last. In the early thirties Hann had very successfully tried his hand at a few dramatic roles, so the management decided to let him prepare the *Rheingold* Wotan. The head of musical preparation at the time, Franz Hallasch, personally assumed the task of getting him ready and told me what had happened in one coaching session. Hann himself wasn't all that sure this was the right role for him; at least, he registered misgivings. They arrived at the scene in Nibelheim, where Alberich stands facing Wotan and Loge and launches into a tirade of contempt at the two gods, whereupon Wotan, more to himself than to his adversary, replies: "Vergeh, frevelnder Gauch." (Begone, blasphemous churl!) As the rehearsal reached this point, Hann briefly stopped and said indignantly: "What!? Ver-geh, fre-veln-der Gauch! I ain't gonna sing that stuff. Ain't nobody gonna understand that!" Hallasch tried to explain to him that this was Wagner, and there was no way it could be changed. "Don't worry about me, just play the piano. I won't sing that stuff. Stupid nonsense!" Hallasch decided not to get involved in any discussions, went right on playing, and marked Alberich's next entrance, when the dwarf calls out: "Was sagt der?" (What did he say?) To which our Schorschi laughed triumphantly, "See what I mean? He don't understand it either!"

Of course there was a whole series of other funny stories about our dear Schorschi, but I'd better turn my attentions to some of the others among my many—mostly new—Munich colleagues. My first choice is basso Paul Bender, who first came to the Munich Opera as far back as 1903, and thus also delighted my parents' and grandparents' generation of opera enthusiasts. For me he was always the quintessence of a mature, yet anything but superannuated artist. I first heard him as a recitalist before I admired his work onstage. I must confess that, as a young music student, I often found lieder recitals horribly tedious, even when the singers in question devoted noble, beautiful voices to the task. Bender was one recitalist who handled language so well and lent such color to his interpretation and characterization of the songs that he turned every one into an artistic and acoustical experience for me.

I felt much the same way about the recital magician Karl Erb. He too, had been a member of the Munich ensemble all the way back in the days when Bruno Walter wielded the baton on the conductor's podium of the opera house. Hans Pfitzner himself was the one who elevated Erb's unique interpretation of the title role in his *Palestrina* to a position high in the heavens of his admiration. The remarkable thing about Erb's song interpretation was that it was not just the sheer beauty of his voice that made all the difference, as with Bender, it was also his interpretive acumen. I had the good fortune to be able to learn and profit from the impressions any number of great recitalists made on me in the course of my long life, but ultimately it was Paul Bender and Karl Erb who sparked my great love for the art song. Bender was, of course, also outstanding when it came to acting, although very much in the style of another time. But as with Chaliapin, one forgot that element with Bender and likewise with many other singing actors. Bender was an uncommonly amiable, universally educated man, who had actually studied medicine in earlier years, and was always willing to give some good advice when you asked him for it. We all loved listening to his stories because he never lifted his mental index finger in remonstration—so often a characteristic of senior vocal citizens.

I also admired the celebrated star of the twenties, Wilhelm Rode, an actor and singer with flawless enunciation (especially in his glory roles in the Wagnerian heroic baritone repertoire) and equipped with a mighty, untiring voice. His Hans Sachs was unforgettable, his Wotan overwhelming, and for years he was my great role model. When, years later, I met his granddaughter at a Munich party, I was proud to hear that while her grandfather did not particularly like speaking of me, when he did it was always with great respect.

Another favorite of the operatic stage and the concert podium in Munich was baritone Heinrich Rehkemper. A brilliant, elegant performer with a distinct, powerfully impressive voice, he gave me many an unforgettable evening in the opera house during the 1920s: *Salome* (Jochanaan), *Don Giovanni* (Giovanni), *Les contes d'Hoffmann* (the four villains), *Palestrina* (Morone). It was in his unique interpretation that I first heard the *Winterreise,* leaving me deeply stirred and close to tears. How lucky I was to be able to stand on stage with him in the years between 1937 and 1943! When I told him how much he had sparked my enthusiasm ten years earlier, he would laugh and give me a friendly slap on the back. After some initial reluctance on his part, we later joined together in a genuine artistic friendship. A great actor on the operatic stage—and sometimes in private life—he was a life-affirming, very witty man. You could clown around like crazy with him onstage when he tried to crack you up right in the middle of the plot.

Of the female stars I first admired from the auditorium I must begin with Elisabeth Feuge. I was really crazy about her, even back in my high school years. In the years before the war she made many appearances in the house on Maximilianstrasse, not to sing, but rather more out of curiosity and perhaps also in a kind of longing for the past. It was then that I could confess my schoolboy puppy love for her.

To this day I can still hear the sweetness of her voice when, as Eva in the first act of *Die Meistersinger,* she sang "wie ihn uns Meister Dürer gemalt" (as Master Dürer painted him for us), describing the famous Nuremberg artist's portrait of the young King David. I don't think I've ever heard a more moving, soul-stirring interpretation of that phrase.

I've already mentioned Hildegard Ranczak. She was my first partner on the Munich stage, in *Salome.* We struck up an immediate friendship. In my early Munich years, we were often on stage together: as Carmen and Escamillo, as Clairon and Olivier in *Capriccio,* as Nedda and Tonio in *Pagliacci,* as Aithra and Altair in *Die ägyptische Helena,* as Aida and Amonasro. She was an unusually endearing colleague, a sometimes incisively witty, charming woman, in private life and onstage. Born in Moravia and raised in Pennsylvania, she had returned to Europe to launch her singing career and got stuck there in the wake of political developments, with which she had no sympathy whatsoever. Fortunately she had managed to retain a kind of no-nonsense Stateside bluntness, which held in her good stead, especially in the troubled war years. As witness the following anecdote.

She was taking the streetcar like everyone else—there were no taxis in those days—and stood, dressed to the nines, on the platform, there being no seats in the crowded vehicle. In the style of the day, she wore a perky little veiled hat, and the bright red of her highly polished fingernails glittered through the gossamer of her open-mesh gloves. One passenger, clearly a Nazi zealot, looked daggers at her and felt obliged to grumble his disapproval, "Disgraceful! Our boys are holding the line in the trenches, while back home these brazen hussies run around with their lips and fingernails painted scarlet!"

To this, she gently raised her veil, and with the most benign countenance imaginable, looked him dead in the eye, cooing in a sweetly acerbic manner she had doubtless picked up on the streets of Pittsburgh, "I could paint my asshole bright red, and it still wouldn't be any of your fucking business, buster!" The gentleman beat a hasty retreat at the next stop, whereupon every face in the crowded trolley car was instantly wreathed in a contented smile.

One of the old guard of highly popular ladies in the theater was alto Luise Willer, a great artist with an outstandingly beautiful mezzo voice. She was a genuine Munich original, outfitted with a delicious sense of humor, soft and appealing in her vocal approach, then ready, at the next moment, to let loose with some heavy-duty Bavarian imprecation, which she delivered with the best of them. I also shared the stage with her many times, and there are very few people I laughed and had fun with as much as with her. When I think of "Luiserl," I can still hear Brangäne's call from the second act of *Tristan und Isolde;* it still brings tears to my eyes and a warm glow to my heart.

When I congratulated her on her fiftieth birthday in 1938, she asked me,

"What do you think I started my solo career with? *Not* with my voice, but with my legs," and appreciatively slapped her thighs. "They were pretty good show pieces in those days. I started singing in the Munich Opera chorus, back in the days when Bruno Walter ran the place. Shortly before the World War, we were getting Mozart's *Figaro* ready. Everybody was ready to go on in act three when Bruno Walter came and inspected the ladies' chorus along with the stage director. The gentlemen's eyes were fixed on the chorines' legs. After a thoroughgoing examination, the gentlemen selected two of us to sing the little duet in the last scene ("Amanti costanti"). One of the girls selected was me. Years later, long after I had become a regular member of the solo ensemble, Bruno Walter once said to me: 'Back then, in *Figaro,* the only reason we took you at first was because of your good-looking legs. Not until afterward did I realize what a glorious voice you have.' Another way of starting a singing career, don't you think?"

The year 1937 was rich in important events and new roles, actually the richest in my entire career. Before making my successful official Munich debut as Wanderer in *Siegfried* in April of that year and spending the month of May preparing my first new production there with *Salome* under Clemens Krauss (which brought with it that important first meeting with Richard Strauss, as I already mentioned), I had already enriched my repertoire with the title roles in Puccini's *Gianni Schicchi* and Wagner's *Der fliegende Holländer* in Hamburg productions. These two roles were joined, also in Hamburg, in September and October, by three new assignments: Cardinal Borromeo in Pfitzner's *Palestrina* under the composer's baton, Wotan in *Rheingold,* and Basilio in Rossini's *Il barbiere di Siviglia.*

Meanwhile, I appeared for the first time in the Munich Summer Festival as Kurwenal in Wagner's *Tristan und Isolde,* also my first collaboration with the great Karl Böhm, another dear and honored old friend I had admired back in my Munich student days.

And then, finally in December, there was my debut in the role of the Grand Inquisitor in Verdi's *Don Carlo* in Munich, also under Clemens Krauss. This was the only role in my repertoire that I would perform more than five hundred times. Last but not least, that same December I made the acquaintance of the composer who was so unjustly ostracized during the Nazi era in Germany, Paul Hindemith. Soon after the beginning of the Hitler regime in 1933, works of certain creative artists that were "not German enough" for the brownshirts were denigrated as "degenerate." Paul Hindemith's works were also blacklisted as "degenerate art" and thus prohibited. He invited me, as had Bruno Walter, to a concert with the Concertgebouw Orchestra in Amsterdam. On the program were concert selections from his opera *Mathis der Maler.* The work was new to me. I sang the role of Mathis with great joy and to the obvious satisfaction of the conducting composer, because he autographed my piano score with the words: *H.H., the essential and ideal image of Mathis, for whom, without his previous permission, I custom-made the role, with sincerest gratitude, Paul Hindemith — December 16, 1937.* That, at least in part, was the actual world premiere. The first staged performance then took place in 1938 in Zurich.

The most important artistic event in 1938 was doubtless a world premiere that attracted global attention: Richard Strauss's *Friedenstag* on July 24 in the Munich State Opera. I, having been entrusted with the leading male role of the commander, stood beside a lady who was then at the pinnacle of her career, the incomparable Viorica Ursuleac. Our roles were vocally fine-tuned by the composer to fit us.

A further, valuable enrichment of my growing repertoire was the character of Sir John Falstaff in Verdi's eponymous opera—a success that came my way unexpectedly for many people. Purely from the outside, the transformation of a quite slender, almost skinny twenty-nine-year-old into the rotund, feisty Falstaff was just as hard to imagine as my successful characterization of this difficult yet ultimately very gratifying role.

The new assignments in 1939 were Mandryka in a new Munich *Arabella* and the baritone role of Francesco in a new Berlin State Opera production of Max von Schillings's opera *Mona Lisa,* a work virtually forgotten today.

Absolutely, the most positive factor of our work on *Arabella* in Munich was the ongoing presence of the composer during the rehearsals and the all-encompassing, powerful personality of Clemens Krauss. Keenly interested, not only in his own musical area but also in everything happening on stage, taking note of the smallest detail as new characters came into being, whether vocally or theatrically, he provided good advice, expressed approval, or registered doubt. Sometimes he presented his counsel with delightful humor, and all of this, time and again, with a mischievous side-glance to Strauss. Simply being there and watching was an educational experience—and then, when the discussion focused on my own interpretation . . . !

Rudolf Hartmann, the stage director, and later also codirector of the theater, with whom Krauss often collaborated, had an anything but easy job; he always had to reckon with being interrupted at one point or another by one of the "greats."

On top of that there was the inspiring presence and artistic radiance of my Arabella, Ursuleac. At that time she was still completely equal to all the vocal challenges of this truly not easy-to-interpret character. This role seemed custom-made both for her larynx and her heart! I say this today with great conviction, despite all her famous successors in this role, including the wonderful Lisa Della Casa, a lady who looked like she might have stepped out of one of the portraits of great beauties in King Ludwig I's gallery.

What a wave of glorious sound emerged from the throat of the 1939 prima donna, when, in act three, she sang: "hat eine große Macht mich angerührt von oben bis ans Herz" (a great power stirred my heart from on high) accompanied by Strauss's E-flat major six-four chord, she crowned the phrase with a breathtaking high B-flat. The mere memory of that sound still brings tears to my eyes to this day.

On August 17, we had a repeat performance of the new *Arabella* production. As, shortly before the performance, I stepped out on stage, already in my Mandryka costume, Strauss hurried over to me, heartily shook my hand and said excitedly, "My heartiest congratulations! I hear you've become the father of a daughter." Then, looking at me from head to foot in my costume, he added, "Well, Mandryka's daughter must surely be called Arabella?"

I replied, "But Herr Doktor, that would be too great a burden for the poor girl. Just imagine, what if she doesn't turn into a real 'Bella'?."

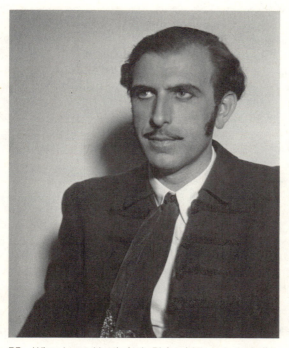

7.3. When I sang Mandryka in Richard Strauss's *Arabella,* the composer paid me the compliment of suggesting Helga and I name our daughter for the title character. That kind hope was finally realized in a later generation with the naming of our great-granddaughter (not co-incidentally Strauss's own great-great-granddaughter).
Photo, © Max Reinhardt Institute, Salzburg.

"A daughter of your lovely wife and yourself will be a Bella, you can count on it!"

Well, today the proud father can say, the maestro knew what he was talking about. If only he might have known that twenty-three years later the "almost Arabella" would one day bear his surname as the wife of his grandson. His wish finally came true in 1995 when his great-granddaughter gave birth to a daughter whom she named Arabella.

The Berlin State Opera inaugurated its 1939–40 season with the aforementioned *Mona Lisa* by Max von Schillings. The title role was sung by my Munich Arabella: Viorica Ursuleac. On the podium was Karl Elmendorff, with whom I joyfully renewed my acquaintance from our collaboration in Barcelona back in 1936. The main attraction of this engagement, however, was the fact that the widow of the composer, who had only died in 1933, the formerly world-famous dramatic soprano Barbara Kemp, was our stage director. She knew the work like the back of her hand, and had often sung the role of Mona Lisa herself under the musical direction of her husband.

I enjoyed the work with her very much. A real "specialist," she had lots of valuable impulses to pass along to us singers. She had lived the greater part of her long, successful life in Berlin and had taken on the character and jargon of this most urban of all Central European cities, with its quick-witted, refreshingly iconoclastic populace. When I think back on her, a smile always crosses my face. Nevertheless, she was very much to be taken seriously in her work. In any case, I learned more from her in a couple of weeks than I did from many another pseudointellectual stage-directing desk jockey over the course of the years.

I think she was quite fond of me, and she loved telling stories of her life in art. In these stories, the name of my old friend from back in Prague, Theodor Scheidl, often popped up. She had sung quite often with him; no wonder she remembered him so fondly as her stage partner. She spoke with great enthusiasm of another baritone, the Portuguese singer Francisco d'Andrade, the legendary Giovanni, a role his painter friend Max Slevogt masterfully preserved on canvas. I was mightily proud when Barbara assured me I reminded her of him in the way I portrayed that role.

Once, in rehearsal, I was sitting in the auditorium next to her. The opera *Mona Lisa* has a subplot: the opening and closing scenes take place in the present day. The characters appear in modern dress. Viorica Ursuleac walked on stage in a chic tailored suit, a sprightly little hat on her head with the veil just a bit out of place, at which Barbara called out in traditional no-nonsense Berlin style, "Hey, get the lace curtain off of your face."[1] We all roared with laughter. The working climate during rehearsals was animated

1. "Mensch, nimm doch die Jardine von's Jesicht!"

with everyone in high spirits. We all learned and profited so much from that great artist and amusing personality.

I also took advantage of my days in Berlin to attend the nearby Theater am Gendarmeriemarkt and spend many an inspiring hour in the company of Gustaf Gründgens and his actor friends.

When, in 1939, the war broke out, I had guest contracts in four opera houses. I would continue to make my home in Hamburg for another year, but I sang regular evenings in Munich, where I hoped to find a new artistic future. To these were added, as of the autumn of 1939, several evenings in the house on Unter den Linden in Berlin as well as performances at the Vienna State Opera.

Traveling from place to place got harder and harder as the war progressed. Soon the only way to get anywhere was by sitting in overcrowded trains by day or night. Flying was still rare, and later it became totally impossible, while sleeping cars began disappearing from the rails. Getting a meal on the train got harder and harder as wartime rationing became more and more severe.

Of course I know all too well that I personally had little cause to complain over the discomforts these conditions brought with them. Thanks to a certain professional cachet, I was in a special position, which spared me an induction into the forces at the front. This preferential status, however, on my many journeys often caused people on trains to treat me with tremendous rancor and hostility.

The year 1939, shortly before the outbreak of the war, brought me the long-desired contact with the Vienna State Opera. I had already briefly noted that I had received an invitation from that institution back in 1937—set in motion by Bruno Walter and recommended by Hans Pfitzner—to sing Cardinal Borromeo in a new staging of *Palestrina*. The whole project came to naught, because Hamburg refused to release me. Then, in June 1939, Vienna was preparing a festival week for music and theater, in conjunction with which a guest performance by the entire ensemble of the Hamburg State Opera in the old imperial city with a production of Händel's *Giulio Cesare* (with me in the title role) was envisioned.

I've already mentioned that Clemens Krauss conducted the first Viennese performance of Strauss's *Friedenstag* in 1938 and brought Viorica Ursuleac and myself from the Munich world premiere cast to the Vienna stage. Before these two events, I had already marked my debut in the house on the Ring as Jochanaan in *Salome*. This was the first link in a long chain of appearances over the course of more than forty years, in which the Viennese audience pampered me with incomparable enthusiasm and affection. Even today, whenever I find myself within the walls of that beloved house, my heart is always filled with a profound sense of gratitude.

These days of my first appearances in Vienna took on an added significance for me, because the incomparable Hans Knappertsbusch was on the podium, and I was making my first appearance under his musical guidance. Knappertsbusch was famous for his aversion to rehearsals, even just a quick brushup rehearsal before a performance. He was an ingenious improviser with the rich background of experience every greatly skilled conductor possesses.

No wonder, then, that I found myself sitting at the makeup table that evening without any prior preparation, a little uneasy over the performance to come, when the dressing room door opened and a gruff voice snarled, "Do you know the piece?" That was pure Kna!

"Well, . . . I . . . ," I stammered, "I think so." "So do I," he replied, and disappeared.

Then I saw him from the vantage point of the stage. The conductor's podium seemed a terribly long distance away.

The next time I met him was a month later in the so-called Direktionsgang, the all-hallowed corridor with doors leading to the offices of all the various department heads, their secretaries and their assistants at the Vienna State Opera. He shot over to me and growled, "You recently said hello to me, and I'm afraid I didn't recognize you. The next time I don't recognize you, kick me in the a––. Terrific Jochanaan, by the way, the other night," and again he was gone. This happy first collaboration would be followed over the next twenty-five years by many other happy ones, mainly in Munich, Vienna, Bayreuth, and in the opera houses in France and Italy.

I have to tell you a bit more about Knappertsbusch. People are always talking about what a powerfully authoritative, almost downright magical aura this aristocratic master of the conducting art radiated, one that nobody who ever worked with him could escape. Even in personal contact, you could feel that power.

The characteristic I always associate with him was his unconditional forthrightness, occasionally bordering on intransigence. He would brook no contradictions and on occasion could even be extremely hurtful. But this was all coupled with a genuine sense of justice toward everyone, including himself. Besides this, he had a certain softness that one would hardly suspect to be lurking behind the famous rough exterior of his brash nature. Most of the classic stories, that became legend even while he was still alive, give testimony to these traits. Spiced with the dry humor of his Westphalian homeland, they will live on, deliciously delightful, sometimes a bit off-color, and often going to the limits of what can be retold—and beyond.

Famous names meant nothing to him. The decisive factor was what these people had achieved. But he always had plenty of understanding for the wants and needs of the so-called little people, who did not stand in the foreground of an operatic institution. The story of a rehearsal accompanist who failed to cue in a stage band on time, for example, is so characteristic of that quality. In the intermission, after the "accident," "Kna," as we all called him, appeared on stage, something he normally never did, and asked irately what idiot had given the wrong cue. He was told the name of the miscreant, a hardworking, quietly modest but somewhat frail pianist, of whom Kna was rather fond. Hearing this, Kna quietly replied, "Well, then don't say anything to him, otherwise he'll just get sick." So saying, he did an about-face. After walking a few steps, he turned back and said, somewhat louder, "But the next time we do Aida, I'll have the fellow locked in the . . ." and mentioned a small facility where people generally lock themselves in.

His opinion of overindividualistic musical interpretations on the part of some of his conducting colleagues is documented in the following: *Tristan und Isolde* was on the bill at the Vienna State Opera. The conductor that evening, one of the house conductors by the name of Leopold Reichwein, who prided himself on his loyalty to the letter of a Wagnerian score, noticed that colleague Knappertsbusch had listened to a part of the performance from the director's box. When the two gentlemen met the next day in the opera house, the conductor, flattered by the presence of his distinguished colleague, inquired self-satisfiedly, "Well, Herr Professor, how did you like my *Tristan?*"

To which Kna replied, "I didn't know you'd composed one, too."

Then there was the malevolently sarcastic exchange with another prominent conductor, who inquired about the qualities of a young conductor, a pupil of Knappertsbusch, "Him? He's good, he's exceptional, he's better than I am, he's almost as good as you, my dear colleague."

Once in a performance Knappertsbusch was conducting, and, of all things, in a role I had already sung at least two hundred times, I experienced something that happens at least once to all of us singers: in a moment of faulty concentration, my memory suddenly went out of commission. I drew a total blank, the prompter wasn't paying attention, and all of a sudden an important phrase remained unsung. From the podium, I could make out a few harsh words snarled in my direction. No complaint over the next couple of days, no devastating reaction on Knappertsbusch's part. The whole thing happened in the Munich Opera. A year later, the Vienna Opera was giving the same work, again with Knappertsbusch on the podium, and I was again among the singers. We approached that spot. This time doubly careful I waited expectantly for the conductor's cue. And what did Kna do? He shot up out of his seat, and with a wide preparatory beat he assumed a savagely threatening stance, turned the baton upside-down with the thick end on top, raised it on high in his right hand, and kept it there until the perilous phrase had been completed. Any more of this, and I might have cracked up so badly I would have been unable to sing.

My favorite Kna story has to do with an audition in the Vienna State Opera during the war. I was present at the occasion myself, as I had come to Vienna for a couple of performances and found out one morning that an audition was scheduled for that day onstage. Partly out of curiosity, partly from boredom, I showed up at the time appointed in the house, where all the so-called heads of the house had assembled: directors, deputy directors, and all the conducting staff, including Knappertsbusch, rehearsal accompanists, stage directors with their assistants, directors' secretaries, a group of soloists, chorus members, and several people from outside. On the completely empty, enormous stage stood an upright piano downstage left, not a grand piano, an upright, and seated at it, with his back to us sat a spindly, unprepossessing little man, but an excellent musician and pianist, by the name of Meid, who had been assigned to accompany the auditions. On the huge stage, he looked even smaller than he was anyway. The audition procedure was in the hands of the opera director, Dr. Kerber.

First came three singers with unattractive, average voices, who were all dispatched with the usual, "We'll let you know." Then Kerber announced: "The next candidate is a tenor, comes from Berlin and works as a civil servant there in the Aviation Ministry. He was personally encouraged by his boss, Hermann Goering, promoted as an especially talented singer and has been sent to audition in Vienna by Mr. Goering for an adjudication of his vocal material." The astonishment among the listeners grew as a short, somewhat bulbous gentleman walked out on stage. He started to sing, and he was ghastly, so awful that Kerber turned to Kna and said: "We can forget this one, I think we've heard enough."

But Kna replied with the most earnest expression imaginable to the astonishment of all and sundry: "Why? The gentleman made a special trip from Berlin, on personal recommendation from Mr. Goering. Now let him give us a proper performance." The little butterball went on singing. It got even worse. By the time he started the third aria, his face had meanwhile turned red, and he began sounding like someone being tortured on the rack. He somehow managed to choke out five selections, while the mood in the room slowly turned from glum horror to amusement.

Exhausted and dejected, the would-be singer departed the scene. For a while, the room was shrouded in total silence. On the stage only the small upright piano remained, with little Meid in front of it, seemingly waiting for the next person to audition. Then Knappertsbusch's voice mercilessly pierced the stillness, "Well, I think the least we can do in return is to send Mr. Meid to Berlin and recommend him to Goering as an air force general."

The "recommendation" triggered torrents of laughter: you needed real courage in those days to let loose a wisecrack like that!

On August 13, 1964, our Kna stood for the last time on the conductor's podium and led one final performance of the opera he loved the most, *Parsifal*. Could he have suspected this would be his swan song? Unfortunately, a collaboration on *Der fliegende Holländer*, planned for the autumn of 1964, which we had all been looking forward to so eagerly, was not to be. It was the first, and regrettably the only staging assignment the directors of the theater ever offered me. My friend of many years Günther Schneider-Siemssen created the settings, and the great Kna was slated to conduct, but he was stricken with his final illness shortly before the rehearsals in the autumn of that year.

To help my readers better understand the following story I must add that Kna had conducted *Die Zauberflöte* at the Munich Opera shortly before in a production staged by the great theater man and longtime director of the Frankfurt Opera, Harry Buckwitz. On this occasion, our Kna left no doubt that he was so disappointed by this production that he hardly ever looked up at the stage throughout the entire performance.

The aforementioned final *Parsifal* was conducted by Knappertsbusch in Bayreuth, and I sang the part of Gurnemanz. During the intermission before the third act, he asked me to come into the conductor's dressing room and told me that a film was being planned on his life and work and asked if I might enjoy narrating it. I was more than delighted to accept, to which he responded in his typically harsh tone (which was totally canceled out by the mischievous gleam in his eye), "Now get back to your dressing room, and sing me a nice Good Friday Spell, and we'll see one another again in Munich on the *Holländer*. How is Schneider-Siemssen doing it? Are you two staging Richard Wagner or Wieland Wagner?"

"No, no, we'll be doing Richard," I tried to mollify him.

"I should certainly hope so," he called out, then threateningly added a little pun on Mr. Buckwitz's name, "I can't handle any more Buckwitticisms!"[2] Both laughing, we shook hands. These were the last words we exchanged on earth, and they still resound in my ears.

From the distance of more than fifty years it is hard to imagine how we artists managed to cope with the problems that came about in our professional and personal lives during the war. The burdens not only came from the many scarcities we all had to face. Granted, the singing profession is a strenuous one, and inadequate nourishment is no great help in assuring the necessary endurance for a long Wagner opera. But this lack was not the only dismal circumstance we had to contend with. Anyone who really thought

2. "Keine Buckwitze!"

7.4.   Strauss wrote the role of Jupiter in *Die Liebe der Danae* for
me, but the war intervened, and I sang it only once, at a public
dress rehearsal in Salzburg.

about it could only come to the conclusion that the whole business was destined to take a bad end. Behind this was the troubling question of whether
and how, once the total collapse finally came about, life would go on, and
whether cultural activity in any form would even be possible.

The constant fear of losing our lives, either in a bombing raid or as a consequence of an evil denunciation, weighed heavily on us all and, in the course
of time, led to a kind of fatalism, which had us all living in a dull, apathy from
one day to the next. Creating anything artistic under conditions like these
was really not easy; above all, we were oppressed by the awareness that
countless numbers of our fellow human beings had been subjected to the
most unspeakable atrocities, while we were forced to look on powerlessly.

While I had the incredible good fortune that a lucky star had brought me and my loved ones virtually intact through the whole war, I know that I must thank destiny on my knees for it. And for the fact that I was able to resume my professional activity outside the country soon after the cessation of hostilities: partly because I was politically clean and partly because, as so often happened in my life, helpful people crossed my path when I most needed them. Perhaps it would be good for today's opera and theater generation to learn a little more about the circumstances under which we had to ply our trade back then.

Even someone who, like myself, was able to work outside the country shortly after the war, had a difficult time ahead of him. After all the terrible crimes we Germans had committed, any citizen of this country was automatically burdened by a guilty conscience. When we looked in the eyes of people in other countries, we felt as if we had been permanently branded with the mark of disgrace. At first, many people outside Germany were anything but cordial, especially the ones who had been forced to emigrate from this part of the world. There was downright hostility, or at least understandable suspicion toward us. How many discussions were held, answers expected, indeed demanded, as to how all these reprehensible things could have happened?

These first phases of a severe test we were all put through were painful to endure, as we were all so horribly ashamed of the accusing words and looks we all received. I remember one Viennese gentleman who had emigrated to London, and who wrote me in English that he had sworn never to have anything further to do with German culture and its exponents. Nor did he wish to speak or hear the language of his one-time tormenters ever again. Then he continued that he had to confess, after he had heard and seen me onstage, that he found himself obligated to violate his oath. The last sentence of his letter was in German: "Ich will es vielleicht versuchen." (Perhaps I'll give it a try.)

I wrote back to him, asking if there were anything I might do to help him. Sometime later, he answered my letter and wrote in German: "I am unhappy and happy at the same time, that I went back on my oath." We then met personally, and he brought me into a group of immigrants. At first I was received with the usual misgivings. Then I made friends with some of them, and they attended some performances at the Covent Garden Opera, where they were happy and longingly recalling Vienna and the time before 1938.

These were positive, moving experiences, compensating us for many a bitter awareness we had to live with.

Chapter 8

In the early summer of 1945, barely five weeks after the Americans had marched into Munich, I was summoned to my first interrogation by a U.S. officer. This process was called "denazification." If, at the end, we were declared "not politically suspect," we received the famous "white paper," a certificate of exoneration (which the locals referred to as a "Persilschein," a reference to a popular brand of laundry detergent called Persil). Holders of those documents were considered politically clean. At this first interrogation, the officers wanted to know why I hadn't left the country as so many others had done if I hadn't been in agreement with the Nazi doctrines. My answer was that I believed, as did a number of other like-minded theatrical artists, that because we had been exempted from military service we had an obligation to the homefront to serve the general well-being of the population, to distract people, to use our art to give them what they desperately needed: a chance to turn their attentions to something more beautiful than violence, brute force, and misery.

But, the other side went on to argue, I must have been very popular with the Nazi leaders. After all, in the Eagle's Nest on the Obersalzberg, Hitler's residence in the Bavarian mountains, they had found my recordings. Fortunately, it occurred to me that I had nothing to do with it; in fact, as far as I knew, the pope had a couple of my records, too. This evoked a hearty chuckle from the officer conducting the interrogation. We soon became close friends. He loved classical music, and even had nothing in principle against singers.

The opera companies to which I had been contracted during the war years did whatever they could to maintain the usual high artistic level of their performances. From the abundance of artistic events, I have selected four main aspects that were significant in my further development and the expansion of my repertoire.

In February 1940, I first essayed the role that would, over the course of years, become one of my most successful ones: Wotan in *Die Walküre*. It says something about my beloved teacher Römer's foresight and his instinct for vocal suitability that, from the very beginning of my studies, he kept reminding me of how significant this role would be for me in my singing career. I have already mentioned the way Römer invariably regarded my future as an accomplished fact rather than merely a possibility. Yet, this was no idle fancy on his part. Nevertheless, he also kept stressing that these things could only happen if I kept my eyes focused on a single high goal.

I myself tended to regard statements of this kind as the stuff that dreams are made of, but it was my great good fortune that the first Wotan took place in Munich and that my boss, Clemens Krauss, was present at the birth of this portrayal as both midwife and godparent. How many suggestions he gave me! Suggestions that would more than surprise some of today's singers! Yet all of his statements concurred with the good advice my teacher had given me along my way.

For example, Krauss would say, "Don't forget that it was never Wagner's intention to have the *Ring* performed outside of Bayreuth, and the acoustics in the Festival Theater are outstanding, not least because of the covered orchestra pit." Today's conductors don't take into consideration that the dynamic markings (*piano, forte,* and so on) were intended only for his Festival Theater and its unique acoustics. In other words: the composer would have altered those markings, modifying them for performances outside Bayreuth. Then Krauss told me, just as Römer had, that Wagner always instructed his singers to interpret his roles, especially the dramatic ones, strictly in Italian bel canto style.

How fortunate I was to be instructed and advised by such mentors! How many *piano* passages, for example in *Die Walküre*, are simply overlooked by so many musical and stage directors, when they should be insisting on the singers interpreting them that way.

While I was preparing for rehearsals in Munich, Krauss imparted to me an especially important insight: "Don't make the mistake of listening to the people who claim that Wotan's narration in the second act is so unbearably long. On the contrary: base your interpretation on the view that this narration, as measured by the many things that happen in it, is actually too short. You must keep thinking to yourself: how am I going to accommodate so much text, how will I make the many significant words understandable to the audience, with so little music? Ergo: the narration isn't too long, it's too short." At first I found it hard to understand such a new approach, but then I gradually began to gain understanding of what I was being told. I am convinced that I owe it to advice like that, when after the experience of more than a hundred performances, people credit me with successfully structuring a diversified interpretation of that dauntingly difficult scene.

Seventeen years later, Herbert von Karajan was conducting a new production of *Walküre* at the Vienna State Opera, doing double duty as stage director. I believe it was the first time he ever staged anything. At the time he said to me, "We'll have to cut a bit out of the narration. It's just too long, and if we cut it down, that will make it less strenuous for you." By dint of considerable diplomacy I succeeded in talking him out of it, by telling him, among other things, that if we were to shorten it, it would bring the three to four heavy vocal climaxes closer together than they are in the original score. Karajan, otherwise generally a dictator, accepted my argument and conducted the greater part of the aforementioned narration so discreetly and considerately that I was able to sing and declaim half of it like a Schubert lied.

In all honesty, I must admit Maestro Karajan had a valid point: while thoughtfully expressing concern for the effort involved in singing that music, I have no doubt that he was even more interested in the sequence of the work, which tends to bog down into stultifying monotony if that monologue is inadequately prepared. This tedium is more than unfortunate: the monologue is not only a pivotal point in the development of the musical drama but also a watershed in Wagner's own creativity, indeed, key to much of what the composer-librettist set out to do in his reformation of musical theater. Of course, all of this is lost if the singer simply delivers this vital material in an incoherent mumble, as regrettably is so often the case when both singer and conductor lack awareness for the importance of the poetic and musical language.

This awareness is why I think it is so important to focus attention on the kind of *piano* singing we learn from presenting lieder, and this approach, as I have already quoted Wilhelm Furtwängler, has nothing to do with falsely equating *forte* with noise or *piano* with weakness. On the contrary, letting up on strength and concentration in those long *piano* passages both weakens the musical statement; if anything, it costs the singer greater effort than concentrating even more intensely on the power of the utterance than in louder singing in which clarity often happens by itself. I often discussed this challenging approach with wind players, who will readily admit that *piano* performance on their instruments is the hardest thing they do because it involves retaining the balance between tension and relaxation: the sound must be tense in the sense that the pressure on the instrument is adequately supported and the articulation clear, yet it must communicate relaxed and comfortably produced sound.

The question thus arises, How do we get there? How do we prepare this narration so that the result is soft singing with clear understanding of expression, making it possible for this scene to assume its rightful place in the dramatic action, where the audience appreciates it as a revealing clarification and doesn't wonder how soon it will be over, so we can get back to the musical fireworks? This preparation calls for an assiduous working process and a total control of the special demands involved with singing Wagnerian *piano*. To elucidate this point, it makes some sense to review the history of declamatory utterance in opera.

Mozart uses recitative passages to advance the plot, and then uses the arias and ensembles as the musical setting for the expression, in other words, the emotional response to those plot events. Wagner, on the other hand, accommodates highly significant elements of the expressive utterance in passages we might regard as recitative. For the singer, this means that even recitative passages must continue to give an *arioso* impression with all the emotional content that term implies. Bruno Walter summed the whole process up with his statement that in the performance of Wagnerian music, recitative and *arioso* singing are actually one and the same. The listener may not perceive it this way, but the singer must nevertheless take both plot advancement and expression into account whatever the dynamic marking. In this regard, Wagner is a giant step away from a composer like Weber, who dispensed with the Mozartian recitative element completely and entrusted his plot elements to spoken dialogue (as Beethoven does in *Fidelio*).

In Wagner, the musical setting sometimes turns the tables on the recitative accompaniment as well, not simply advancing the harmonic structure but also inserting reminiscences of earlier moments, harbingers of future events, and what acting teachers might call "sense memories": recollections of how a character may have emotionally perceived a moment in the previous action, which is now the subject of the narration, then interweaving these elements into the vocal part (for example, the recollections of building Walhalla and the early history of the Valkyries, which goes over into moments of *arioso* drawn from the orchestral impulse).

One clue to these new demands of recitative: throughout the *Ring* action to the point where the narration begins, the audience has only experienced Wotan as a character involved in interaction with others. Now, for the first time, while he may be physically speaking to Brünnhilde, as he tells her himself, the god is essentially alone with his thoughts. In Wagner's words "mit mir nur rat ich, red ich mit dir" (I confer only with myself when I speak with you). As the scene progresses, he not only tells us things we have already witnessed; he also gives us the new perception of what he was thinking and feeling as these events unfolded. As such, this narrative is essential to an understanding of both the thrust of the story and its place in the creator's artistic agenda.

In the previous scene with Fricka, he tries to explain to her some of the things he has done and some of the decisions he has made. She understands nothing. Her only guiding force is the sanctity of tradition and the concern that new approaches will dilute the authority of the gods. Wotan, and Wagner speaking through the character, communicates to us that without new and daring approaches, we are doomed to stagnation; yet, as with anything untried and venturesome, there is always the peril of making mistakes and having to live with the consequences of those mistakes. In this sense, Wagner might even be talking to his first wife, Minna, a former actress who was constantly urging her husband to build his artistic canon on past successes rather than take bold new steps—and to steer clear, both personally and creatively, of political issues. As Wagner saw it, her whole approach was like telling the wind to stop blowing, and his effort to explain things to her was no less futile. In his words: "nichts lerntest du, wollt ich dich lehren" (you learned nothing of what I wanted to teach you). In this context, it is interesting to note that the composer's own grandson, Wieland, always referred to Fricka as "Minna."

In Brünnhilde, who sees herself as a manifestation of his will, Wotan has a more sympathetic listener, and so he can confide his innermost thoughts to her knowing she will comprehend his yearning for things that never existed before; in other words, his belief that there are no overarching moral rules applicable to every creature. This absence does not mean an expurgation of morality, but rather a morality born of exigencies, in which laws were not made to be followed eternally. Laws call for ongoing reevaluation, amendment, and expansion, a morality of the heart, free of exclusive adherence to what we are accustomed. All the so-called rules are merely human creations subject to modification as the learning process advances. In all of this, Wagner makes the valid point, both verbally and musically, that new approaches call for familiarity with everything that has gone before. As Richard Strauss once put it, "Artistic freedom is meaningless without background knowledge." Or, even more succinctly, in the words of operetta composer, Sigmund Romberg, "To break the rules, you have to know the rules."

And it was with a full awareness of this expansion of things as they had been that Wagner also invented this intriguing style of declamation in which all the techniques that had gone before enter into a symbiotic interrelationship: recitative and musical *arioso* delivery hold equal sway, presenting the singer with a new and thrilling challenge. This way the audience will not yearn for an end to the story, but will be surprised when it ends so soon.

We know historically that Wagner originally conceived the *Ring* tetralogy from back to front, so to speak, beginning with the events of the final drama and then moving forward as the story germinated in his mind to create the text for the three preceding operas. This historical fact has led to a rather brainless exegesis to the effect that if the composer had started with *Rheingold,* he would have left out all these extended descriptions of previous events. Nothing could be farther from the truth. Every time one character or another, be it Loge, or Wotan, or Waltraute in *Götterdämmerung* relates past histories, they add the element of subjective perception to the events they are relating; as such they heighten the audience's perception of the drama and what it seeks to communicate.

All of this led me back to the need I felt to give this important moment in *Walküre* its full weight by singing the softer passages without losing any clarity of articulation or emotional expression, and I embarked on the quest for the technical tools to make this possible. The technique I developed—with significant help from qualified experts—was remarkably simple. I merely learned the music over again with no regard to the original dynamic markings, singing the whole narration loudly as if it were an aria in its own right, intentionally overstressing the alliterative components in the poetic composition. For instance I would sing "listig lockte mich Loge"—playing with these *l* sounds as I almost imitate the cunning of the other character luring Wotan into some ill-considered ploy—with no consideration for any recitative elements or the need for subtlety that goes with them, following Richard Strauss's suggestion to start out with an old-fashioned, unabashedly overemotional performance as a point of reference to guide me to my artistic destination. Then, taking care to note all the significant dramatic points, and bearing in mind that alliteration is not a banal poetic device in the hands of a master but rather an ingenious way of making symbolic music with words, I would trim off the ham by reducing the volume while retaining the intensity of tone and the clarity of articulation until I had the level the composer needed to communicate the desired compound of urgency and intimacy.

The result was a *cantabile* recitative, a technique we can trace back to that moment in operatic development, yet one that continued to develop in virtually every work that followed, whether we're talking about late Verdi, Puccini, Strauss himself, or all the others. As such, I acquired not only a fresh approach to this Wagnerian character, which even modern-day commentators stress when they review my performances, but also one that gave me insight into many other communicative tools for subsequent works.

This technical development had nothing to do with magic or mysticism. I simply took the material the creator had given me and tried to understand the motivations he must have felt in developing that material as he did. I don't know if Wagner himself was a good teacher, but the way in which he crafted the work is the ultimate clue to the interpretation; as such I could build the character using much the same methodical approach as my grandfather did when he made his horseshoes.

Using this craftsman's insight, I developed an even greater appreciation for the whole Wagnerian concept of *Gesamtkunstwerk* (synthesis of the arts), a concept Wagner gave us without ever really defining it. In my effort to comprehend this new artistic development I began to realize it goes far beyond a mere coming together of different skills and crafts. It also involves a philosophical union of statement and all the factors that cause a statement to be articulated in a certain way. In a sense, this concept gives the artist an awareness of his or her responsibility to approach the exercise of his or her performance backed by an exhaustive fund of knowledge coupled with the determination to continue the learning process in the realization that nothing impacting on the art is ever tangential.

I already indicated that when people ask me which role was my favorite I don't automatically mention Wotan in *Die Walküre*. Of course I know that nature had endowed me with a number of prerequisites for this portrayal. But just because this role brought me such unequivocal success that people went so far as to use expressions like "predestined," over the years I began to fear that I might become stereotyped as this kind of character. How often I was reminded of my conversations in Prague with the famous actor Max Pallenberg, who told me about the problems that arise from being forced by certain successes into a specific direction of artistic activity. This is the kind of success that leaves you feeling inescapably trapped. Fortunately my wonderful Matthäus Römer had seen to it from the very start that perils like these would not happen in my life. Starting with my first lessons, he had warned me not to get too one-sided. "Your voice and your stature have you cut out for the dramatic parts, but be careful not to spend your entire career on a single track. It may very well happen before you know it that people will take advantage of your lack of experience and force you into a period of nothing but dramatic singing. Then withdraw into a room and seek, before it's too late, the salutary route to the lyrical element, to the world of the art song and the oratorio." This was a bit of advice I have never forgotten throughout my artistic life and one that I have passed along to many a colleague and pupil. "Then an evening will come when you have a dramatic role to sing, but you're not feeling very well and aren't really sure you might not have bitten off more than you can chew. Then have the courage, while already in your costume, to walk over to a piano and try to sing a couple of bars from the Schubert lied 'Ich hört ein Bächlein rauschen' *piano,* but very *legato.* If that works, then you're all set." Often enough I have taken a detour over to that piano because I knew I just couldn't do it otherwise that evening—and how much happier I was when everything worked out all right anyway just one more time.

In February 1940 it was Clemens Krauss who carefully guided me through my premiere around all the pitfalls, as well as onto the peaks of ecstatic enthusiasm, and thus to a huge success. In 1957 it was Herbert von Karajan.

Another amusing experience came about in that first performance in 1940 and shortly afterward was repeated twice. My first Brünnhilde back then was Erna Schlüter, an adorable, helpful colleague with a glowingly beautiful voice. Erna was probably the most "weighty" in the long series of all my "daughters." When, at the end of the third act, I embraced her with paternal affection, my arms were just long enough to make it around her circumference. In the third performance, shortly thereafter, the slender, graceful Helena Braun was my "wonniges Kind" (lovely child). When I embraced her at the end, my arms suddenly seemed overlong and somehow dangling behind her back. In more than four hundred performances, in thirty-three different productions, I have stood on operatic stages all over the world in this role.

In the autumn of 1941, Clemens Krauss opened the season at the Munich Opera with a new production of *Don Giovanni,* the title role of which gave me the opportunity to add another important characterization to my repertoire, a thankful but not simple challenge to my dramatic abilities. At the time I began attending performances in Munich, Heinrich Rehkemper had fascinated me in the role. My earlier problems with "elegant characters" on the stage dating back to my Prague years were still all too clear in my memory, but meanwhile I had undergone a healthy learning process in Hamburg and Munich. Besides that, there was an extensive rehearsal period. For five weeks we worked under the tutelage of stage director Rudolf Hartmann and our boss Clemens Krauss day in and day out on one of the most brilliant works of the entire operatic literature.

My Zerlina was the pulchritudinous Hilde Gueden, a guest from Zurich, who was successfully introduced to the Munich audience in that role. Further highlights in the cast were Helena Braun as Elvira, Viorica Ursuleac as Donna Anna, Georg Hann as Leporello, Ludwig Weber as the Commendatore, and a longtime favorite of the Munich public, my friend Julius Patzak, as Don Ottavio.

At the end of the long weeks of rehearsal, we were all a bit "overrehearsed." I can still remember that everything was a bit too mechanical. Then a rather typical incident came about at the first dress rehearsal. One of the many difficulties for the person portraying the title role is that he has a lot of costume changes and not very much time. Added to this was the understandable nervousness over a new role, and as tough a one as this in the bargain. In any event the intermission before the second act was certainly too short for the costume change and the necessary conferences. In short, when I heard over the dressing room loudspeaker that Krauss had already started the second act with the opening duet between Giovanni and Leporello ("Eh via buffone!") without waiting for me, I blew my top. I stormed out onstage and grumbled, "This is unpardonable, I've got a costume change, on top of which I'm doing this part for the first time."

"Curtain down. Second act again from the top," came Krauss's voice, cool as a cucumber from the podium. Afterward, his musical assistant, who had sat directly behind him in the auditorium told me that Krauss had turned around to him and said with a grin, "Well, that finally woke him up!"

8.1.   Motivating Don Giovanni's passion was no problem with a pulchritudinous partner like Hilde Gueden as Zerlina.

In one of the subsequent performances, something indescribably funny happened. My darling wife, who had attended this performance, always claimed it was the funniest thing she had ever seen on any stage. For a better understanding of the situation it should be recalled that in the third year of the war there were all kinds of problems acquiring suitable fabrics for the costumes. The gentlemen's tights were not, like today's garments, made of a thin elastic material, but rather of coarse yarn. Now the director had decided that Giovanni, during the dialogue with Leporello before the party scene at the end of the first act, would have his servant exchange his shoes for a more elegant pair to be worn the next scene. For this purpose Giovanni was to swing his right, unshod foot, covered only by the tights, elegantly onto a footstool. In the course of this action, my big toe, cramped inside the narrow, unyielding tights must have forced its way out into the open. At any rate, it was clearly visible in a gigantic hole in the tights just at the moment when I demonstratively set my foot down, calling out, "Bravo, bravissimo!" The audience roared with glee, along with Leporello Hann. The seconds before the shoe was put on seemed to pass in an endless slow motion, but we continued our dialogue as gracefully as we could, and the performance resumed its animated course. In successive years, I did some 150 performances of this role in nine different productions around the world. How often on such occasions did I find myself remembering the *Giovanni* performances in Prague in which I sang Masetto and had my problems with elegant characters!

On the whole, there were three stage directors whose understanding and experience gave me the most support in laying the dramatic groundwork

8.2.   In the tough postwar years, my family provided invaluable emotional sustenance. This picture from 1953 shows Helga and myself with our daughter Gabriele and our son Peter.

for Giovanni and then working in the fine points: Rudolf Hartmann, Oscar Fritz Schuh, and Günther Rennert. Musically, the greatest and most valuable inspiration, as with many other roles, came from Clemens Krauss, who had been on the podium in my debut performance and saw to it with the full glow of his artistic personality that I was properly introduced to the ingenious musical drama of this Mozartian tonal miracle right from the beginning, so that I could use the formation of words and vocal sounds to interpret it in a manner that would do justice to the requirements and concepts of the composer. These men were ultimately the supporting pillars of my artistic conscience and my sense of responsibility toward the will of the author, who strengthened me in the gradual development of my final artistic thinking and feeling.

It was from Clemens Krauss I learned the precepts from which I later developed my attitude toward such concepts as sense of responsibility in artistic matters and the assessment of artistic freedoms. Then Richard Strauss's golden words on the aforementioned topic were then added, so to speak, as confirmation.

If today I sometimes find it hard to agree with certain new opera productions, it is because of the period of apprenticeship and education that shaped me and not some kind of narrow-mindedness or senile stubbornness. The very thing that makes the figure of the Spanish grandee so interesting is that it can be correctly interpreted in so many different ways. He isn't just the elegant seducer who knows how to use every trick in the book to score his conquests. He also has a kind of demonic, Mephistophelean power at his disposal, which seems to make him irresistible.

As long as he lived, the unforgettable Ezio Pinza was my great role model for this characterization. I met him in 1951 during my time at the Metropolitan Opera when his operatic career had already drawn to a close, although he continued to enjoy a few additional years of triumph in the musical *South Pacific,* where his performance of the rapturous "Some Enchanted Evening" regularly brought down the house. During my Met years (1950–54) I met him at the home of the great German soprano Elisabeth Rethberg. She spoke of the "unique fascination" Pinza radiated both on stage and in private life.

About the same time I brought my first "Don" (as theatrical jargon in the United States calls him) to the stage in Munich, I undertook a role in Hamburg for the first time, one that would fascinate me throughout my long stage career both as a singer and an actor: the police chief Scarpia in Puccini's *Tosca*—initially, as was the custom in those days, in German, then later in the original Italian.

A couple of years later there was another German-sung performance of *Tosca* at the Vienna State Opera, one that took a rather questionable course.

My partner in the role of Tosca was the Hungarian prima donna Maria Németh. She was a frequent guest and, thanks to her glorious voice, a very popular one, a real diva in the traditional sense of the word with all the peculiarities thereunto appertaining, plus a pronunciation in any language that made it clear that Hungary was her homeland.

It was one of those no longer new productions that everybody knew backwards and forwards. The performances were scarcely rehearsed. The fact that the participants generally saw one another for the first time onstage added a certain piquancy: as we could never be completely certain what our partners would do next, a kind of inspiring, sometimes amusing mixture of the joy of improvisation and curious expectation came about, which often produced a welcome atmosphere of excitement.

A darling colleague from the legitimate stage, with whom I was close friends for decades, the Viennese actress Jane Tilden (we had both been engaged at the German Theater in Prague back in 1932) had always been a great opera fan, like so many of my actor friends. So she was sitting in the audience. Afterward we planned to meet. Of course I was eager to hear what my colleague thought of my acting skills. Playing Scarpia certainly gave me ample opportunity to display them.

It was the second act, in the scene between Tosca and Scarpia. Tosca had just discovered to her horror that her beloved Mario was being tortured in the next room. Scarpia has the torture stopped for a moment. A henchman reports, "He's lying there like a corpse." Tosca races over to Scarpia, blind with rage and hisses, in the Italian original, "*Assassino!*" But what came out of Mme. Németh was the German equivalent of "ASSasin!" My eyes were fixed on Tosca, my face visible only in profile to the audience. The corners of my mouth were quivering, but I kept my cool. Then a laugh emerged from the audience, quite short but immediately recognizable to me as emitting from Jane's throat. Nevertheless the plot continued to move along onstage until Scarpia, stabbed by Tosca, sinks down to the floor.

Here I must note that it was always my intention to make the stiffness of the body, which came about as a result of the dramatic event, quite clearly visible. That means, the minute I lay on my back, the spectator must think of me as dead. To create this illusion I used all my self-control to breathe as calmly and uniformly as possible and not give away the game by allowing my abdominal muscles to move up and down. I was succeeding quite well, as Tosca, scanning the letter of safe conduct, began to speak. The words should have been "And all of Rome once trembled before that man!" But what I heard was something along the lines of "And all de rooooom vunce trampled beforr dot men!" My breathing technique went by the boards and (as Jane later reported) my abdominal muscles began to oscillate; not because I was out of breath, but because I was laughing. And out in the auditorium, that laugh could again be heard, only this time louder and longer.

A major music-historical event was planned as late as July 1944, when it was decided, as a kind of belated gift for Richard Strauss's eightieth birthday, to present the world premiere of his opera *Die Liebe der Danae* in the Salzburg Festival Theater. This work certainly deserved a more favorable inauguration than it received; in view of the master's advanced age, however, we were all determined to fulfill his wish that he might still witness a performance of the piece. None of us could have envisioned that political developments—the failed attempt on Hitler's life—would preempt our world premiere.

Only with great reluctance would the Nazis finally consent to a public dress rehearsal. The atmosphere during the rehearsal period was on a high level of inspiration thanks to the constant presence of the master with his youthful elan. But there was no way we could summon up any real enthusiasm. The times were just too oppressive for that.

Ineradicably etched upon my memory are the words Strauss spoke at the end of that rehearsal in a firm voice, although it was choked with tears, words that have meanwhile taken on historical significance: "This is the end of Western culture. I hope we may see one another again in a better world." None of us was ashamed of the tears glistening in our eyes. I don't believe anyone was aware of the fact that here one of the greats had mustered the incredible courage to take such obvious issue with the dogmas of a regime that had only another ten months to continue in power. In any event, the role of Jupiter, which Strauss had in fact conceived with me in mind, remained a precious memory, even though it had been vouchsafed to me to sing it only this single time.

In the early 1940s an event that also happened as if by itself and without advance planning marked the beginning of my career as a recitalist. I'll go into it later in greater detail but for the moment I would like to relate briefly how it came about. As already often mentioned, my teacher Römer devoted the greater part of his active career to singing oratorios and song recitals. Unfortunately, in his boundless modesty, he hardly ever spoke of this activity. Nevertheless, he placed the greatest stress in my training on his own domain, especially as he soon realized that opera meant less to the musician in me. When I then got my first steady contract at the age of twenty-one and slowly began growing into my stage assignments, I was totally absorbed by this new world. In the realization that there were still considerable imperfections in the use of my voice and that I was furthermore having problems bringing together the combination of singing and acting, I devoted all my energies to these tasks and had no time for anything else. I did occasionally sing a few lieder but strictly for my own personal amusement. The thought

8.3.   When composer Richard Strauss spoke of "the end of Western culture" we had all we could do to hold back the tears. *Left to right:* tenor Horst Taubmann as Mercury, the composer, soprano Viorica Ursuleac as Danaë and myself as Jupiter.

of a public appearance in recital never entered my mind, because my ideas about the interpretation of lieder along with the poetry of the authors' words could not be accommodated with what I was capable of forming at the time. I believe it was not only good, but also necessary to find my initial approach to lieder when I began understanding and using my voice as a musical instrument.

The occasion came about quite by coincidence. One evening in a private home I was asked to join forces with my friend, conductor Meinhard von Zallinger, and give an ad hoc rendering of a couple of songs from Schubert's cycle *Die Winterreise*. I had frequently worked with Zallinger in the opera, and we always got along splendidly. But now we suddenly discovered such a shared approach in the formation of words and music that we spontaneously decided to do a public recital as well. And so it happened that an operatic tyro with eleven years onstage to his credit, to the surprise of many, made his debut as a recitalist in Hamburg on an overcast November evening in 1941 with a performance of Schubert's *Winterreise*. I had no way of knowing then that I had begun a brand-new segment in the development of my singing career with this appearance, one that would not only give me a high level of personal and artistic satisfaction but, in contrast to the massive demands of the dramatic stage figures, would also provide me with an extremely healthy and vital balance for my vocal resources.

Things did not turn out so badly for musical culture as the grieving Maestro Strauss had feared back in July 1944, but one must try to place oneself in the position of us young, hopeful artists: for years we had helplessly looked on as everything around us descended into rubble. When, at the end of the war, despair and bitterness were stronger than hope and ambition, wasn't it obvious to believe in the dark prophecies of the greatest German composer of our time?

Political events had cut a deep swath through all of our lives. This insight only occurred to us, however, after a certain period of time had elapsed following the long awakening from the bad dream.

Reality began when the U.S. Army moved into our half-destroyed Munich on April 30, 1945. This is how it happened for us in the northern section of Schwabing, near the English Garden. A German private car, commandeered by some young American officers, stopped directly in front of our house. As the car door opened, a voice called out, "Anybody in there speak English?" My wife replied, "Yes, I do" from inside the building. Thereupon one of the officers explained that they needed someone to show a column of vehicles the way to another part of town. My wife volunteered and was placed in the car. A steel helmet was popped on her head, because bullets were still flying in the area they were headed toward.

After an hour of nervous waiting I saw the auto return. My wife jumped out of the car and said, "Mobilize a few friends. They'll be coming back in two hours, and they want to have a party with us." That was the first time I ever heard the word "party," which has since become an integral part of the German language. I would soon hear it far more often. "They'll be bringing the refreshments and the drinks," Helga casually added, as if this were an everyday event. And that's just how it happened. A friendly star had guided the young Americans to our house. From then on, they showed up every evening, sometimes even during the day, behaved themselves like well-brought-up guests, grateful to be visiting a home that had fortunately remained untouched by the bombs, and not like enemy occupation forces. As if by a miracle, we were spared having our house requisitioned. We can only surmise that people probably thought the large numbers of jeeps parked outside our door meant that our house had already been taken over—which was anything but the case.

These were not easy weeks for us. We seldom got to bed before two in the morning, but nobody did us the least harm. The young GIs behaved irreproachably, they were courteous and considerate and hauled in food, alcohol and, most important, cigarettes, which at the time were less something to smoke than a means of payment or barter. Long since totally weaned from alcohol, cigarettes, or coffee, our lives in those first postwar weeks were anything but healthy. We found ourselves in somewhat of a whirl; we were benumbed by the unaccustomed freedom from being forbidden to speak our minds freely, from disturbed nights, from the fear of brutal occupiers who would chase us out of our home. Instead of this, we got to know some young people who were just as happy as we were that their war was over.

To this day we are grateful for the fate that had dealt so kindly with us that we were spared all forms of those wrongs that many others had to endure at the war's end. Of course, there was no point in even thinking about any kind of artistic activity in those days, and so I took advantage of all this free time to expand my sketchy knowledge of English. I devoured every form of reading matter I could get my hands on. My goal was to learn thirty new words each day and then to use them in conversations. Later on, when I taught my singing lessons in this language, I was grateful for this almost forced grounding during the postwar period.

Through our American guests I came into contact with the CIC (counterintelligence corps), an institution of the U.S. Army for control purposes. This group brought me, along with a number of other artists, to our first performances in a kind of private situation until I could be recruited for entertainment events for U.S. soldiers at the Landestheater in Salzburg. My friend, motion picture composer Lothar Brühne, had succeeded in putting together a show featuring a group of prominent actors, among them Margot Hielscher, Bruni Löbel, Paul Dahlke, and many others. The actors played funny sketches, and a little dance group provided an excellent change of pace. Margot Hielscher and I sang some popular songs that brought me into the world of "Stardust," "Deep Purple," and "Old Man River."

The absolute highlight of my presentations, however, was my appearance as Carmen. In an operatic parody, I sang the "Habañera" in a countertenor voice, in the original mezzo-soprano range, in high-heeled shoes, and a spacious Carmen costume, with a high wig and an even higher comb atop it. All these elements together brought me to an aggregate height of $7\frac{1}{2}$ feet. The GIs howled and guffawed. They were having the time of their lives—and so was I!

When I was singing at the Met in New York five years later, members of the audience were constantly asking me to confirm whether I had been the same person who appeared as Carmen in the summer of 1945 in Salzburg. In addition to the personal pleasure, those weeks brought me a small daily fee—I wasn't earning any money anywhere else in those days—and the usual, very welcome cigarette cartons.

Occasionally we would get together with some of the American officers after the show and enjoy a pleasant evening with our "occupiers" telling stories or just kidding around. On one such evening, one of my German colleagues prevailed upon me to give a repeat performance of my Hitler imitation that had got me into such trouble with the embassy authorities in Prague before the war. After howling with laughter, just as the audience in the Czech capital had done, one of the CIC officers revealed to me that this Hitler imitation in Prague had been reported to Berlin by the embassy diplomats, where my name was promptly placed on a blacklist of politically unreliable individuals. When this list was found among the documents "liberated" by the U.S. Army after the war, it had a positive effect on my denazification hearings, enabling me to continue my career so soon after the cessation of hostilities.

One more benefit developed from those Salzburg activities. There was a temporary director in the Landestheater at the time by the name of Egon Hilbert, the later head of the Federal Theater Authority in Vienna, and later yet, together with Herbert von Karajan, director of the Vienna State Opera. Dr. Hilbert summoned me to his office and vented his indignation at the nature of my activity at the time, saying it was "undignified for a serious artist." He also wanted to know what plans I had, and asked if I would be interested in returning to the Vienna Opera, which would soon be reopened. I assured him I would be delighted to do some guest performances there. That pleased him, and he promised he would soon be getting in touch. It was easier said than done; at the time there was no postal or telephone contact from Bavaria to "foreign" Austria. But it was again a first contact with the Vienna Opera, and soon I heard more from there—about which I shall subsequently report.

We didn't have long to wait for the Munich Opera to go back into operation: as early as November 15, 1945, the curtain went up for the first time after the end of the war at the Prinzregententheater. Beethoven's *Fidelio* was on the program. Never before were we more aware of the significance of the words the prisoners' chorus sings in the first act: "What joy to breathe easily in the free air." Günther Rennert was staging his first production in Munich. Soon the house had a regular performance schedule. I remember the production of *Les contes d'Hoffmann,* music that many of the younger people on stage and in the auditorium had never heard before.[1] There followed *Otello, Le nozze di Figaro,* and many others. Puccini's *Tosca* was also on the schedule, to the delight of the audience, where the sight of many American uniforms became a regular event, as was their presence among the autograph seekers who waited at the stage door after the performances.

In this *Tosca* production, the stage director wanted Scarpia in a fit of rage

---

1. The work had been banned under the Third Reich because the composer, Jacques Offenbach, was Jewish.

to hurl his wineglass against the wall where his henchman Spoletta was standing. Our property master, however, made it clear to him that this bit of business could only be carried out once—in the first performance. There weren't any more glasses in the storeroom, and there were none to be secured anywhere else.

After one of the subsequent performances, a U.S. officer visited me and wanted to know what had become of that effective business with the glass. I explained our precarious situation to him, and shortly before the next performance there was a knock on my dressing room door. An outstretched arm with a wineglass in its hand appeared in the door opening; it was the officer from a few days before, who smilingly handed me the prop. From that evening on, there were no *Tosca* performances at which my glass supplier failed to make his appearance right on schedule.

Very soon afterward, the young Georg Solti joined our ensemble as general musical director. Then someone else promptly kept his promise: Egon Hilbert contacted me and saw to it that I could get to Vienna, on adventurous journeys in American military vehicles or by train, which often took eight hours and more for the stretch from Munich to Vienna, because we had to stop and put up with long hours of controls at the Enns Bridge near Linz, where the Russian occupation zone began.

Hardly had I resumed my Viennese career, when an unexpected friend got in touch with me. I was overjoyed that he had not only made it through the war unscathed, but also held more than one position of great importance back in Prague. It was Dr. Paul Eckstein, who had miraculously emerged alive from the Warsaw ghetto! We immediately arranged to get together at the home of a mutual friend, and he told me the story of his intervening years. Shortly after arriving in Warsaw, he told me, he had advised the administration of the ghetto of his skills as a streetcar driver, and he was immediately given the grim assignment of driving the trolley that transported the corpses of persons murdered by the Nazis from their place of execution to a site on the outskirts of town where their remains were disposed of. It was a hideous task, but it did keep him alive.

He went on to tell me about how he and a group of his cohorts had somehow managed to smuggle a radio into an abandoned fireplace, where they would secretly listen to various radio stations, both from Germany and other countries, thus keeping abreast of the status of the war during the four years he spent in Warsaw. On one such occasion, he told me, he tuned in a music program on which he heard my voice, and for him this became a kind of omen that he would somehow manage to escape from this terrible place and go on to live a useful life in the service of the arts.

The big break came during the ghetto uprising in 1943, during the confusion of which Paul and his wife somehow managed to escape from the confines of the ghetto, going on to live for a couple of weeks on the land, spending the nights in barns and abandoned houses, eating roots and berries and somehow surviving two Polish winters before they managed to make contact with the Red Army, which rescued them and arranged for them to be returned to Prague.

The initial years back home, however, were anything but salutary for Dr. Eckstein. Very much his own person, he was not at all interested in knuckling under to the Stalinist regime that took over the country shortly after the war. Somehow his cunning, his incredible musical knowledge, and his indomitable will for survival prevailed, and soon he began assuming one post after another on the highest level. In 1948, he became a member of the secretariat of the Prague Spring Festival, and served for many years as secretary and head of the foreign division of the Union of Czechoslovak Composers, doing much for both Czech music and for cooperation between his homeland and other countries.

A gifted writer, with close to native fluency in a number of languages, he served as Prague correspondent of several prestigious music magazines, including *Opera News, Musical America,* and the *New Yorker* in the United States, *Opera* in Great Britain, and the German magazines *Opernwelt, Oper und Konzert,* and *Musik und Gesellschaft,* as well as serving as editor of the Czech music magazine *Hudební rozhledy* from 1951 to 1955. He was artistic adviser to the Prague National Theater, where he and I had enjoyed so many performances of that nation's finest operatic masterpieces together back in the thirties, and served on the ISCM (International Society for Contemporary Music) presidential committee as a member of that prestigious body and as secretary of the national committee of the International Music Council. On top of this, he wrote a number of learned books on subjects ranging from Mongolian music to the operas of Mussorgsky, Richard Strauss, and Paul Hindemith, and lectured on music throughout the world—while continuing to maintain a flourishing law practice!

We met from time to time on the Green Hill in Bayreuth, where he often lectured to sessions of the Jeunesses Musicales there, and we kept in regular contact until his death on July 21, 2000, at the age of eighty-nine. Whenever we were in the city, we would get together with our wives for an evening of good food and wine, excellent conversation, and often enough, any number of his inexhaustible collection of Jewish jokes, still told, after all those years and all those appalling events, in his inimitably captivating style.

Shortly before he died, I sent him a copy of the German edition of these memoirs, and I was surprised to note that he was one of the few recipients who wrote back frankly that he felt the book had missed the mark somewhat by not going into greater detail on matters of artistic substance. The reason for this was that the original publisher had been somewhat wary of a general reading public's being interested in a book on opera with a lot of technical detail. He begged to disagree, stating that mine had not been an average career that could be related exclusively in anecdote form. And so when our American publisher expressed similar reservations about the original text of the book, my translator/collaborator and I were more than happy to expand the English edition to include a more serious discussion of substantial musical matters. I only regret that Dr. Eckstein, whose English was as good as his German and Czech, did not live to see the results of this cooperative effort, to which he doubtless would have had a great deal to contribute.

In the spring of 1947, another old friend unexpectedly got in touch with me, someone I had known in 1937 in Berlin, where he had been the secretary and right-hand man of the English conductor Sir Thomas Beecham: Walter Legge, who later married Elisabeth Schwarzkopf, and who for many years was the highest artistic authority, the heart and mind of the English record company Columbia–His Master's Voice. Legge was a genius in the art of recording technology, beyond which he was unbeatable in his familiarity with the entire musical literature. "We all learned from him," confessed John Culshaw, who was for the English competitor firm Decca what Legge was for Columbia: a brilliant sound recording expert, who made a name for himself with the famous complete recording of the *Ring* under the direction of Georg Solti (*Ring Resounding*) in the early 1960s. With "we all" he meant the generation of prominent conductors, instrumental soloists, singers, musicians in general, as well as artistic and technical sound recording experts—all of whom had worked together with Legge. I consider myself fortunate to have belonged to Walter's inner circle of friends, and I owe him much inspiration, advice, and other thoughts worth knowing on the subject of music. He was also the one who offered me a contract with his record company and motivated me to record some lieder at the BBC, thus laying the foundation for my many years of artistic activity in Great Britain and beyond in many other parts of the English-speaking world.

That same summer of 1947 I was already back on the stage of the Salzburg Festival as *Don Giovanni* with Karl Böhm in the pit. The excellent stage production was in the hands of Günther Rennert. Afterward, I went to Lucerne, where I had been entrusted with the baritone solos in a festival performance of Brahms's *Ein deutsches Requiem* under Wilhelm Furtwängler. To this day, I still have the celestial sound of Elisabeth Schwarzkopf's voice in my ear as she sang: "Ihr habt nun Traurigkeit" (And ye now therefore have sorrow) and then "eure Freude soll niemand von euch nehmen" (your joy no man taketh from you). The trip to Lucerne was the first journey to Switzerland for my wife and myself in a long time. We felt as if we had arrived at the Big Rock Candy Mountain as we had our breakfast served to us in bed every morning at the Schweizer Hof hotel. I can still remember our chagrin at ordering ham and eggs even though we weren't all that eager to eat them. We didn't want to give the room waiter an opportunity to turn up his nose at the starving, emaciated Germans. Once, as we were strolling around downtown, we stopped outside the window of a toy shop and looked at the abundance of playthings on display. Then we both had to cry, because it became clear to us how long it had been since we were able to give our children, then seven and nine, any of these things.

The following year I made my first trip to London to make those lieder recordings at the BBC. I was staying at the Rembrandt, a small, cozy hotel in Kensington. I had read a great deal about English customs, but now it became reality: driving on the left side of the road; the patient queues of passengers waiting at the bus stops; the people who reacted with calm superiority to any excited "foreigner" and would talk to anyone without exception in the hotel lift, and who invariably started their conversations by remarking on the weather. It was also a new experience for me to have the daily paper delivered to me along with breakfast. On that first morning, as I immediately tried to use my sparse knowledge of English to figure out the contents of the news, my eye fell on a bold headline on the front page. With incredulous amazement, I read, "Hotter in London, and More to Come." Nonsense, I thought, that's impossible. Not a soul here knows me or knows who I am, and I then set the paper aside. But then my vanity took hold of me: might Walter Legge have . . . ? I picked the paper back up and began deciphering the article beneath this unusual headline. It soon dawned on me that this was nothing other than the usual weather report. Of course I told this story of my comical misunderstanding to the great glee of everyone in London. When later my name was somewhat better known in the country, the story continued to get a good laugh, especially in musical circles, as I was to discover almost fifty years later, when I was invited to attend Georg Solti's eightieth birthday celebration in Buckingham Palace, where the Queen's sister, Princess Margaret, with quite un-English directness took me aside and asked, "Did that story about 'Hotter in London' really happen?"

My first trip to England for the lieder recordings at the BBC in the spring of 1947 was followed in the autumn of that same year by a second one: this time in conjunction with a three-week guest appearance by the Vienna State Opera. I believe there were three roles altogether in which I made my first appearances on the stage of the Royal Opera: Don Giovanni in Mozart's eponymous opera, Count Almaviva in *Le nozze di Figaro,* and Pizarro in *Fidelio.* In one of the *Don Giovanni* performances there was an unexpected encounter with an old friend from my Prague days, Richard Tauber, who was substituting for the indisposed Anton Dermota as Don Ottavio. As I men-

8.4.   Postwar visits to Vienna brought about an
enriching collaboration with one of the native-born
stars of that city: Anny Konetzni, who often sang
Brünnhilde to my Wotan.

tioned in the first chapter of these recollections, it would be his final appearance on the operatic stage: the great tenor died, only fifty-seven years old,
shortly afterward, in January 1948. He had a remarkable singer's breathing
technique, and I have never heard Richard Strauss's *Freundliche Vision* sung
with such technical perfection as it is in his recorded rendition.

Back to my lieder recordings at the BBC. I was quite surprised when
David Webster, then the director of the Covent Garden Opera, asked to
take advantage of this occasion to come to the studio and listen to me. Obviously he took a liking to my voice, because after the session was over, he
walked over to me and asked if I would like to join the Covent Garden ensemble for a couple of months during the coming season (1948–49). Not
suspecting what I would soon be facing, I spontaneously said yes. It had
been decided, once the war with Germany had come to an end, to revive
Wagner's *Meistersinger* and *Walküre*. Not in the original German, however,

but in English! That meant I would have to learn these monster roles all over again and sing them in a foreign language, a downright impossible proposition. The role of Hans Sachs, the dream of every baritone, would have to be swallowed in this first outing along with that bitter pill. And on top of that, *Walküre*. For all of this, learning the English text wasn't the hardest part; forgetting the German words was appreciably harder.

As I fortunately had the *Meistersinger* premiere behind me, and had digested the English words (not without some gastric distress—of course, the critics found my English inadequate), I emphatically addressed myself to Webster and attempted to pressure him into at least allowing *Walküre* to be sung in German. He just wrinkled his brow and said with great calm, "I have complete understanding for your situation, but, my dear chap, presuming I were to give in, what do you think I can tell my darling Kirsten (Flagstad) when she finds out that she had taken on the onerous task of learning the whole English text for nothing. No, no, I'm going to have to ask you to leave *Walküre* in English."

Most unwillingly I resigned myself to my fate. The rehearsals began, and the famous Wagnerian heroine, whom I had been very eager to meet, appeared. She was a pleasant lady and not at all difficult. We got along splendidly and liked one another from the first moment on. During a rehearsal break she took me aside and said, "Tell me, why in heaven's name did you insist on having this thing sung in English?"

"Whaaat?!" I exclaimed, "what ever gave you that idea?"

"Well, a week or so ago I asked Webster if we mightn't sing the whole thing in German, to which Webster innocently replied, 'I do understand, darling Kirsten, but what do you think I can tell my friend Hotter when he finds out.'"

"That two-faced con man!" I expostulated disrespectfully. When we both then approached him about his disgraceful swindle, he apologized with the words, "Unfortunately my hands were tied by the political authorities." So we had no choice but to knuckle under to this pressure, knowing full well that the language barrier would inevitably have an effect on our performance.

Then in the premiere there was an anything but everyday incident. The production had been staged in such a way that father Wotan takes his daughter Brünnhilde onto a little raised area, representing a rocky cliff, about five feet above stage level, where he must bed her down in a cramped area for a singularly uncomfortable slumber. After I had guided the rather sizable Kirsten, with some effort, up to the place appointed and kissed her good-night, I was just about to start down when a spotlight suddenly glared right into my eyes so harshly that for a moment I could not see a thing. I lost my footing and in full stage regalia, complete with a heavy solid metal helmet, chain mail, and spear, tumbled down onto the stage floor. Fortunately, the landing was reasonably soft; I had obviously not suffered any serious injuries. During the few bars until the descent of the curtain, an audible murmur emerged from the auditorium. As fortunately only a faint light fell on me, I quickly grasped my spear, scrambled to my feet and, in hopes of rescuing some residual modicum of godlike dignity, I spread out my arms with a majestic swing of the spear. Meanwhile I was again fully lighted, and slowly and decorously the curtain mercifully fell. That evening, of all people, Queen Elizabeth and her two princess daughters, Elizabeth and Margaret Rose, were among the spectators. The next morning, Her Majesty did me the honor of having her secretary send me a couple of lines inquiring how I was faring and expressing the hope that I hadn't done myself any serious injury.

The successful premiere ended in understandable confusion, both on the stage and in the auditorium. Well ahead of the reviews, the newspapers printed a report of the sensational event, generally on the front page: "Queen Sees Opera Star Fall, Foreign Singer Double Pitfalls on Stage and Language."

Wagner has Wotan, in his total breakdown in the second act, cry out in despair, "Nur eines will ich noch—das Ende" (I want just one more thing—the end). As the word "end" has only one syllable in English as compared to the two in the German "Ende," the English translation replaced it with the word "downfall," whereupon one critic wittily remarked, "Wotan, the god, was able to predict the events of the third act."

A couple of days later Webster told me with visible delight that one of the dignitaries on the board of the opera company had wanted to make sure I hadn't really hurt myself in that "downfall." After Webster had assured him that I was well and in the best of fettle, the worried gentleman replied, "Well, I don't know, I saw he had something over his left eye," to which the opera director told me mischievously, "I had somebody send him a *Walküre* score."

Apart from the two Wagner roles, I also sang a third part in English, the Speaker in *Die Zauberflöte*. The translation was not good; it sounded like a kind of biblical English.

The year 1950 took me for an entire season to the Met in New York, about which I will report later in greater detail. At any event, I returned from my stay in the States directly to London's Covent Garden Opera, to sing the "English" Speaker, among other things, there again. Primarily because of the English text, I had a rehearsal with my old friend, the coach Norman Feasey, who had given me immeasurable assistance in learning Hans Sachs and Wotan in English for the previous season. Things worked out a bit easier with the Speaker; after all I had spoken a fair amount of English during the past year, and learned a great deal of new vocabulary.

8.5.   My first appearances at London's prestigious Royal Opera House Covent Garden, obligated me to relearn Wagner in an English translation that has Wotan yearning for "the downfall"—but there was one downfall in that production, in the presence of royalty no less, I could have lived without. Photo © Erich Auerbach, London.

Nevertheless, I asked Norman to tell me candidly how my English sounded. His answer was classic British humor. "Well, it's not bad. As a matter of fact it's quite good." He added with a broad grin, "Only, there is a sprinkle of Coca-Cola in it now." I've never heard a better description of the difference between British and American English.

Nobody, least of all myself, could have suspected the degree to which the misunderstood weather report on my first London morning would prove true. "More to come" was an understatement: in the thirty following years, I went to that country so often and on so many different professional occasions that it became my second artistic homeland. Opera performances, song recitals and concerts, stage directing assignments and, later on, teaching activities and recording sessions there followed in rapid and colorful succession.

In the course of all this I met many, many people and forged friendships, which have survived over the long years. One special place was accorded to the many immigrants who had fled here from all over the European continent, many with gruesome stories to tell. As an artist I could only try to provide at least some small compensation for the many hardships they had suffered, and make a small contribution toward rebuilding bridges. As a guest in England, so briefly after the end of the war, my eyes were really opened to the horrible effects of the injustices that had been heaped on so many innocent persons. It was all too grotesque that those very individuals whose clean bill of political health had made it possible for them to travel to other countries had to pay bitterly for the privilege with the almost unbearable burden of the many justified reproaches that rained down on them. How infinitely worthwhile were all the friendships, which again, even under such circumstances, slowly and carefully grew. Our first contacts were made with those opera and concert fans among the German immigrants, and their enthusiasm for the arts rapidly built a bridge of reconciliation across the barriers unholy political compulsion had once erected. To this day, it warms my heart when I remember how those people, who only a few years before had been robbed of the safety and comfort of their homes, exerted their every effort to offer us artists, in place of living out of our suitcases in hotels, the family atmosphere of their newly gained homes in this adopted country. Their generous hospitality really put us to shame, and the brutal suffering forced on them in Germany seemed all the more subhuman in our eyes.

To make clear what I mean, I would like to relate an incident that took place at the beginning of 1948 in London. At this juncture the English were faced—as were we—with the strictures of food rationing. In this context it should be mentioned that we foreigners were apportioned the same ration as the local citizens. One day my wife gave me a couple of oranges to take along for the rehearsal breaks. When I offered a few pieces to my colleagues they asked in astonishment how I had gotten my hands on some of that particular fruit, which had been earmarked exclusively for children under the age of six. I then went straight over to the fruit market where the oranges had come from. "Is it true that oranges are only available to children under the age of six?"

"Yes, that's true."

"So how come you gave us some?"

"Oh, you had to go through so much misery in your country, sir, we thought you deserved having someone do something nice for you." The saleslady smiled pleasantly, and we left the shop speechless and deeply moved.

❧ Chapter 9 ❧

The years of my professional activity in England after the war were also marked by my first meeting with a great musician whose name I had first heard as a music student in Munich: Otto Klemperer. In the 1920s he had attracted a great deal of attention as general manager and musical director of the Krolloper in Berlin, with that theater's modern, provocative stagings, many of them featuring works by contemporary composers. We worked together on record productions for the British recording company Columbia. Afterward he engaged me for concerts both in England and then later in Vienna. Right from the start he impressed me with his almost rigorous musical approach, permeated with absolute loyalty to the score and an imperturbable determination to have the work interpreted in accordance with his ideas. Once I heard somebody ask Herbert von Karajan, during his period at the Vienna State Opera, what, in his opinion, were the qualities that made a good conductor, to which he replied quite spontaneously, "Being able to communicate his understanding of the music *before* it reaches a performance."

Klemperer was the very embodiment of that trait. I first met him when, partially paralyzed by a stroke, he could only conduct with his left hand and without a baton. He was—viewed from the vantage point of the soloist directly next to the podium—fascinating to observe, as he occasionally raised his right hand with the lower arm, quite unconsciously, as if the arm had forgotten about his disability. He had a rather grotesque nature and occasionally got on the nerves of the people he worked with by making completely unexpected remarks just to see if they had caught his drift. I liked him very much, because he was direct and straightforward, both in personal and professional relations. And that somewhat bizarre sense of humor of his was always good for a few surprises. No wonder so many indescribably funny stories are invariably told whenever anyone mentions his name. I experienced the first two of these anecdotes personally. The rest came from totally credible eye- and ear-witnesses. I'm passing them along in the face of possible claims that they might have occurred quite differently.

The scene of the first event was a London concert hall, where Klemperer was conducting a recording session with the London Philharmonic Orchestra, at which I was present as a listener. I just happened to witness a conversation between Klemperer and the music librarian (this is the man who sees to it that the musicians get their orchestra parts on time). Klemperer expressed a desire to go through the various scores with the librarian, checking for mistakes, which they would then correct. He suggested they schedule the get-together for the following Saturday at 2:00 P.M. directly following the rehearsal. The librarian replied, "A proper Englishman spends Saturday afternoons at the football game, especially when the team he supports is playing." Klemperer laughed amusedly and said, "Well, well, football, hahaha, the football game, eh?" I was again present that Saturday and observed how the librarian crouched down behind the musicians trying to sneak out of the building. Klemperer interrupted the music for a moment and called out to the escapee, "I hope you lose!"

The next amusing episode took place in Cologne in the large hall of the West German Radio network. Klemperer was conducting Beethoven's Ninth. I was present with my daughter Gaby, at the time eighteen years old and a very attractive young lady. Naturally she came along to the rehearsals and was quite taken with Klemperer, the way he conducted, his general manner. She was very impressed. Of course, I had filled her in on some of his eccentricities, which made her all the more curious. She sat in the second row of the almost empty hall; I, as one of the four soloists, was positioned directly beside the imposingly tall conductor. Needless to say, a loving glance I exchanged with my daughter didn't escape Klemperer's notice. He went on conducting, turned halfway around to the auditorium, saw the attractive girl, turned back to me and in the middle of the music made comical sounds, such as "Aha!" "Well, well!" and so on, looking back several times at my daughter. After the rehearsal, she was at first a little reluctant to join me in his dressing room, having observed his rather odd behavior, but finally came along anyway, to find the maestro settled comfortably in an armchair. "May I introduce my daughter, Herr Doktor?" I began. Klemperer snarled back categorically, "No!" My daughter was initially shocked and turned to leave the room. I held her back and said somewhat louder and more decisively, "Herr Doktor, this *is* my daughter, and she would like to make your acquaintance." When still no reaction came from him, I put my arm around Gaby and repeated, "But Herr Doktor, this really is my daughter." To which he extended his left hand with a friendly smile and purred, "What do you know? I thought she had some other function in your life."

In the twenties the Vienna Opera was rich, not just in beautiful voices, but also in great stage personalities. In the dramatic soprano category there were primarily three artists vying for public favor: the Moravian Maria

9.1. When I brought along my beautiful daughter, Gaby, to a Klemperer rehearsal in London, the conductor with his overactive imagination misread the smiles we exchanged and thought we had another kind of relationship.

Jeritza, the Hungarian Maria Németh, and the German singer Lotte Lehmann. These ladies provoked quite a number of little tales and anecdotes—always a sign of great popularity. Lotte Lehmann enjoyed one success after the other in the theatre, primarily as the Marschallin in *Der Rosenkavalier* and Leonore in *Fidelio*. Following a guest appearance in Los Angeles as Pizarro in *Fidelio* in 1956 I had the good fortune to meet the great singer and convince myself personally of her great charm and the strong aura of her personality, qualities that made a sizable contribution to her teaching activities at the Music Academy of the West in nearby Santa Barbara.

It was in this function that, soon after the war, she returned to the scene of her former triumphs—Vienna—where she was welcomed by old and young with open arms. By chance, she happened to be staying in the same Vienna hotel with Otto Klemperer, with whom she had made music in that city's great theater for many years. Now, in the years before the war there had been a silent agreement in the initiated circle of leading conductors to make one concession to the celebrated and universally honored Leonore. Despite their reluctance, they allowed her to sing the first-act aria, notorious because of its exposed upper register, a halftone lower—in musical terms, in E-flat major instead of the original key of E major. Klemperer, who had not seen Madame Lehmann for many years, was quite amazed to be running into her again in Vienna, "Well, what are you doing here, Miss Lotte?" "Hello, Doctor," she replied, amused, "fancy this, today I sang the Leonore aria again for my pupils. Of course, an octave lower . . ." "But still in E-flat major instead of E major, right?" wheezed the cantankerous old man, as his daughter Lotte later told me.

My favorite Klemperer anecdote takes place in Switzerland. I'll pass it along as it was told to me. Paul Hindemith was not only one of the foremost composers of the twentieth century but also a distinguished practicing musician, on top of which he was a high-ranking musicologist, who wrote several extremely interesting books and gave lectures on musicological subjects, which, because of their highly specialized content, were not always easy for the average listener to understand. One of these events took place shortly after the war before a select audience in a Zurich lecture hall. In the printed program, it was noted that Professor Hindemith had kindly agreed to answer some questions from the audience following his presentation.

The eminently scholarly treatise had been completed, and the lecturer then politely inquired if the audience had any questions. Most of the people out front, however, were visibly still busy trying to make head or tail of what they had just heard, and so the inquiries at first came forward rather tentatively and sparsely, and were fairly superficial in the bargain, if not downright stupid. The mood in the hall was a little nervous and impatient. Hindemith was looking somewhat helplessly around the hall for further questioners when he recognized a familiar face in the middle of the second row: Dr. Otto Klemperer. Seeing him encouraged the lecturer to extend an inviting gesture toward the well-known conductor, because he expected the famous musician would doubtless ask an interesting and substantial question. Otto Klemperer actually did rise to his full, considerable height and asked in a loud, universally audible voice, "Where's the men's room?"

The effect was indescribable, and the incident concluded with a tortured smile crossing the face of Hindemith on the podium. For all of this I am convinced that Klemperer had no intention of turning this serious event into a comedy hour, but simply wanted to liberate Hindemith from a very uncomfortable situation.

⮞⮞ Chapter 10 ⮜⮜

Besides my travels to England, beginning in the spring of 1948, I began making regular appearances at the Vienna State Opera. As the House on the Ring still lay in ruins, we were fortunate enough to have found a temporary venue at the Theater an der Wien, similar to the way the Prinzregententheater in Munich served as the opera house until the reopening of the Nationaltheater.

Nobody looking at the theater from the outside, wedged in between apartment buildings in the fourth district of the city, would suspect that, with its 230-foot deep stage, it has an amazingly large playing area. Living conditions at the time, sparse to say the least, engendered an incredible sense of community, which in turn had a very favorable effect on our work together. Although, figuratively speaking, we naturally often found ourselves treading on one another's toes, we were simply closer, in an artistic sense; a condition that no longer exists in the present-day theater with its working atmosphere getting cooler and cooler with everybody jet-setting from place to place.

Not for at any price would I have wanted to miss the period when the Austrian composer Franz Salmhofer was running the opera house. During that administration, we were all taking part in an event that made operatic history: we had succeeded in presenting to the creator of *Palestrina,* Hans Pfitzner, his favorite work one last time shortly before he left us forever on May 4, 1949. Josef Krips was on the podium, Josef de Witt sang the title role, Ferdinand Frantz was Morone, and the role of the prince of the church, Borromeo, which I had already sung in the big theater during the war, was again entrusted to my care.

The composer, almost completely blind, his face etched by his approaching death, was happy once again, and took part, as much as he was able, in what was happening on stage. To my great joy, one of the first famous interpreters of the cardinal from the world premiere in 1917 showed up for several rehearsals and performances: it was the great singer Dr. Emil Schipper. I was enjoying success in my own interpretation of this role we both loved so dearly and, with ungrudging collegiality, he shared my pleasure.

During the rehearsal period and the first performances of this opera, there was an incident I still remember with great amusement. To understand this story, you have to know that in the third act Cardinal Borromeo recognizes the terrible injustice he has committed against Palestrina; with a sense of deepest repentance and contrition, he kneels down before his composer friend and begs his forgiveness. I must admit that I always played this short, emotionally laden scene with great inner involvement. During one rehearsal, Director Salmhofer took me aside and remonstrated, "Now then, this business of kneeling down in front of Palestrina, a distinguished cardinal in front of a secular musician, and on top of that in full clerical regalia. We'll just leave that out, don't under any circumstances do that again, otherwise I'll have the whole Catholic Church in Vienna at my throat. I need those priests like my daily bread . . ."

"But, Director," I interrupted him, "this is a very special situation. I've always done it everywhere, in every production, and that's also the way Pfitzner wants it."

"A Hotter doesn't kneel in front of a tenor, remember that! You owe that much to your Viennese reputation!"

I was certainly not prepared for that kind of argument. I helplessly lay down my rhetorical weapons and launched a feeble attempt to get Pfitzner involved. He, however, reacted with unfamiliar leniency, "Stand, my dear friend, kneel, do whatever you want—just sing." So there was no help to be expected from that quarter. From then on I either knelt or didn't, depending on whether Salmhofer was anywhere around.

At the premiere, Pfitzner was as pleased as punch when we stepped before the curtain with him, practically carrying him, as he could barely manage to stand on his own feet.

At the end of the third repeat performance, I was on my way back to my dressing room, happy finally to be getting out of my heavy costume, as my dresser came bounding into the room and excitedly said, "Keep the regalia on. You've got a distinguished visitor." At that moment there was a knock on the door, and in wafted a very soigné gentleman, greying at the temples, wearing a dark vestment with a high red-and-white striped border. "Grüss Gott, Herr Kammersänger! My name is Jachim, I'm the Archbishop of Vienna," adding, while cordially shaking my hand, "My heartiest congratulations on this evening's performance." I involuntarily winced, finding myself totally out of place in my cardinal's robes, which he expertly checked out and then said with a mischievous grin, "Superbly turned out, I must say, you make for some uncomfortably dangerous competition!"

I had not yet digested this high praise when there came another knock, and our director Salmhofer entered, hastily crossing himself and whispering

10.1.   Although I had prepared the role of Cardinal Borromeo in Hans Pfitzner's *Palestrina* and sung it in many different productions under the supervision of the composer/ librettist himself, Vienna opera director Salmhofer was keenly disturbed by one bit of business, until a real prince of the church cleared matters up. Photo, © Foto Fayer, Vienna.

"Praised be Jesus Christ." His bowed his head low over the hand with the ring. At that moment a brain wave flashed through my cranium: "Tell me, Your Eminence, did it bother you to see the cardinal kneeling down before Palestrina?"

"Why, not in the least," the prince of the church replied, "he isn't kneeling before Palestrina the man, but rather before the divine spark in him. He also clearly says: 'God speaks through you'—and I didn't even realize it!" Thereupon Salmhofer turned triumphantly to me and intoned: "What did I tell you? You've got to KNEEL! KNEEL!"

Chapter 11

When, in the hot summer months, our opera companies sent their artists along with the rest of the workforce on vacation, the largest opera house in South America, the Teatro Colón in Buenos Aires, with its nearly 3,600 seats, would open its gates for the Temporado, the annual large-scale cultural event for opera fans on the southern hemisphere of the globe. I mentioned this season somewhat earlier.

On this occasion, from time immemorial, well-known singers from Europe and North America have been coming down to the Argentine metropolis to swell the ranks of the local ensemble. Internationally renowned conductors were also engaged, and they shaped the local orchestra into a first-class ensemble as they led their performances in the Italian, German, and Slavic repertoire.

The famous Austrian conductor Erich Kleiber, well known from his activity as General Music Director of the Berlin State Opera from 1923 to 1934, had departed the European music scene before the war and acquired a whole grove of laurels for his contribution to the development of musical life in the Argentine capital. For the 1948 season, he resumed contact with the operatic institutions in Vienna and London and brought over a varicolored vocal ensemble to the Teatro Colón. Back in those days, we members of the Vienna State Opera were, of course, more than delighted to take advantage of the opportunity to spend time in a country far distant from the war and its devastation. I believe it is hard for younger people to realize what it was like for us in the years after the war. Life back then was pretty horrible, and then suddenly this: we found ourselves walking down the streets of a wealthy, modern city with four million inhabitants. We looked in the shop windows and could contemplate buying anything our hearts desired. Or, we could sit down in a restaurant and, for very little money, order from a vast array of treats we had only been able to dream about for a long time.

It all began aboard the Italian ship that sailed under the Panamanian flag to bring us in nineteen days from Europe via Rio de Janeiro to Buenos Aires. We felt like regular gourmets, who had been magically transported to a dreamland of delectable Italian cuisine. On this enjoyable sea journey we had an experience that deserves recounting here, because it was typical for that time. On trips across the Atlantic, there was an amusing traditional entertainment called the Equator baptism. This was a jolly ceremony, to which passengers were subjected if they had never crossed the Equator by ship before. To the cheers of the others, a member of the crew would appear dressed as the great god Neptune, Lord of the Ocean, who would conduct the baptismal ceremony, accompanied by a merry assemblage of fauns and mermaids. Every novitiate had to step forward individually, kneel before the god Neptune, who would offer him or her a pinch of flour or salt on a spoon, which the novice would then have to swallow. As the crowning glory of this ceremony, a raw egg would be broken on the initiate's head, which of course led to the onboard hairdresser being blamed for staging this little farrago, as all the baptized females would have to seek out his services following the ceremony. In our case, every one of the passengers on board—some seventy in first class and a good two hundred in tourist class—took part in this baptismal parody.

No wonder, then, that many of the passengers from Austria had second thoughts about 270 fresh eggs being broken just for the fun of it, when they realized that back home eggs were still regarded as a precious rarity; at the time, we all got a ration of one egg every two weeks. And so it was understandable that in the face of this wastefulness our thoughts went back to our hungry compatriots, and we stood there, amid all the merrymakers, with earnest, pensive expressions on our faces. Two young Frenchwomen had observed us; they shared our emotions, because there was also a terrible food shortage in their country. Then a couple of Brazilians joined us and asked us about the cause of our gloomy expressions. We were unable to make clear the reasons for this, because they simply refused to believe our story. Shaking our heads, we parted company, each side totally misunderstanding the other—all of us absorbed in our own thoughts.

The rehearsals on the gigantic stage of the Teatro Colón were in full swing. My first view of the stage from the auditorium put me into a slight panic: How would I ever fill that enormous hall with my voice? But my worry proved to be unfounded. In the hotel lobby I ran into my friend, pianist Walter Gieseking, who was on a concert tour through South America. In the course of our conversation, I immediately mentioned my worries about the acoustics in the Teatro Colón. He smiled comfortingly and said, "Tomorrow evening I'll be giving a piano recital there with plenty of Debussy on the program. Come to the concert and take a seat in the top balcony. You'll be amazed at the acoustics!" I followed his suggestion and experienced a real miracle. So what he had told me about the dream acoustics was really true! The softest tones rose from the stage like individual pearls.

The music seemed to be coming from any number of different directions. Gieseking walked out on stage. Beside the large instrument, and despite his powerful stature, he seemed tiny when viewed from the top balcony. The experience of this concert gave me the necessary assurance. When, still a bit skeptical, I myself stood singing on the stage, I was able to confirm what I had heard before. Sixteen years later I sang the *Winterreise* in the same hall, a work that couldn't be less suited to such a huge room. But the unique acoustics didn't leave me in the lurch.

The performances in 1948 and 1949 were marked by Erich Kleiber's powerful musical authority. We discovered a surprisingly pleasant contrast in his work method: while he could be a meticulously demanding and often hurtfully severe despot in rehearsal, during performances he was a helpful, paternal, and considerate master of the situation. Nothing and no one could rattle his calm. Here's an example: our first production was Wagner's *Tristan und Isolde*. I was cast as the loyal Kurwenal, one of the most human, moving characters the poet-composer ever created. Wagner has Kurwenal make several entrances in the first act, concluding with his appearance to announce the arrival of King Marke to his Lord Tristan.

To understand this story, you need to know that in the vast open spaces of the Teatro Colón, the singers often had to cover sizable distances from their dressing rooms to the stage, and communication between the stage and the dressing rooms was only possible via loudspeakers. The stage manager on duty thus had to summon the soloists early enough for them to start on their long walk to the stage in plenty of time to make it on cue. As I sat in my dressing room, the thought suddenly crossed my mind that it must be about time for that final entrance. So on my own, I started on my way to the stage. When I arrived there I discovered to my not inconsiderable horror that the curtain had already fallen. I had completely missed my entrance! Obviously there was something wrong with the loudspeaker system. There was great agitation and much loud screaming on the stage, in which I agitatedly joined, when a hand gently descended on my shoulder. It was Erich Kleiber, who pleasantly said, "Easy does it. It's happened, and now it's over. But remember you still have the third act ahead of you, and I'm looking forward to that. Now go back to your dressing room and try to calm down a bit." I was confused and thought I hadn't heard him correctly. Any other conductor would have thrown a fit in that situation.

Only recently I read a review in an English newspaper discussing a newly released recording of *Tristan und Isolde,* featuring the 1949 cast at the Teatro Colón in Buenos Aires. Obviously, this was one of those pirate recordings. The critic expressed considerable annoyance that at the end of act one, the voice of Hans Hotter was virtually inaudible. If only he had known why!

My partners in this *Tristan und Isolde* performance were Swedish tenor

Set Svanholm, with whom I often stood on the stage of the Metropolitan Opera in New York, as well as the incomparable Kirsten Flagstad as Isolde. Shortly before that, she had been my Brünnhilde in *Die Walküre* at the Royal Opera House, Covent Garden, in London. Following the *Tristan* at the Teatro Colón, there was a production of *Götterdämmerung,* again with Svanholm as Siegfried and my beloved Kirsten as Brünnhilde. I was Gunther. Kirsten's immolation scene was overwhelming; at every performance I would stand backstage, enraptured by the beauty of the miraculous sound of that voice. This is truly a memory of one of the most gorgeous female voices that ever was. Even now, as I commit these reminiscences to paper, I am still profoundly stirred by it.

In 1962 I again sang in Buenos Aires, this time as Wotan in two entire *Ring* cycles, and in 1966 I made my final appearance in the Argentine capital and gave a song recital at the Mozarteum there.

That same October, I began rehearsals on a new production of *Meistersinger* at the Prinzregententheater in Munich, which, as already mentioned, had become the temporary quarters of the company until we could return to the reconstructed building on Maximilianstrasse in 1963. To my great joy, there was a new encounter with Eugen Jochum, who had conducted the opera fifteen years before in Hamburg when I was still singing master baker Kothner. And now we were slated to work together in Munich, where I would finally be singing my first Hans Sachs at home in Germany, uncut and in the *original German!* This may sound peculiar, but I really did have to debut this role in the unfamiliar English language. And now a long-held dream was finally about to come true. This once-in-a-lifetime work of the Bayreuth master, which had received its world premiere in 1868 under the direction of the composer at the Royal Bavarian Court Opera in Munich, had already had a profound effect on me as a schoolboy: the music, and especially the character of Hans Sachs, had always deeply moved me. There were a number of meaningful reasons for this: first of all, the maestro on the podium, the all-commanding Hans Knappertsbusch. Then there was the casting of the leading roles, I still remember their names as if it had all been yesterday: Fritz Krauss as a glowing Stolzing, the captivating Elisabeth Feuge as Eva, Luise Willer as Magdalene. What a feast for the ears! Beckmesser, Emil Geis—what a performer! Paul Bender's personality in the part of Master Pogner, and as the crowning glory, the towering interpretation of the cobbler-poet by the great singing actor Wilhelm Rode. His embodiment of this role of roles was an optimum guiding light and a role model for me for many years. This seemingly endless part calls for a sizable measure of endurance and vocal economy and can only be taken on successfully by an experienced, mature singing personality. It also makes the most extraordinary demands on the actor! You can't just "play" Hans Sachs in the usual operatic style; you have to move and behave as if in everyday life, and yet with every note, from the first to the last word, uninterruptedly radiate a very personal authority.

The *Meistersinger* rehearsals in the autumn of 1949 were pleasant and lively. Eugen Jochum exuded a healthy, natural joy of music-making, so that we all enjoyed a pleasantly productive working atmosphere. The staging was the work of the house director, Heinz Arnold, a man well versed in the theater, who left no doubt that he was the master of his craft. The audience and the press welcomed the new production with unanimous enthusiasm.

At this point in the narrative, it would be satisfying to relate, as I have with several other characterizations, that this role became yet another staple in my repertoire, one that I sang for decades all over the globe. But such was not to be. Today, long after the conclusion of my career, I cannot but reflect back on the advice my teacher gave me when he warned me about false evaluations of my own abilities, telling me to be brutally honest in judging my own limitations. And so I now have to confess that the role of Hans Sachs never suited my voice as much as the other Wagnerian figures I portrayed, such as Wotan or the Dutchman. The heroic dimensions of those characters were better suited to my physical proportions than was the character of the sensitive cobbler-poet with the big heart, much as I loved the brief period during which I sang the part.

At the time, however, everyone was just happy to have the beloved *Meistersinger* back in the repertoire, whatever my limitations may have been in the interpretation of the protagonist. Nobody indulged in the luxury of exaggerated expectations. There was still an unrestrained sense of gratitude to the destiny that had allowed us to survive, and all of us performers, in our everyday activity at the opera house, stood closer together than ever before as we coped with the large and small problems that came along. Perhaps, after all the brutality we had been through, our usual tendency to gripe about this and that was somewhat blunted. My family and I had been spared the worst fate. As so often in life, our lucky star had not abandoned us.

Chapter 12

Perhaps this is the right moment to talk about something many singers would rather keep to themselves, but which I would prefer to discuss: the subject of vocal crises in the life of a singer. Accounts of such periods of vocal weakness are told in quite a few singers' biographies. We can even read that the great Russian basso Fyodor Chaliapin was forced to stop performing for several years. My own observations have shown that every singer sooner or later in the course of his or her career has had to face a period of diminished abilities, sometimes even without the individual even being aware of it. The reasons for this generally transitory disability can be many and varied. Most frequently the cause is an overburdening of the vocal material as a result of too much stress or improper vocal technique. The person most likely to help here is the right teacher; and the best way out of the dilemma is to maintain regular breath control in one's teacher's studio. In my own case, it was in the years 1950 and 1951 that I had trouble and occasionally noticed signs of vocal exhaustion during performance.

I particularly recall two evenings in Munich, both of which I had all I could do just to complete. Soon the rumor was out that Hotter had lost his voice. My long time adviser and resident vocal expert, throat specialist Dr. Rudolf Zimmermann spoke of a weakening of my respiratory and vocal organs caused by the annual attacks of hay fever and asthma during the pollen season, along with the physical aftereffects of the war years and the period thereafter. Fortunately I managed to find my way out of this low point by doing some intensive vocal-technical work on my own. In conversation with expert professionals, along with my memory of many of the things my teacher Matthäus Römer had said, I began to realize that I was one of those singers to whom nature had given many things other singers have to work fiendishly hard to acquire. But this gift also lures one into the trap of neglecting the necessary regular vocal exercises. If recognized early enough, this neglect can be remedied. The more intensive work can even bring about improvement and a more mature application of the vocal means.

I always wondered why, of all performances, my debut at the Metropolitan Opera in New York in the crisis year of 1950 in the title role of

Der fliegende Holländer turned out to be a success nobody had expected. And, why of all things, in the second crisis year of 1951, I probably turned out the top recording of my life with a performance of the Bach cantata "Ich habe genug."

To conclude this "crisis commentary" I must mention what happened on one occasion when I had to fight vocal exhaustion toward the end of a performance. It took place during the Munich Festival in the summer of 1950. Kna was pretty livid and told me so in no uncertain terms.

In the autumn of 1951 I again sang in Munich, in a performance of *Walküre* under his musical direction. To my great amazement he came out onstage (which was certainly not his usual practice) at the end of the second intermission, took one of his typical little bows, and said in front of the other members of the cast, "That sounds splendid. I really must sincerely beg your pardon; I behaved like a pig. I'm sure you know what I'm talking about." This happened after the end of the first postwar Bayreuth Festival, which took place in the summer of 1951 without my participation.

From 1952 on I then spent every summer singing on Bayreuth's Green Hill, working hand in hand with Kna and spent many a post-performance evening with him playing skat in the Eule, the tavern where the singers continue to gather after the show to this day. What impressed me the most was that he found the courage to admit that he had been wrong and had behaved inappropriately.

There is no other opera house in the world that, from time immemorial, has exercised such a magnetic attraction to singers as the Metropolitan Opera in New York—even though it is generally known that this attractiveness is attributable neither to a transcendent artistic level nor especially lucrative rewards. After the war, the prospect of standing on the stage of that theater was the great dream of every individual to whom the ownership of a "golden throat" had been vouchsafed. My contacts with this famous institution went back to 1938, when I received a letter of intent for the 1939–40 season—which, however, had shrunk into a worthless scrap of paper in the wake of political developments. It took until 1950, when the longtime director of the Glyndebourne and Edinburgh Festivals, Rudolf Bing, was appointed general manager at the house on Manhattan's Thirty-Ninth Street, for me to be engaged, that same year, and I was on the soloists' roster there for the succeeding four years. I have already mentioned that I was in the middle of a vocal crisis in 1950, and so it was no wonder that friends and well-meaning individuals on the operatic scene tried to talk me into canceling the engagement or at least postponing it to a later date. I can't really say what provoked my thickheaded determination to honor my contract. In any case, in the autumn of 1950 we found ourselves boarding the SS *United States* in the English port of Southampton. My wife was fairly anxious, as she later confessed, but heroically suppressed her fears and misgivings during the five-day, rather storm-tossed crossing, so as not to upset me. We still had no inkling of the dramatic events that would delay our arrival in New York.

To explain what happened then, I have to take a little detour into American political history at the time. During the period between 1950 and 1954, the junior senator from Wisconsin, a tinhorn demagogue by the name of Joseph R. McCarthy, was acquiring a nefarious reputation for his take-no-prisoners battle against both real and imaginary Communist elements in American society. The same severity was applied in the scrutiny of arriving foreigners who might be suspected of any imaginable connections with the Communist cause. Exactly during the time we were crossing the Atlantic that severity was extended to cover anyone suspected of fascist or Nazi associations.

The immigration officer who exercised his office on our ship accused me as a member of the *Deutsche Bühnengenossenschaft,* (The German Theatrical Association, the labor union repesenting all artistic and technical theatrical employees in German-speaking countries), which from 1933 had been subjected to the authority of the *Arbeitsfront* (Labor Front), of having belonged to a Nazi organization. So there would be NO ENTRY PERMIT! It made no difference to him when I explained that I had been a member of the union since 1930; the membership was obligatory, just as I was required to join AGMA (the American Guild of Musical Artists) before being allowed to set foot on the stage of a Stateside opera house, a requirement I thoroughly endorsed. The officer insisted on keeping us out of the country, and so we were shipped by ferry to the notorious immigrants' holding area on Ellis Island. There we spent two nights in barracks, sleeping in a dormitory along with several hundred others, whose entry permits had also been denied. It was a weekend.

The Metropolitan Opera had meanwhile been anything but inactive. It intervened in Washington, and we were finally released the following Monday morning. The whole thing was only half as bad as was later reported in the local media. American friends, former officers in the U.S. occupation forces in Munich back in 1945 were more than touching in their concern for our well-being and begged our pardon time and again for the rough treatment we had undergone while uttering some fairly X-rated imprecations at Senator McCarthy.

We still had no idea of the effect this whole business was to have on my first appearance in the United States. There was still a considerable uproar, with newspapers printing long articles on the subject. The rehearsals for my debut began in the loveliest harmony. My Senta was Astrid Varnay, who had been my London Brünnhilde back in 1949, and the small role of Mary was sung by Jean Madeira, who would shortly afterward advance to the status of a major star in several European opera houses. On the podium was Fritz Reiner, a crackerjack professional of the old school.

One week before the premiere, stories again appeared in the press detailing our involuntary stay on the immigration island. The general public mood had been aroused, and it was becoming clear that the whole episode was being turned into a publicity stunt of the first order—and all this despite the fact that I had not yet sung a note in a public performance there. Opening night was a huge success for all parties concerned. The sad story of the poor unfortunates whom cruel fate had briefly barred from entering the country was exaggerated out of all proportion. The most important thing was that I was vocally at my peak. My wife and I both heaved sighs of relief, and every thought of a vocal crisis was consigned to the past. A Munich paper wrote, "An unexpectedly great success," and informed friends could not believe their eyes.

The days and weeks in New York went flying by. The unfamiliar atmosphere of friendliness and accommodation on the street, in the subway, in the theater, in shops, even in government offices seemed unreal to us and taught us the lesson of keeping our eyes open and exercising more tolerance ourselves. The American colleagues at the opera behaved like good old pals. There were Regina Resnik, Rose Bampton, Margaret Harshaw, Jerome Hines, and all the others. The Italian basso Cesare Siepi arrived at the Met about the same time as myself; he was an adorable colleague with a dream voice. And then one of the most glorious tenor voices that ever was: the Swede Jussi Bjoerling, a refreshingly shy, diffident artist. His "Ingemisco" in the Verdi *Requiem* is one of the most moving renditions of any music I have ever heard from a human voice.

The season in New York opened with Verdi's *Don Carlo.* In later performances I sang the role of the Grand Inquisitor, a part in which I was cast possibly more than any other in the course of my career. This time, too, it was a great success! In the following season this role brought me the "Best Operatic Performer of the Year" award from some magazine, I can't remember which. Today this impresses me as being on a par with "Best Soccer Player of the Year." With all due respect to soccer, it bothers me that the quality ratings that have found their way into today's artistic life have no business there in the first place.

There followed concert engagements in places like Cleveland, where my former Prague musical director George Szell had formed that city's orchestra into one of the best in the country. He brought me to Cleveland and we reveled in reminiscences of the good old days in Prague. I became acquainted with his large collection of recordings with the orchestra, which I soon grew to love. To this day, I still believe these recordings can hold their

12.1.   My interpretation of the Grand Inquisitor in Margaret Webster's Metropolitan production of *Don Carlo* so impressed one magazine that it named me "Operatic Performer
of the Year"; at the same time Rudolf Bing became convinced that I was made for secondary roles—as if the Inquisitor were a secondary role!! Photo, © Metropolitan Opera Archives.

own in comparison with any other of the same works by his most illustrious colleagues. After Cleveland we continued on to Chicago, San Antonio,
and San Francisco.

During my time at the Met, I also began giving song recitals, mainly in
colleges and music academies. Soon, as had been the case in Great Britain,
I began meeting Jewish people who had immigrated to this country from

Europe. Many of the things that had stirred my heart in England repeated themselves here. Here as there, new friendships began to develop, and we soon became involved in discussions over the injustices that had befallen so many of them. These new friendships also introduced us to a new lifestyle, with a different attitude toward everyday things, one which initially struck us as very unusual. However, we soon found ourselves taking on attributes that had fallen by the wayside back in Europe: first and foremost the virtue of tolerance in matters of taste, especially artistic taste.

One key experience began with a ride on the New York subway where I discovered a billboard showing two hands folded in prayer over a light blue background. At a gathering that evening I was chatting with a Catholic priest and told him what I had observed on the subway. "That's quite an impressive image, isn't it?" he said. "Yes," I agreed, "but who pays for that billboard?"

"We do," was his terse reply.

"You mean the Catholic Church?"

"No, no, all of us, all the churches that want to take part pay for it." I began thinking this over and tried to imagine if anything like that would have been possible in Europe.

Once, at another get-together somebody asked me the meaning of the Dutch word "kitsch," which had long since also found its way into the German language and was then just beginning to make inroads into English as well.

"Well, kitsch, that's . . ." I stuttered, "that actually means something tasteless."

"You mean something *you* think is tasteless. Do you believe you have the right to rate your taste higher than other people's?" I kept further argumentation to myself. In a silent moment, I asked myself how far fairness and endurance of someone else's taste has to go. To this day I have found no answer to that question.

My activity at the Metropolitan Opera only covered four seasons. After my almost tumultuous initial success with the Dutchman and the Grand Inquisitor there were two Richard Strauss operas on the schedule: *Salome* and *Elektra*. The Salome was Ljuba Welitsch from the Vienna company. She had an incredible success with this role. Provocative in her portrayal, she was a master in the craft of characterization, yet she always managed to hit all the right notes, which is certainly not the story with many other interpreters of this part. The great Wagner tenor of the 1930s and '40s, Max Lorenz, gave Herodes the full weight of his interpretive art. I particularly liked him in this role and always found that the decadent tetrarch was one of the best parts in his capacious repertoire. I had been entrusted with the role of Jochanaan.

As Orest, I was the beneficiary—as I had been in *Holländer*—of the special enjoyment of an exceptionally adjustable partnership in the form of Astrid Varnay's Elektra. It was during the preparatory phase of this production that I intensified my friendship with her and her husband, Hermann Weigert, who had been a conductor at the Berlin State Opera before 1933. Astrid showed me the way to a better understanding of the American mentality, including its relationship to the arts and the artists who practiced them.

We met again in the European summer on the stage of the Bayreuth Festival and then later in guest performances in France and Italy. I've already mentioned her tremendous adjustability. Nevertheless she possessed sufficient artistic instinct to inspire her partners enormously. Beyond that she had a wealth of one of the most important traits anyone in our singing profession can call his or her own: a delicious sense of humor. I always found that, in the tangle of easily exploding emotions, nerve-racking tension and vexatious hypersensitivities, a humorous remark or a funny story is the best way to get back to reality. And with Astrid Varnay, you could really enjoy a hearty laugh, even during the performance, secretly, clandestinely, like being back in school. The more serious and solemn the mood on the stage, the greater the temptation to indulge in a little clandestine nonsense. Sometimes we would make bets as to whether we could crack one another up. Once we were singing Wagner's *Parsifal* together in France. Astrid was Kundry, and I was Gurnemanz. Now, Wagner has only given Kundry two words to sing in the third act of his opera, or more specifically the same word twice. To Gurnemanz's reproach she only replies humbly and subserviently, "Dienen" (service), and shortly after that, repeats it for emphasis' sake, "Dienen." I was standing with my back half turned away from the audience. After the first "Dienen," I bent over slightly toward her, as if I were hard of hearing, and mumbled, "Huh?" The second "Dienen" almost dissolved in frantically suppressed laughter.

Back to more serious Wagner: after the *Holländer,* I sang Master Pogner in *Die Meistersinger,* King Marke in *Tristan,* Gurnemanz in *Parsifal,* Wotan in *Rheingold,* and, surprisingly enough, in *Walküre* I generally sang Hunding. One single time I sang, as I did everywhere else in the world, Wotan in that opera. In 1954 my relationship with the Met ended rather abruptly.

Here's how it happened: Rudolf Bing, who had brought me there with great interest in 1950 and had always been extremely well disposed toward me, suddenly said my strength was in the smaller character roles (thinking perhaps of the Grand Inquisitor in *Don Carlo*). He felt I should stay away from the major Wagnerian roles. To this day I haven't a clue what gave him that idea. It may have had something to do with the fact that, in his heart of hearts, he didn't care for Wagner. In any case, that was the end of my days

For Hans Hotter, the people who are the friendliest and nicest folks! Affectionately, Astrid Varnay 1952

12.2.   I first worked with Astrid Varnay in London, then in her hometown of New York and in many other theaters. She is shown here hugging one of her favorite conductors, Joseph Keilberth, in Bayreuth. Astrid is an authentic tragedienne, but she is not averse to some harmless onstage clowning, as long as the audience doesn't catch on. Photo reprinted with the kind permission of the Bayreuth Festival.

12.3.   My favorite operatic venue in the United States was the San Francisco Opera. Here Helga and I join tenor Ramón Vinay and his wife to celebrate the twenty-fifth anniversary of the theater in 1979, along with the company's director, Kurt Herbert Adler. Photo, © 2005 Ron Scherl, San Francisco.

at the Metropolitan Opera. I only saw the stage of the new theater on Lincoln Center from the auditorium.

This somewhat inglorious departure from New York was followed more than twenty-five years later by the greatest of successes in my usual Wagner roles at the Chicago Lyric Opera during the administration of Carol Fox and especially in the War Memorial Opera House in San Francisco, when Kurt Herbert Adler still wielded the scepter. It was his successor Lotfi Mansouri who brought me back to the West Coast to portray Schigolch in his *Lulu* production. To this day I have remained loyal to the house with its amiable, personal flair—yet another reason why that beautiful patch of ground by the Golden Gate was always my favorite spot on the American continent.

⇜ Chapter 13 ⇝

On one of my many visits to the United States, I discovered the entertainment community in the throes of one of those odd, peculiarly American crises that frequently leave us Europeans somewhat baffled. It all began during the war years, when "feel-good" movies, intended to help maintain high spirits on the home front, were very much in vogue. Leo McCarey, one of the top producer-directors in Hollywood, had written a short story called *Going my Way,* which Paramount thought would be an ideal contribution to the effort of keeping people's sunny side up in the turbulent 1940s, and they certainly didn't spare the horses when it came to casting the film, a tale about a happy-go-lucky singing priest in an underprivileged neighborhood. The part of the crusty old Irish curate was assigned to Barry Fitzgerald, a veteran of Dublin's prestigious Abbey Theatre, who had been the Hibernian of choice in America since the early 1930s. The female lead was played by a moonlighting star from the Metropolitan Opera, one of the most glamorous ladies on the roster of any theater, operatic or otherwise, Risë Stevens. In the leading role of Father O'Malley, the singing priest, Paramount cast one of its top drawing cards, Bing Crosby, who turned in a truly heartwarming performance, singing several tunes that topped the charts all over the world, including one still popular standard, "Swinging on a Star," which was number one on the hit parade for nine weeks and won the Oscar for best song that year.

The prize for that popular ditty was only one of the many Academy Awards heaped on the movie, including a golden statuette for Fitzgerald as best supporting actor, for Crosby as the best actor in a leading role. Further accolades included best screenplay, best direction, and best film, plus a stack of other honors and nominations, including three Golden Globes.

Building on the success of the Paramount hit, RKO decided to bring back Bing Crosby as Father O'Malley the very next year in a sequel called *The Bells of Saint Mary's,* also produced and directed by Leo McCarey and this time costarring one of the hottest stars in Hollywood, Swedish actress Ingrid Bergman as the most pulchritudinous mother superior ever to grace a convent. While not so highly honored as its predecessor, *The Bells of Saint*

Mary's did receive several Academy Award nominations; most important, it advanced Bing Crosby, a fine actor apart from his singing talents, from the status of a popular crooner to that of a superstar. Oddly enough, when Crosby, himself a devout Roman Catholic, was initially offered the role, he wasn't sure playing a goodtime priest was really an appropriate task for him to undertake. But there is no quarreling with that level of fame, and from then on Bing Crosby was a household name, inexorably linked with the kind of ultravirtuous character he had played in these two hit films—and it was that status that sparked the crisis.

Some ten years later, back at Paramount, Bing Crosby did a complete about-face in a film called *The Country Girl,* George Seaton's heavy-duty drama based on the Broadway hit by Clifford Odets, in which the former interpreter of the too-good-to-be-true Father O'Malley played a down-at-the-heels song and dance man, destroying his own life and oppressing his long-suffering spouse (an Oscar-winning performance by Grace Kelly) with his alcoholic excesses.

This portrayal in *The Country Girl* was arguably the finest acting performance Bing Crosby ever turned in, and the film, unlike the two Father O'Malley pictures, which are now looked upon as hopelessly dated, has become an authentic classic, holding the screen as effectively today as it did when it was released more than a half century ago. But Bing Crosby had meanwhile become so inextricably associated with that kindhearted priest character that several women's religious organizations went on a rampage over his later movie, demanding that any motion picture showing "their" Father O'Malley in such an unsympathetic characterization ought to be banned from the nation's movie houses. Fortunately for cinema lovers then as now, the ladies did not achieve their objective. But their protest is an interesting case in point.

Life may occasionally imitate art and vice versa, but audiences are ill-advised to see the character of an actor or singer as a kind of clone of the roles he or she performs. Much of casting has to do with the luck of the draw: in theater and motion pictures, physical appearance and apparent personality are major determinants. In musical theatre, especially opera, it is, of course, the range and nature of the voice even more than appearance or personality that have the most to do with who sings the villains and who sings the heroes. This explains why, for example, it was the quality of my voice that predestined me to play, among many other roles, many of the foulest fiends in operatic literature. As each of these came along, starting with Tonio in *Pagliacci* during my earliest year in Troppau and moving on to a long line of other blackguards, it became my job as an interpretive artist to try to understand each of these characters. I undertook to portray them as plausibly as I could, largely through an assiduous study of the musical and verbal text and an observation of the human condition as it affects the motivations of those individuals toward good or evil—*not* by plumbing my own personality for characteristics that may or may not have jibed with those of the character on stage. My goal in all of this was never to become one with the character but rather to convey that character's emotions believably to my audience. My teacher put this attitude into a wonderful aphorism when he warned me: "Beware of ever stirring your own emotions." He went on to illustrate this with a slightly scatological observation: "Should you find yourself taking on the emotion of your character, you can always retire to a safe distance by imagining the people out front sitting on chamber pots in their nightgowns." Discretion prevents me from mentioning any specific events in which that course of action became necessary.

The Bing Crosby episode in America came to mind a couple of years later, when I was preparing to sing in a new production of Wagner's *Parsifal*. In the course of rehearsals, the tenor singing the title role made a remark that I think missed the point of his assignment on the stage: he suggested that his religious upbringing and his profound Christian faith made him virtually predestined to portray the supreme knight of the Holy Grail. With all respect to that artist, who certainly did give the audience a deeply moving portrayal, I beg to differ. It was his understanding of the character and not the singer's own personal mind-set that made him as effective as he was in the role of Parsifal. I have seen and worked with tenors both before and since who did not have that background or those religious convictions, yet who, in their own way, have been equally effective in the same characterization. Having said this, I would like to relate a few of my own observations in the process of creating some of the characters, both malign and virtuous, with which I have become associated in my stage career and try to shed some light on how I made them believable for my audience.

A prominent music critic once stated there are a few operatic villains that are not motivated by anything but the archetypical evil that imbues their personalities, mentioning in this context three specific roles I myself have sung: Don Pizarro in Beethoven's *Fidelio,* Jago in Verdi's *Otello,* and the ultimate rogue in that opera of operas, the title role in Mozart's *Don Giovanni*. To my way of thinking, this eminent writer on music underrated three of the greatest composers who ever lived by suggesting that their characters are so monodimensional that we cannot create believable human portraits drawn from those factors in their lives, which, if convincingly portrayed, ultimately explain to the audience the origin of the terrible evils the characters visit on others.

Don Giovanni has to be one of the most complex characters ever created for the theater by simple virtue of the fact that he is tragically driven to do whatever he can to achieve his ends, and he derives his greatest satisfaction from gratuitously subjugating virtually everyone he encounters to his will, whether the individual is a servant he must force to do his bidding or a woman he is uncontrollably compelled to seduce. On top of this, he possesses the almost magical quality of being able to convince just about everyone he encounters, at least initially, of his sincerity, whether in his offers to marry Donna Elvira and Zerlina or in his pledges of heartfelt support to Ottavio and Anna to help them track down the miscreant who ravished Anna and killed her father—in other words, himself. Even though the audience knows, in both cases, that he is lying, both his words and his music are so reassuring that his motives come across as being of the noblest. Bear in mind, these are not gullible dolts: all of them, including the unsophisticated peasant girl Zerlina, have been around, and it is this skill of taking people in that makes Giovanni so fascinating.

In this artifice he has been magnificently aided by Mozart's music, which gives him the gift of treating everyone just a little differently as he lures them into whatever trap he wants to set for them. In the case of Zerlina and Masetto, for example, the Don wins over Zerlina by singing her one of the most captivating folk tunes imaginable, a ploy he repeats in his tantalizing serenade to Elvira's servant girl, while a simple imitation of his servant Leporello, using the music characteristic of that character, sets Masetto's posse off looking for the villain so that Giovanni can give the poor bumpkin a vicious thrashing. His approach to Anna and Ottavio stresses his aristocratic manners, feigning deep concern for "poor mad" Elvira, whom he then brings around in the second act with a siren song, only to dump her into the arms of Leporello, while he goes off in quest of greener pastures. Whoever the victim may be, the chameleonlike Don finds a remarkably characteristic language for winning them over, to the point where at least Elvira is firmly convinced that her own love for him can turn his character around, a misapprehension that has proven the tragic misfortune of many a lady. Were he not such a driven, compulsively hurtful person, this gift would certainly render him a totally ingratiating chap we would all like to know better, but the devil, in a very literal sense, is in his details.

As I see him, Giovanni is someone who probably would like to mean well with people, but who invariably gives in to his baser nature in a hopelessly desperate quest for love and loyalty, and who in the final analysis can be perceived as a tragic figure because, in the course of the entire drama, he fails to realize that he himself is totally incapable of loving. Giovanni has, for whatever reasons, become so experienced in achieving his intermediate objectives by whatever means he has found effective that he is utterly unable to reach any of his ultimate human goals. This may seem a simplistic observation, but I honestly believe this facile quality in getting his almost childish way is what sets the whole machinery of the man's character in motion and makes him concurrently contemptible and pitiable. In another sense, he is further accursed by having the kind of intelligence that turns into cunning, enabling him to rationalize everything he does and feels—without, however, the wisdom than that might force him to confront himself on some kind of realistic level and find his way out of the dilemma that eventually proves his undoing: that of carrying things too far in every instance and then in the final analysis being totally rejected, if you will, by man and God.

I was greatly helped in creating this role by knowing that the original Giovanni in Mozart's Prague premiere was a very young Italian singer-actor named Luigi Bassi, who, while strikingly handsome, wasn't as accomplished a singer as the rest of the cast; and so Mozart never gave him the kind of vocal challenges he presents to the others. This way, while the other characters delve into the intricacies of Mozart's bel canto writing at its most sophisticated, Giovanni is always able, vocally, to keep his distance, devoid of any vocal obstacles the average baritone might be unable to surmount (such as the ones, for example, that Count Almaviva encounters in the score of *Le nozze di Figaro*). This knowledge helped me remain detached or, paraphrasing Rudyard Kipling's words (admittedly in a totally different context) to keep my head while all around me were losing theirs. It gave me a particular malevolent nonchalance while retaining the illusion of innocence vis-à-vis the other characters, which shows why it's always a good idea to know what (and often whom) the composer and librettist had in mind when they wrote the piece in the first place—especially when you're singing Mozart.

This insight, derived from the circumstances of the first performance, also gives us a deeper understanding of what this opera is all about. In many ways its message is every bit as revolutionary as the aforementioned *Le nozze di Figaro,* its "scandalous" predecessor. Destiny has given Giovanni every imaginable advantage—noble birth, a privileged upbringing, chivalrous manners, intelligence, charm, wealth, physical agility—and yet he is utterly lacking in those essential human qualities without which his other privileges are meaningless. On the contrary, instead of practicing anything vaguely akin to noblesse oblige, he believes that his privilege is a free ticket to help himself to whatever pleasures happen his way. Clearly, Mozart and da Ponte were making a sociopolitical statement that was not lost on their noble patrons, and that speaks eloquently to us today on a number of levels.

It is often sad to note that so many productions, not just in our own time, misperceive this character as a stock villain, a humorlessly leering, lecherous monster with none of the appealing attributes that make him so fascinating to everyone on both sides of the footlights—which of course totally invalidates the telling message of the opera, besides being illogical on

13.1.   The title character in Mozart's *Don Giovanni* abuses his privileged status and his sophisticated manners to achieve his corrupt ends, making this opera an early example of incisive sociocritical theater.

the face of it. One salacious leer from a character like that, and any of his victims would waste no time heading for the nearest exit.

Don Pizarro, the cur in Beethoven's only operatic work, *Fidelio,* is quite a different story, and presented me with a challenge that gave me greater insight into all the villainous characters we are called upon to portray. Taking gratuitous, "pure" evil as a point of departure will not really get us very far in helping an audience understand the dimensions of the character on stage. In many cases—Giovanni is one; Shakespeare, Verdi, and Boito's "honest" Jago another—villains captivate by using their wiles to appear far more well-meaning than they are. In the case of Pizarro, whose every utterance is a study in malignity, the singer must guard himself against overstressing the qualities that are already there. In many ways, Pizarro is almost a pitiable creature, a man who has woven a fragile web of intrigue without taking the most significant variables into consideration.

What is his dilemma? Discovering that a friend of the minister of justice, a nobleman by the name of Florestan, has revealed his corruption to higher authorities, Pizarro has hastily arranged to have the man secretly arrested to prevent his accuser from giving further evidence, having him hurled without due process of law into the dungeon of a prison over which he, Pizarro, is the governor, expecting that the darkness, isolation, and starvation of that confinement will soon destroy the man, driving him to either death or insanity and thus ridding him of an adversary who could seal his doom, but he is forced to realize that he has vastly underestimated his opponent's durability or the valor of his remarkable wife.

This all takes place before the curtain rises. As Don Pizarro enters into the action of the drama on a routine inspection, he is informed that the minister himself is on his way to the prison on an inspection tour, which means he will have somehow have to get Florestan precipitously out of the way or face disastrous consequences. Of course, he is totally unaware of the fact that Florestan's aforementioned wife, Leonore, dressed as a young man, has taken a job as warder in this very prison in hopes of discovering her husband and securing his release. What follows is a fascinating study in the development of human desperation as one scheme after another fails to materialize. Pizarro begins his action in full control of the situation, almost reveling in the "revenge" he believes to be his, and seemingly convinced of the justice of his cause. As he says in his frantic aria in act one, the moment has now arrived in which he himself can destroy the murderer, but we never find out who, if anyone, Florestan has ever done to death. Maybe Pizarro is reflecting on his own probable fate should he not manage to put his adversary out of commission at the last minute. He tries to bribe the jailer, Rocco, into murdering the prisoner in the dungeon, even calling the crime by its name, murder, never even suggesting this might be a justified execution.

13.2.   Yes, Beethoven's Pizarro is evil incarnate, but he is
also a man trapped in a predicament of his own making,
running away from his own past. Miss that element and
you have only half a portrayal.

But Rocco adamantly refuses, claiming that taking human life is not one of
his duties. So Pizarro decides to take the man's life himself, ordering the
jailer to go down to the dungeon and dig a grave there in a cistern, where
he can hide the corpse. Once he is in the dungeon and face-to-face with Florestan again, we become keenly aware of his total loss of self-control. A
cliché villain, unconscionably unaware of his own guilt, would probably try
to do the man in quickly and clandestinely, but Pizarro is determined to reveal to Florestan the identity of his killer: "Pizarro, den du stürzen wolltest"
(Pizarro, whom you wanted to topple), thus also exposing to Rocco and his
assistant, whom Pizarro has yet to recognize as Leonore, the reason for the
crime he had been plotting and the illegitimacy of his undertaking. It is at
this point that Leonore intervenes, and the game is up for Pizarro, although
he even tries to plead his case with the minister, who for his part is unwilling to lend any credence to conduct that is clearly indefensible.

My task in interpreting this character was not to convince the audience of Pizarro's fiendishness, which is more than obvious anyway, but rather to stress what the character believes himself to be: that is, not someone who has perpetrated a series of infamous misdeeds but rather one who sees himself as the victim of injustice with every right to take revenge against his accuser.

Jago is another character who feels totally justified in the evils he perpetrates. I do not see him as a man who commits foul deeds for their own sake. He does what he does because he is a monumentally ambitious individual, consumed by envy and resentment that another man, someone alien in race and nationality to the exclusive society of which he esteems himself a privileged scion, has "usurped" a higher position than he has been able to acquire. Enormously gifted with an abundance of cunning and the ability to feign sincerity and loyalty, he uses these gifts to chip away at Otello's self-confidence bit by bit until the poor man is driven to the murder of his own beloved and unshakably loyal wife. In this sense Jago, too, is somewhat of a tragic figure, plunged by his perception of what he believes to be his cruel fate into the nihilistic beliefs he articulates in his credo aria.

Baron Scarpia, the chief of police in Puccini's *Tosca* is a figure we initially encounter, for all his severity in the face of what he regards to be crime, as a seemingly decent, charming, elegant, deeply religious gentleman, one hundred percent on the side of the law. In his eyes, and actually by the letter of that law, Mario Cavaradossi *has* committed a real crime by hiding the Bonapartist "traitor" Angelotti in his garden well. Were it not for Scarpia's determination to use his persecution of Cavaradossi to have his way with the man's paramour, the singer Floria Tosca, he might be considered over-harsh in his pursuit of justice but certainly not in any way corrupt. My motivation in the portrayal was not to stress the man's evil character but rather to underscore the façade he tries to present to the outside world, allowing his baser nature to penetrate slowly, totally motivated by what happens in the words and the music. I stressed this by placing great emphasis on Scarpia's chivalrous good manners and hypocritical religiosity vis-à-vis the initially unsuspecting Tosca, until, of course, push comes to shove, and Scarpia reveals the ugliness of his true nature.

Fortunately, I did not have to spend my entire career portraying one miscreant after another, although many of the most interesting and challenging of the more virtuous characterizations I was vouchsafed came from the pen of an author-composer whose own personal life can be regarded as more than a little unsavory: Richard Wagner. I think the genuinely decent human beings he created may very well have been an expression of a longing in his imagination to acquire a level of humanity he was never able to reach in his earthly existence. This hypothesis sheds interesting light on one of the most enigmatic figures in the history of the arts. I don't think we will ever know for certain if compensating for his own frailties was his basic intention when creating these figures, but there is no doubting their sincerity. For this reason I cannot but believe that many of their attributes derive from a desire on his part to incorporate those characteristics into his own personality. Whatever the case, and in the final analysis these parallels are tangential to the consideration of his characters, it does make for some interesting speculation.

One excellent example of my theory is the figure of Kurwenal in *Tristan und Isolde,* whose human qualities are on the highest plane. The thing that makes Kurwenal so fascinating to me is the mixture of an absolutely healthy, solidly anchored loyalty and a profound sense of inner security in his own being. In portraying this role, I think we need a very firm sense of reality and an ability to see things as they truly are. Kurwenal is not a philosopher-knight reflecting on things as they might have been. He is a battle-hardened broadsword who witnesses the fatal attraction between his own commander and the lady destined to marry the king and realizes the utter impossibility of the situation in common, earthly terms. Yet he holds fast to his lord because, come what may, that is the stuff he is made of, a quality I find endlessly inspiring. He is the one who comes to tell the suddenly impassioned Tristan it is time to greet the king, to which the other man bluntly replies, "What king?" That moment, when it becomes clear that Tristan has lost all touch with reality, might have sent a lesser man into flight, if not out-and-out betrayal in the name of loyalty to the king. In the case of Kurwenal, however, it marks the beginning of a remarkable human development, one that ends in his own demise in defense of what he must know is a lost cause but nonetheless Tristan's destiny. It is Kurwenal's task not to try to undermine that destiny, or use some kind of rational argument to turn him away from the path he is fated to follow, but simply to stand beside him and be there for him wherever that destiny may lead.

This is not the kind of portrayal we can make happen by simply responding to instructions from a director and carrying out certain specified stage motions. We need to plumb the character's elemental humanity, which comes particularly to the fore in the third act when he has become transformed from a brash braggart poking fun at Isolde's emotional anguish to the caring companion, who for all his deep concern is still powerless to heal the affliction consuming the hero to whom he is so selflessly devoted. I find this unquestioning acquiescence to the will of the man he serves a fascinating illustration of an individual who is totally at one with himself and, who, even in the face of hard fate, retains a positive attitude toward life. It is what motivates him to live, fight, and even die in the service of another human being: not because he is under any kind of outer compulsion to do so, but because his integrity is a self-explanatory manifesta-

13.3.   I always had a special affinity for Wagner's Kurwenal because of his unswerving, unquestioning loyalty.

tion of his fundamental nature—which tells us a great deal about the ability of the hero to inspire this level of fealty. I believe Kurwenal is definitely
older than Tristan, and has probably made a major contribution to his upbringing, which lends a certain parental quality to the character.

Of course, this devotion on Kurwenal's part (and in a parallel sense the
loyalty of Brangäne to Isolde) tells the audience quite a bit about the need
of two people caught up in the unfathomable mystery of an all-consuming
love, which is concurrently a blessing and a curse, to have the understanding support of caring individuals who are in closer touch with reality than
either of them can be in the throes of their passion for each other. In this
sense, Wagner is fulfilling a wish-dream not only to have friends like this in
the face of his own unorthodox lifestyle but also to *be* that kind of loyal
friend, a friend he was able to place on the stage even if he was never able to
bring those qualities to bear on the confused reality of his own life.

The title character of *Der fliegende Holländer* represents the quintessence of the never-ending Wagnerian longing for redemption, yet at the same time remains driven by pure egoism. Not once does he ever utter a word about loving or wanting this woman Senta, or any of the others who have "failed" him over the decades; he simply states his need for her to love *him*. Ironically, though, he finally unites with her not by virtue of any kind of subterfuge or the bribery he offers her father, but through the honesty of openly admitting who he is and the curse he is under—to which Senta is able to respond that she has known this all along, and that she does not love him despite his terrible destiny but rather because of it. Thus it is her strength and resolution that give him the ability to surmount his own egoistic needs and return the love she offers him.

This early example is one of many that come about in Wagner's stories in which a hero can only be a hero, much like the protagonists of classical times, if there is some kind of fatal flaw in his character, or, stated in theological terms, some form of guilt, the awareness of which drives the thrust of the drama forward. For a long time Wagner wanted to write an opera on the life of Christ, but he finally realized that the project was impossible because there was no theatricality in the story of an individual without any form of guilt—which ultimately gave rise to his use of Christian elements devoid of the actual biblical story in his *Parsifal,* in which the hero, unlike many of Wagner's earlier characters, finds redemption in his ability to overcome his own guilt through awareness and suffering. In this opera, we also find the fascinating character of Gurnemanz, who begins the story as a teacher of others and ends it with the realization that he has indeed found the leader who can take his community out of the devastation that has befallen it and thus becomes his follower, perhaps a deeper realization of elements we find in the Kurwenal character.

It was primarily the influence of stage director Wieland Wagner that contributed to my attempt to clarify certain elements in the characterization of Gurnemanz to prevent his sometimes rather long-winded expostulations from being downright tedious, (as was also the case with the Wotan monologue I mentioned earlier in these recollections). A certain stress on harshness, indeed coarseness, with the members of the younger generation entrusted to his care, both with the squires and then later with Parsifal, brings liveliness into the long monologues without in any way reducing the image of the highly authoritative sage in his claim of primacy in the realm of the Grail.

It was the unique atmosphere up there on the green hill of the Wagner city that, fairly late in my operatic career, brought me closer to the figure of Gurnemanz and awakened my interest in the depiction of this role, especially as it suited me so well vocally. This is why, today, I am still grateful to

13.4.   When I first began singing Gurnemanz in *Parsifal*, many listeners said they could hear elements of Wotan in my interpretation. Photo reprinted with the kind permission of the Bayreuth Festival.

Wieland Wagner. It is his accomplishment that I was able to find so much more in this figure than the beautifully singing, dignifiedly striding, yet often fairly tedious "Stehbass" (a basso who just stands there and sings). In the twilight years of my operatic career, Gurnemanz became one of my favorite artistic assignments. Perhaps it is not uninteresting to learn that after my first Gurnemanz performances, several members of the press and public claimed to have found a fair amount of Wotan in my interpretation. A year or so later, they began finding elements of Gurnemanz in my Wotan.

Wotan in the first three *Ring* operas is possibly the most complicated role I have ever had to interpret, a character that has been subjected to such colossal misunderstanding on the part of superficial "concept" producers—far more interested in commenting on contemporary society than in mak-

13.5.   Later the same people began hearing characteristics of my Gurnemanz in Wotan.
Photo reprinted with the kind permission of the Bayreuth Festival.

ing a valid statement about an everlasting masterwork—that he is often de-
picted as a self-serving opportunist and reduced to a mere critique of venture capitalism at its worst. This is such utter nonsense, I see little point in
wasting time discussing these tiresome theories on these pages, except to
note that the poor crackpots who espouse them clearly have no knowledge
or awareness of the music this character has been given.

Wotan's music is Wagner's creativity in its noblest and most majestic
form; the ultimate proof of the character's basic humanity can be found in
his readiness to realize, accept, and indeed suffer from the many mistakes he
makes along the path he has chosen. Again he has an awareness of guilt, but
for all of this, his motivations are always on the highest plane, even if his actions do not always reflect the sublime level of integrity that prompted
them. At no point does he make any pathetic excuses for his weaknesses and
mistakes. On the contrary, his tragedy is in the realization that many of the
things he does simply fail to give correct expression to his own ideals. He is
a dreamer, a greathearted being with unfulfilled visions of supreme dominion over all things; but this dominion, this ruling over others in a kind of
benevolent condescension is never, in his eyes, an end in itself. On the con-

trary, he sees himself as a supreme ruler called to the exalted task of somehow leading this world and the people in it, all of whom he regards as his
children, to a greater good—an impossible goal he tragically fails to
achieve, perhaps because of his inability to perceive that even the most exalted ends never justify questionable means.

Is this a critique of the short-sightedness of capitalism? An analysis of
human nature? Insight into contemporary political developments? A kind
of aesthetic journalism? To be perfectly honest, it has never entered my
mind to try to draw parallels between the characters in these symbolic operas and common, earthly events. I do not see opera as a mere reflection of
elements in everyday life or a way somehow to come to terms with our
undigested political past, as is so often attempted in written commentaries
and misbegotten stagings with all their obsession with rehashing yesterday's newspapers (which, as we all know, ultimately wind up lining the bot-
toms of tomorrow's birdcages). This kind of literalism for all its pseu-
dosymbolic trappings has all the profundity of the Stateside clubwomen
mounting their protest against casting Bing Crosby in an unsympathetic
part. And it certainly has nothing to do with opera. Opera is a mystical
dream that stands above these things in a reality all its own.

A wise Berlin critic by the name of Oskar Bie once wrote a book about
opera, in which the first sentence states the case perfectly: opera, he says, is
an impossible artwork, and this is why all attempts to "relate" operatic expression to normal reality, even when the operas in question are based on
real historical events, are doomed to failure. Opera is a dreamworld, a fabric of fables with a reality all its own, propelled forward more by the ab-
straction of the music than by the words. And this is why we love opera so
much: in its lovable imperfection, it takes us beyond the pedestrian realities
of our material existence to a realm that can only be experienced by the sublime imagination of the spirit.

While this higher level of perception does not abrogate the singer's obligation to give plausible expression to the nature of the characters he or she
portrays, it nevertheless goes to prove why so many of the great operas,
most particularly those in the Wagnerian canon, have continued to retain
their full meaningfulness long after many dramatic works have become
hopelessly outdated: as Wieland Wagner so profoundly realized, their musical communication goes beyond time and place, turning the characters
that music depicts into archetypical creations with an everlasting validity.

In my view, this quality comes about not so much because the composers
wanted to act as tonal psychoanalysts or current affairs pundits but because
they successfully sought to comprehend the cosmic essence of human beings at their core and had the consummate inspiration and skill to turn that
essence into a transcendent form of musical expression.

Chapter 14

At the height of the Clemens Krauss era in the late thirties, we often saw a young man watching the performances from the director's box. He looked like a graduate student and followed the proceedings on the stage with visible interest. I once asked Krauss who he was. "That's one of Richard Wagner's grandsons. His name is Wieland. He comes to our performances quite frequently, don't you know him?" I had to admit I didn't. During the war, I once did a guest performance as the Dutchman at the Nuremberg Opera House. The settings were unusually solid, massive, and impressive. In the intermission, that same young man from the Munich director's box walked over to me and wanted to know if I was managing all right on the sets. Afterward the stage manager told me they had been designed by Wieland Wagner. He was also able to add the information that the Wagner grandson was a magnificent photographer and an impassioned artist, with the emphasis on painting.

In the spring of 1951, Wieland Wagner came to see me at my Munich home. His words, the pronunciation of which clearly reflected his Franconian upbringing, communicated his profound sense of disappointment: He confessed that he had waited for years for the moment he could tell me, "The time has come, we're finally going to get started again in Bayreuth," and that I would of course have to be there. Now, however, he had the sad duty to inform me that Hans Knappertsbusch had expressed misgivings as to whether I should be included in the 1951 reopening of the Bayreuth Festival after his experience with me in the summer of 1950. "Come to our opening performance of *Parsifal*," Wieland added, "say hello to him in intermission and then make it clear that Bayreuth can't possibly continue without you." That's exactly what happened. Considering his usual gruff manner, Kna was downright amiable when he growled, "Make sure that you're the old Hotter again by the time next summer rolls around. You belong here."

In the summer of 1952, it was Herbert von Karajan who wanted me as Kurwenal in the new *Tristan,* and then I sang my first *Walküre* Wotan and *Siegfried* Wanderer in the house on the green hill with my much-revered

14.1. Vocal problems precluded my participation in the first postwar festival in 1951, but I was doubly happy to join the company in 1952 with my old friend Kurwenal in a *Tristan und Isolde* conducted by Herbert von Karajan. Photo reprinted with the kind permission of the Bayreuth Festival.

Joseph Keilberth. Meanwhile that memorable *Walküre* in Munich had taken place in the course of which I discovered what an honorable character Kna had.

The 1952 *Tristan* performances marked my debut at the prestigious Bayreuth Festival but not the first time I had been asked to sing there. In 1939, only weeks before the outbreak of World War II, the management there planned several performances of *Der fliegende Holländer* in which Jaro Prohaska had been cast in the title role; as Prohaska would only be available for the first four performances, however, I was asked if I could step in on the remaining evenings. At the time, the direction of the Richard Wagner

Festival had been taken over by the composer's English-born daughter-in-law, Winifred Wagner, one of Adolf Hitler's closest friends and most ardent advocates since he first burst on the scene in the early 1920s, an advocacy she continued to maintain long after the most horrible facts about that man and his regime became general knowledge, indeed, right up to her death in 1980, many long years after the war. By the 1930s she had converted the festival into a temple of adulation for the Führer, and the whole city followed suit. When festival time rolled around, the streets were festooned with swastika banners, and brown-shirted Third Reich satraps strode ceremoniously in droves into the theater, where they dominated the audience. Quite frankly, I wanted no part of that atmosphere, which, in my opinion, had nothing to do with anything artistic, and I eagerly sought a way to get out of this unwelcome invitation with relative impunity.

So I went to see Clemens Krauss with my dilemma, and he was more than delighted to be of assistance. It seemed that Winifred Wagner had designated Heinz Tietjen, the head of Berlin's theaters at the time and a notorious Machiavellian intriguer, as artistic director of the festival. Tietjen had once cunningly maneuvered Krauss out of his position as general music director in the capital city, and Krauss still had a score to settle with him. So he said he would simply see to it that my binding contract with the Munich Opera would obligate me to rehearse and perform in the concurrent Munich Festival and thus be unavailable to Bayreuth. "If I know Tietjen, and believe me I do," he went on to add, "he'll then try to cast you in the premiere, but I'll see to it that you have to sing in Munich that evening, too." Sure enough, Tietjen promptly offered me the premiere, whereupon Krauss scheduled me for the same evening, thus enabling me to advise Bayreuth I would not be free for the engagement.

Years after the event, I happened to be chatting informally with Wieland Wagner, and the subject of the 1939 Festival was raised, to which he said: "My mother knew exactly why you didn't come here then, and she has never forgiven you." Although I fortunately had nothing to do with that fearsome lady professionally, we did meet; on those occasions, she always dealt with me correctly but with a marked degree of aloofness, which I frankly never regretted. She did, however, express her gratitude to me in a courteous letter when, after Wieland's death, I took over the stage directing chores for his *Ring* production.

Parenthetically, it should be mentioned in this context that a number of artists who later loudly claimed their revulsion at the Nazi regime were more than willing to cull some of the prestige that came with a Bayreuth appearance. There is no need to mention any specific names here; the interested reader is welcome to look them up in any number of other sources.

I hardly think there was anybody after the reopening of the Bayreuth

14.2.   Unlike his mother, Wieland Wagner did not take it amiss that I was reluctant to appear in the overpoliticized 1939 Bayreuth Festival. Here he is in discussion with me and baritone Toni Blankenheim.

Festival who had so much as an inkling of what a watershed it would be, and what an epoch-making influence the "New Bayreuth Style" would exert on operatic production everywhere, not just on the interpretation of Wagnerian works but on the craft as a whole. One need only recall to mind the revolutionary clout with which this radical reform struck the tradition-bound, conservative Wagnerites (for that matter the whole musical public) with something akin to an electric shock. And all of this at the very source of that tradition: in the sacred temple of the muses itself!

For the avant-garde of the early twenty-first century, at the dawn of this new millennium, this radical approach may be hard to comprehend; the present generation regards the revolutionary ideas of that period as part of the classic tradition of operatic staging. Today, at a reasonable chronological distance, we know at least that it was the undeniable influence of the Wagner grandsons, Wieland in particular, that brought about a new understanding for acting on the Wagnerian stage in the eyes of the operatic audience, and consequently for the dramatic approach to all opera. The "innovation" that was then being fostered also brought about the need for

14.3. New Bayreuth dispensed with extraneous paraphernalia, and that included the usual hair over Wotan's missing eye. In this photographic experiment, I simply kept one eye shut; in actual performance, the open eye remained uncovered. Photo reprinted with the kind permission of the Bayreuth Festival.

a total readjustment on the part of us performers. The fact that Wieland primarily called on the younger generation of singers to implement the successful realization of his ideas is understandable. This revolution is what brought artists such as Astrid Varnay, Leonie Rysanek, Wolfgang Windgassen, George London, and Gerhard Stolze—to mention just a few—as then unknown quantities in European Wagnerian circles into his directorial care.

But he also wanted a troupe of artists who had still grown up with the tradition-bound approach to Wagner, among them Birgit Nilsson, Martha

Mödl, Ludwig Weber, Gustav Neidlinger, and myself. We had learned to act in accordance with conventional Wagnerian tradition, many of us against the grain of our natural sensitivity. It was this artificiality that had somewhat dulled my enthusiasm for the world of opera in my younger years. In my insecurity I had taken over many elements from my artistic forerunners, and, in reverence for my admired role models had also become dependent on certain approaches, even if I was still not entirely convinced they were the right way to do things.

And then along came this young prophet from the Wagner family, who said of himself that he had no staging experience and demanded that we express ourselves almost motionlessly, without gestures, solely with the impact of the sung word. And all of this on a stage that, compared with the old days, was virtually empty. "If there are no superficial trivialities bothering us," he said fervently, "we can manage with a minimum of stage motion."

Wieland taught us to use these subdued gestures and forms of expression economically and sparsely. This recalls to mind one of the greatest classic actors I ever saw, Werner Krauss, the master of the economical and yet so effective use of stage gesture. I was fascinated by his ability to listen: he seemed almost totally motionless to me, his glance unerringly fixed on his partner for a long, long time, and we could not take our eyes off him because of the magnetic force of that sorcerer's radiance.

Slowly, very slowly, I began to sense the possibilities this innovator had inspired me to explore. The collaboration with the Wagner grandson was so fruitful because he was willing to discuss things further between rehearsals, something that was only possible in a place like Bayreuth. It wasn't always easy to bring our own opinions to bear in his productions. He could be radical and unyielding. I recall, for example, his great revulsion toward the word "pathos": "I can't stand that on the stages anywhere in the world." "But," I interjected, "what you mean is the phony, artificial pathos, which I find as repugnant as you do. But there is also a genuine, sincere pathos in ancient Greek tragedy, and in the powerful heroic outbursts in your grandfather's music." Then he gave in, smiling, "Yes, perhaps when you do it I can accept it, but not from the others."

And so we scuffled our way to a greater understanding of each other in the course of the Bayreuth years. I know for certain that he let me get away with a lot of things he wouldn't have stood for from others. When today I make a résumé of the years that followed, I realize that my conception of "interpretation," not just in terms of stage action, but also in the use of diction in speaking or singing, the importance of correct pauses and the ability to keep still—all of these things were first really revealed to me in my work in Bayreuth. The process of maturation took place relatively late, and it is still not over.

Over the years Wieland developed into a true guide of stage action, particularly in the psychology of his direction of the individual actors. What I sometimes missed with him was a certain sense of humor—especially at work. He could really lose his temper when we occasionally started cutting up; he could laugh, but more in a satirical, mocking way.

I know hardly anyone who worked as hard as he did. If he wanted something unusual or surprising, he always had a justification for it (evidence from his grandfather's spiritual heritage in hand). He worked untiringly in rehearsals, right down to the minutest detail. Self-assurance or satisfaction with the results of his work were strangers to him. I can remember premiere evenings, when in the midst of a boisterous after-theater party in Haus Wahnfried, as the grey of dawn began to take possession of the skies, he would suddenly announce, "Now I'd like to rehearse the same piece again tomorrow morning, because I can't bear to look at it again the way it is now."

He brought out everything we had in us. Because he was a painter with a trained eye, he saw all the action on the stage in correlation to the setting and the way it was lit. He loved the idea of living pictures. Just think of the first scene of his 1956 *Meistersinger* production, in which the chorus at the rise of the curtain gave the audience the illusion of an actual Dürer painting.

He had his problems with the virtue of patience. Once the rehearsal schedule read: "*Rheingold*—rehearsal with orchestra in costume and make-up, scenes 1 and 2 in the morning, scenes 3 and 4 in the afternoon." In the morning Wieland was still not satisfied with Wotan's beard and wig, and so changes were discussed with chief makeup man Willi Klose, with whom he collaborated very closely. As Klose had promised to have everything ready by afternoon, the wig and beard had to be redyed and dried rapidly. (They use ether to accelerate the drying process.) Willi proudly showed me the new hairpieces and applied everything to my face with spirit gum. It was a hot July day. I sat down on my seat in Nibelheim. Then the heat of the thick costume and the muggy afternoon air released the ether from the beard and wig and numbing fumes began creeping up into my nose. At first I felt light-headed and almost giddy until I suddenly blacked out right in the middle of the rehearsal.

When I came to, I found myself lying on the stage floor with my colleagues and the stagehands gathered around me. The first sounds that penetrated into my ears were from Wieland's voice, yelling, "Mr. Klose, you're fired!" This dismissal, however, only lasted a half hour. After that the two men were again sitting tranquilly together, lost in discussion.

What has engraved itself most indelibly on my memory from my activity on the festival hill in Bayreuth is the first years after the reopening. At that time all the evil of the recent past was still very close to us, and the joy and pride of being present at the creation of something new and clean was so overwhelming that it never occurred to anyone to impose conditions for our presence there. I think fondly back on the wonderful community we all belonged to. We spent all our time together, from the end of June until the end of August, rehearsed, and· watched the others rehearse. And how we enjoyed being treated like kings and queens whenever we walked into a Bayreuth tavern or restaurant! Nevertheless, we weren't all that interesting once the performances began. Then there were new monarchs—the members of the festival audience.

Our fees back in those days sound pretty pathetic to modern ears. There were no star wages for selected individuals. The top performance fee was 1,000 marks (around $250.00 by the rate of exchange back then). Fees went gradually down, depending on the importance of the role, to 800, 600, and 400 marks. But the ones with the lower salaries were ultimately better off, because they might be doing twenty-five performances, which put them in a position to treat us, who perhaps had only five appearances that season, to a good meal.

In my fifteen Bayreuth years I mainly sang under Herbert von Karajan, Joseph Keilberth, Clemens Krauss, André Cluytens, and Hans Knappertsbusch. As already mentioned, Herbert von Karajan conducted the opening performance of *Tristan und Isolde* in which I sang Kurwenal, while I was cast as King Marke in later *Tristan* performances. I'll have more to say about my collaboration with Karajan, primarily in his Vienna years from 1958 to 1964, later on in this narrative.

I enjoyed many years of close friendship with Joseph Keilberth, and making music with a friend is especially good when the basic concepts of musical understanding gibe—as was the case with us in the 1952 *Ring* performances.

In the summer of 1953, Clemens Krauss infused the *Ring* with the full authority of his powerful personality on the podium. As the conductor in Bayreuth cannot be seen by the audience, the singers on stage often enjoy some interesting speculation as to whether or not this invisibility to the audience prompts any changes in the respective monarchs of the baton. Clemens Krauss, in any event, remained the lordly figure he always was, with or without the audience. Twelve years previously I had already enjoyed the benefits of his stage experience in my first *Walküre* Wotan back in Munich. We, the members of the cast, all sensed the way that, especially in his 1953 Bayreuth *Ring,* his commanding style revealed the full scope of Wagner's drama, guiding us through the performances with an impressive tranquillity, yet generously allowing us all the freedom we needed to delineate our roles as we felt them—almost as if he had some premonition that this would be his swan song at Bayreuth. Even the sensitive Wieland noticed the

14.4.   While Wolfgang Wagner never ventures beyond the confines of the Festival Theater, Wieland often took his revolutionary ideas to theaters around the world. Here we see him at the Teatro San Carlo in Naples demonstrating a fine point (I hope!) to soprano Anja Silja while I look on. Photo, ©Foto Troncole, Naples.

special quality that our revered Clemens emitted. At the end of the festival summer, he said *en passant* to me: "That man, I'm sure, is going to play an important role in Bayreuth's future". Unfortunately that was not to be, but indirectly Wieland was right after all: fortunately, there is a universally lauded CD recording of that 1953 *Ring,* a challenge to all subsequent Bayreuth recordings.

André Cluytens, the sensitive maestro from Belgium, was an experienced, deep-feeling advocate of Wagnerian tradition in the 1956 and 1957 *Meistersinger* performances.

And finally, anyone who had the good fortune to sing in a Bayreuth *Parsifal* under Hans Knappertsbusch will never forget the experience for the rest of his or her life. As one of the great Bruckner interpreters, and well acquainted with that composer's majestic, solemn breath, he was, like few others, in a position to bring together the full profundity of Wagner's tonal consecration with the problems of the last mysteries of the Grail and their elucidation to form a single integral unit. Anyone who has difficulties understanding the music and poetry of this final Wagner work has never heard it in Knappertsbusch's interpretation. The joy of having portrayed Gurnemanz in the cast of his final *Parsifal* in his beloved Bayreuth Festival Theatre (indeed, his last appearance anywhere) even outweighs the sorrow over his death on October 25, 1965, in Munich.

It may be interesting to learn that I indirectly brought about the first contact of two fine singers from a later generation to the renowned festival. I refer here to Gwyneth Jones and James King. I drove both of them in my own car to Bayreuth, where I recommended that Wieland Wagner audition them. I'll never forget Wieland's initial reaction when I first mentioned the given name of the then totally unknown soprano from Wales, "What's her name? Gwyneth? You can't have a name like that and sing in Bayreuth!" Well, you most certainly could, as we later discovered.

I didn't used to believe the sorcery that emanates from just mentioning the magic word "Bayreuth" almost anywhere in the world. Wherever I happened to be during my Bayreuth years, whether in the United States, in Canada, South Africa, Argentina, Australia, Japan, or in any European country, when I was called upon to give an interview, the questions invariably arose: "What does Bayreuth mean to you? What was your last role there? What's the next thing you'll be singing there?"

When Wieland Wagner left us forever in 1966, he left behind a gap that will never be filled. I believe there was a great deal more he might have communicated to the world and its theaters.

⋙ Chapter 15 ⋘

When, in the autumn of 1954, the London office of ABC, now the Australian Broadcasting Corporation, asked me if I would be interested in doing a concert tour through that very distant continent in 1955, I answered, after short reflection, that I would be delighted. My London agent thought this inquiry had come about as a result of my activities at the Royal Opera House, Covent Garden, in London and the Metropolitan Opera in New York. As I later found out, it was primarily the reports of my appearances at the Bayreuth Festival since 1952, which had also reached the continent on the other side of the globe, that had prompted the interest of the concert managers there. At that time I knew next to nothing about musical life in that corner of the world. I had only heard, more or less in passing, from a few British musicians who had some knowledge of the fifth continent that, soon after the war, the ABC had taken upon itself the task of furthering what at the time was the fairly fallow development of general interest in classical music there with all the means at its disposal and was seeking to win over well-known artists to perform in concert there.

At the time, there were any number of obstacles to overcome. To begin with, there was virtually no tourism in Australia; the country was much too far away from the centers of artistic (or, for that matter, cultural) development. The planes were still equipped with propellers, and they only flew in the daytime. Passengers had to spend the nights in hotels, and often only fairly primitive overnight barracks were available near the equally primitive airports. There were hardly any roads leading to the interior of the country. The various towns were vast distances from one another. Nowadays people find it hard to believe that passengers on fully booked Australian domestic flights were weighed, as the planes carried not only people but also cargo and mail. That meant that passenger transportation actually had to be adjusted to the amount of cargo on any given flight. The selection of hotels in the country, especially in smaller towns (and it was there that most of the musical events took place) was not very large, and most of the accommodations were anything but commodious.

15.1. Wherever in the world my travels took me, Helga shared the travails and triumphs and eased my path with her clear sense of logistics and her refreshing sense of humor.

As my wife and I were sitting in the plane from London to Sydney in mid-August, even before the end of the Bayreuth Festival, we had no idea what to expect over the next three months in this fifth continent six thousand miles away. This whole undertaking we had frivolously let ourselves in for had a touch of adventure to it. We first had to adjust to a three-day air journey, but we were used to a lot of things from our travels in the United States.

That trip is now almost fifty years in the past. Two impressions still cleave to my memory. After we had spend the night in a hotel near Karachi, we were accommodated on the second night in a hotel in downtown Singapore right on top of the equator. Because of the seven-hour time difference, even though it was already midnight, I was totally unable to fall asleep, and so I decided to take a little walk. The hotel was so still, you would have thought nobody was staying there. After the hot day, the air was now agreeably warm and growing pleasantly cool. With great relish, I inhaled the slightly sweet air as I strolled along the edge of a park. There I heard music that was alien to my ears. It sounded like a dance melody. I calmly strolled on for a few minutes and found myself walking right onto a dance pavilion. About thirty to forty local residents were silently observing dancing couples, who, in totally relaxed postures, gracefully moved to the music. Their faces and bodies close together, barely moving, their arms at their sides, they moved their hands gently, delicately in time with the beat. They were all smiling, almost as if in a blissful trance, nobody spoke a loud word, and over the whole scene lay an almost solemn stillness. When the music ended, they applauded, bowed slightly to one another, and separated. As the music began again, other men joined them. And now I noticed them give all the girls some money. So these were taxi dancers, who were being paid for dancing with the men. But nowhere was any sign of impropriety or brazenness to be seen; everybody behaved decorously and pleasantly toward the girls. I was incredibly fascinated and felt strangely attracted by what to me was a totally alien atmosphere. Lost in thought, I strolled back to the hotel, eagerly inhaling the almost intoxicating night air with its strange fragrances. A remarkable, pleasantly relaxing sensation came over me, coursing through my whole body and allowing me, on my return, to fall fast asleep. This was an experience I have clearly retained in my memory. It never repeated itself in this form again.

The next day, after we had flown over the whole Polynesian island realm, we landed late that evening, for the first time on Australian soil, in the extreme north of the continent, in Darwin. In the immediate proximity of the airport, we spent the night, along with the other first-class passengers, in a huge public dormitory. The air was muggy and oppressive despite the unceasingly humming fans. Once again I had a hard time sleeping in these unfamiliar surroundings and spent part of the night outdoors. From there as well, I have retained a keen memory of the heady aroma from the exotic tropical foliage along with the odd cooing of the local birds, which began early in the morning even before the sun came up.

After our first night in Australia we arrived the following day at the first intermediate destination on our long journey, in Sydney. We had been quartered for the first week in a small Swiss hotel with a somewhat private character, so that, despite the eleven-hour time difference, we were able to sleep well for the first time since we left Munich.

I have never attempted even vaguely to calculate how many days of my life I have spent in hotels and how many hotel beds I have slept in. It may seem fairly banal to many people that anyone would ask himself a question like that. In any event, a sensitive individual would understand how much one's mood, the mobilization of artistic creative elements, and one's physical and mental condition in general is dependent upon the direct surroundings in which one finds oneself. I am convinced that the much heavier requirements placed on all the globe-trotting international stars these days are directly responsible for so many hopeful careers partly or totally fizzling out after a relatively short time. And because I have myself experienced how much conditions in our close and direct environment can influence our artistic performance, I believe deeply in the importance of these allegedly inconsequential elements.

After this slight digression into ancillary conditions let me return to our temporary "homestead" at the Hotel Swiss Cottage on the morning after our arrival in Sydney. When we woke up, the sun was already shining in our faces. The weather was magnificent, and we were delighted to discover that it was Sunday, and I had no obligations waiting for me that day. We soon decided to take a stroll to check out the neighborhood a little. Obviously we were in a pleasant upmarket area. We still didn't know that Sydney, largely situated on the seaside, had a population of three million, and that half the residents lived not in apartment buildings but in attractive private homes.

A half hour later we arrived at a square where we saw a huge poster on which to my great surprise I discovered my own face, bearded and made-up in the costume of the god Wotan, taken directly from the second act of *Walküre*.

Moving in a bit closer, I noticed a woman chatting with a little boy. When I heard the woman speak, I could hardly believe my ears: in authentic Bavarian German, the kind the natives speak in Alpine country towns like Lenggries and Waldau on the Isar banks, she said: "Lookee here! See that there fella with the beard. Thirty years ago, he carried your daddy around on his shoulders back home in the old country when he was jes the same age you are now."[1]

"You don't say?" I interjected amusedly, adding that "the fella with the beard" was standing in front of her. Great surprise and delight on both sides. I had just happened to run across some compatriots on my first day in Australia. They had emigrated here from Bavaria back in 1928. In the course of the next three months, I met a goodly number of other Germans and Austrians.

When today, at a chronological distance of almost fifty years, I think back on Australia, my memory first conjures up things that were totally new to me. First of all the weather: on eighty-eight of the ninety days we spent there, the sun shone. And we had arrived there in the middle of the local winter. The constantly blue sky is an integral part of my recollections of those days. In the course of those three months, I gave no fewer than thirty-eight concerts, most of them song recitals (all in all, we had prepared four different programs), and made six to eight appearances in orchestral concerts in the larger cities such as Sydney, Melbourne, Adelaide, Brisbane, and Perth. But most of the events were recitals in smaller towns, some of them in places where no recitals had ever been given before.

To do this we covered hundreds of miles, by car or plane. Far more than I had in most of my other professional travels, I had more opportunity here

---

1. "Sixtas, der Mann da mit 'm Bart, der hat vor dreissig Jahr dei'n Vatta, wie er so alt war wie du jetzt, bei uns dahoam auf die Schultern rumgetragn."

than elsewhere to meet the local citizenry. How often people envy me because I have seen so much of the world on my travels! Yet all I ever actually saw in so many of the great beauty spots on this earth were often only cold, impersonal hotel rooms with tasteless pictures on the walls, rehearsal rooms, dressing rooms in theaters or concert halls, waiting rooms in railroad stations or airports. Because of my contracts as a permanent member of large opera ensembles, time off for engagements elsewhere were few and far between. This pattern began with activities at the festivals in Bayreuth, Salzburg, or at the Munich Summer Festival.

At the end of June, when performances were still running at the contracted houses, in Bayreuth and Salzburg the stage directors began groaning loudly if they had to start rehearsals without all the singers present. When, on the other hand, the last curtain had yet to fall at the festival theaters, the conductors and directors on the stages of the various home houses were all snarling about the damned singers who, in violation of their contracts, were absent from rehearsals. In other words, during my Bayreuth and Salzburg Festival years, I never really had a summer vacation. At the time, an all-too-true saying was making the rounds: "What can be said against the career of a prominent singer?" Answer: "Three important things: *June, July and August.*"

That was different in Australia; there were at least four free days between appearances there. Even on the concert days, if the weather was fine, we could spend plenty of time outdoors.

Another not insignificant plus in the tour planning was the incredibly thoughtful way the travelers were looked after by the representatives of the Australian Broadcasting Corporation. Any artist who works a great deal outside his own country can really appreciate it when, in addition to the nervous stresses, the constant fear of colds, and other things, his fairly delicate mental state is not further burdened by problems large and small having to do with travel—all of which can expand into uneasiness and overexcitement. That situation had been clearly recognized and taken into account in faraway Australia. I feel deeply obligated to recall this most gratefully to mind in today's not only fast-living but also fast-forgetting world. Advance planning for concert appearances, flight bookings, drives to the concert sites, from the hotel to the concert hall and back, whether for rehearsals or concerts, preparations for the physical well-being of the artists and lots more—everything was placed in the tried and true hands of the ABC's tour escorts.

When, shortly after my arrival in Sydney, I promptly picked up a tracheal catarrh, the ABC people instantly organized a Japanese ear, nose, and throat specialist whom they praised as a miracle worker. Fortunately I still had three days before my first appearances. Promptly before my opening concert, my "Asclepius from Kyoto" had not only seen to it that I could perform, but also that my larynx remained healthy for the remaining twelve weeks.

With a sequence of so many concerts, there were of course plenty of comical occurrences. Once my partner at the keyboard, an Englishman by the name of Harry Penn, who had lived most of his life in Australia, brought along the sheet music for another program. He said, "We won't make any announcement, but just go on as if nothing had happened." Although the members of our audience had another program in their hands, there was no reaction in the hall. On the contrary: it was a great success. Ladies in the audience often bring along something to do while the music is being performed, such as their knitting, which enjoyed their undivided attention—or their offspring, whom I often felt I had to drown out to be heard at all. On one occasion, however, I was absolutely powerless. We had a concert in a place that was well known for breeding ostriches, and where a military rifle range was also located. We had already completed the first half of the program when target practice began right around the corner. It was impossible to compete with that. The program was interrupted, and my ABC companions immediately initiated diplomatic relations with the officer in charge of that exercise.

Of course our skilled negotiators were successful. The people agreed to take an hour's break. Meanwhile the audience whiled the time away over a cup or two of tea and returned to the hall, where our officer, obviously curious as to what had brought all this about, also repaired along with some of his recruits. The newly arrived listeners seemed to enjoy what they were hearing. We invited the officer to the reception, whereupon he promptly canceled target practice for the rest of the day and graciously joined the guests at the reception. Somewhat later on, he rather shamefacedly confessed to me that these were the first Schubert lieder he had ever heard. "But they certainly won't be the last," he solemnly pledged. The following day he arranged for us to attend an ostrich race. Until then I was totally unaware how fast those birds can run.

When we appeared in Melbourne, an ensemble from London's Royal Shakespeare Company was also in town. Prominent actors such as Australia's own Robert Helpmann were in the cast along with an American actress we knew back home from her many films, Katharine Hepburn. Of course we didn't miss the opportunity to see one of our screen favorites on stage, attending a performance of Shakespeare's *Measure for Measure* and admiring the powerful stage presence of the Hollywood celebrity. After the performance, our friends from the ABC were on the spot to take us backstage to meet the star. We found her totally unaffected and cordial. After that we spent a delightful hour with her. As it happened, we also ran into her a few more times on our flights as the theatrical troupe was also on tour throughout the country as we were.

On one of our joint flights I was sitting with Katharine Hepburn chatting about Australia, which she had already visited several times before. I saw and heard nothing more from the famous actress until, in 1992 (in other words, thirty-seven years later), she was sitting in Tel Aviv Airport across from a Munich friend of mine, who recognized her and got into a conversation with her. In the course of this he asked the lady, now over eighty but still outstandingly sprightly, if she could remember meeting a singer by the name of Hans Hotter in 1955 in Australia, to which she replied in the affirmative and sent her very best wishes to me.

There was one experience in Melbourne that had more to do with tennis than with music. Regularly at the end of each concert, ABC always arranged a reception, always featuring speeches by local dignitaries, generally the local mayors. The audience took eager advantage of the opportunity to make direct contact with the artists, without thinking they might perhaps be tired and would rather be left in peace. If I was occasionally somewhat less than charming, I would invariably receive a discreet elbow in the ribs from my wife ("Be a little nicer to the people, they expect you to chat with them. It comes with the territory"). So I would be a good boy and answer their questions, "Yes, we like it just fine here." "Oh, yes, this country is very interesting." "Yes, the weather is just magnificent. We hadn't expected it to be so nice." "Yes, yes, I really enjoyed taking pictures of the flora here. Quite different from what we're familiar with back home." "The audience is so interested and grateful, really terrific." Finally they always wanted me to make a couple of extra remarks, and I ultimately got used to that as well. "Tennis? Yes of course. That's what's so special about this country. Whenever we can, we always watch the great, famous players. We know them all, because we've seen them play in Europe, but seeing them all in their homeland, that really is something special." The newspapers picked up on the subject of tennis and would ask me highly technical tennis questions in their interviews.

Tea was always served at those receptions, accompanied each time and place with the same white bread—it tasted a little like cotton—covered with slices of fish, cheese, or tomato and festooned with a little garland of watercress on the top. As one is always a bit hungry after singing, and it was generally well past ten in the evening, we weren't fussy and enjoyed whatever we got. Speaking of white bread: as we were more used to heartier dark bread at home, after a while we began getting pretty tired of that white stuff. Our yearning for a lovely slice of rye bread was gigantic. Judge of our great delight when, fairly close to the end of our tour, already slightly afflicted with homesickness, we wandered through the grocery section of a department store in Melbourne and happened upon some real German dark bread and right next to it a genuine veal liverwurst. We immediately purchased those delicacies along with a bottle of beer and hurried back to our hotel room for a real dining orgy. I have seldom eaten a liverwurst sandwich with such joy and relish. In a reverie, I looked out the hotel window at the blue Melbourne sky, and then over at my wife—is this really possible?—and realized that tears were suddenly welling up in our eyes. The spicy aroma of a liverwurst sandwich was the thought association that relieved our homesickness for Munich.

My rather casual remarks about tennis, also on a radio broadcast, had quite a powerful effect. One day a pleasant gentleman called me at our hotel in Melbourne, introduced himself as a member of one of the hundred or so tennis clubs in the city and said that he had listened with great pleasure to my radio interview in which he discovered that I was interested in the Australian national sport, tennis. He then asked if I wouldn't perhaps like to swing a racket while I was in the country. The reason for his call was to invite me to his club so we could perhaps play a friendly match with one another. At first I declined, I hadn't really played in ages, besides I was certainly not a very good player, but he replied courteously that the joy of the game was the main thing. I was still reluctant, but he wouldn't let up, and so I finally let him talk me into it. The following Sunday, he said, he would pick the two of us up. "And whom have I had the pleasure of speaking to?"

"My name is Jack Harper."

"What?" I expostulated. "The former Davis Cup player who often played with Gottfried von Cramm?"

"Hell, no," he reassured me, "I just happen to have the same name."

Of course it *was* the well-known Australian tennis star who picked us up on Sunday. I recognized him immediately and was thrilled and impressed to meet such a prominent athlete and clearly delightful person. "My goodness," I thought to myself, "this could be some experience."

"Everything's ready," he assured me with a smile, "I've invited two other club members to play with us. We should be a jolly little foursome." I had no alternative but to put a good face on it.

There I stood then, large as life, on the court, and the ball began whizzing past my head hell for leather. I made a feeble attempt, a very feeble attempt to keep up with the others, and lo and behold, all three of them hit the balls so spot-on toward me that all I had to do was hold out the racket. Somehow or other I managed to cheat my way through the challenge. Jack played against me; I got a little braver and tried my best. Then it happened. Afterward I could only vaguely remember the sequence of events. In any case, it was my serve. Jack stood facing me, I slammed the ball over the net, my opposite number was obviously not ready for it, and then my partner called out: "Ace! It's an ace!" I can still hear the sound of his voice. He was a dyed-in-the-wool Aussie, so "ace" came out sounding more like "ice." All three of them applauded, and I don't know what got into me, because a couple of minutes later it happened again, another ace, only this time the former crack player helped me out a bit and just let the ball go by.

At the end, the whole experience was pretty embarrassing. We went to the bar and drank to my two aces. Two days later I opened the newspaper, and there on page one, it said: HANS HOTTER, THE FOREIGN SINGER FROM GERMANY, SERVED TWO ACES TO JACK HARPER LAST SUNDAY. Afterward I was made an honorary member of Harper's tennis club. From then until the end of the concert tour there were no more interviews, whether on the radio or in the print media, in which those two aces were not mentioned.

Whenever we returned to Melbourne or environs, we always met our friend Jack and spent many a happy hour in the company of that great athlete.

I made two return trips to hospitable Australia to which I had become attached with many happy memories: once, to give more concerts; the second and last time, to teach voice classes. Several young vocal talents found their way to Munich to continue their singing lessons with me. Some of them returned to their homeland as voice teachers, and a few of them now hold teaching positions or professorships at local music institutes.

Chapter 16

A short time ago, I finished reading a book that impressed me enormously. Penned by English-born writer and broadcaster Richard Osborne, *Herbert von Karajan: A Life in Music,* a critical biography of the legendary Austrian conductor, is an incredibly evenhanded and honest treatment of one of the most controversial figures in twentieth-century musical life. Speaking as someone who had ample opportunity to collaborate with von Karajan, I can only say this book really tells the whole story as I also remember it.

My first contacts with the maestro went back to the year 1937, when, as I mentioned before, he heard me sing Jago in Verdi's *Otello* in a performance at the Hamburg State Opera and somehow heard qualities in my voice that indicated I would be well suited for the baritone solos in the solemn *Ein deutsches Requiem* by Johannes Brahms, in a performance he was planning for Aachen, where he served as general music director. The Verdi opera and the Brahms *Requiem* are really two compositions that could hardly be more diverse, but Karajan's perception proved totally accurate, and the Brahms work subsequently became one of the staples of my repertoire. After the aforementioned prewar concerts, we were again reunited on a single evening in 1942 at the Berlin State Opera for a *Fidelio* performance, in which he conducted, and I appeared as a guest in the role of Pizarro. Not until 1947 did we again meet to record the Brahms *Requiem* and then again in 1952 in Bayreuth.

Our collaboration proceeded in a spirit of mutual artistic harmony, clearly to the full satisfaction of us both. Fortunately in my experience with "the greats" on the podium, this sort of atmosphere was not unfamiliar. This is why it is somewhat puzzling and hard to understand why my contacts with Karajan, for all their intensity and mutual satisfaction, were largely sporadic. In 1952, shortly after my so-called vocal crisis, I again sang under Karajan's baton as Raphael, the bass soloist in Haydn's oratorio *Die Schöpfung* in a Vienna concert. This work begins, as the reader doubtless knows, following a short prelude, in which Haydn first describes total chaos then tapers down to a hushed *pianissimo,* with the voice of Raphael.

Karajan got the idea of having the first voice to be heard in the oratorio continue to spin out the *pianissimo* of the orchestral passage until, suddenly, there is a contrasting effect depicting the creation of light, with a *forte* chord celebrating its victory over darkness. "Do you have the courage," he asked me, "to sing the beginning of the oratorio in an absolute *pianissimo?*"

"Of course," I assured him, and that's just what I did on the evening of the performance. The consequence was that a friend out in the hall heard a lady in the row ahead of him whisper into this total pianissimo: "Now Hotter's lost his voice completely!"[1]

In the summer of the same year, I was initiated into Richard Wagner's Bayreuth world at the season opener of *Tristan und Isolde*. Karajan sat at the podium in a short-sleeved polo shirt, hidden from the audience, and I sang Kurwenal. Once again I felt the Wagnerian breath wafting up from deep down in the pit, and again I enjoyed this almost incomprehensible miracle of simultaneously experienced consensus and fulfilled reality.

The summer of 1952, which had brought me so many new and beautiful things, came to an end. The following year Karajan did not return to Bayreuth. To this day, I'm not exactly sure what happened between him and Wieland. In any event, with his departure, my brief contact with this great artist was again interrupted.

In 1957, much to the surprise of operatic circles throughout the world, Herbert von Karajan unexpectedly decided to come to the Austrian capital as general director and musical and artistic head of the State Opera; and, in a development that less surprised the initiated, he also undertook the joint functions of conductor and stage director to wield a significant, trailblazing influence on the development of the lyric theater. After all, whenever and wherever he had assumed the musical direction of a new production in the years since the war, he had also shown a keen interest in the dramatic action on the stage, effectively putting across his own ideas and concepts, even when they didn't exactly gibe with the stage director's approach.

When, to my great joy, the Karajan era in Vienna began in 1957, fair weather again prevailed between the two of us, and that excellent cooperative spirit was restored to life. But this was strictly an artistic understanding. In interpersonal relations, he seldom let anyone anywhere near him. He was reserved, in fact downright diffident toward other people. At any rate, I never penetrated into his private, personal sphere.

He inaugurated his administration in his double role as conductor and stage director with a completely new *Ring* for which he engaged the highly experienced Emil Preetorius as production designer. He also took no risks in his casting of the principal roles, bringing in a full complement of established professionals, most of whom had already completed Wieland Wagner's withdrawal therapy from the narcotic of moldy convention and tradi-

---

1. "Jetzt hat der Hotter sei' Stimm vollständig verloren!"

tion. In his directorial work, he spent a great of time and effort on the element that became his stock in trade over the coming years: the lighting.

The positions of the performers were oriented around the so-called light flats. It was unmistakable that the new ideas from Bayreuth had fallen on fertile ground here as well—with the sole difference that in Bayreuth brightness triumphed, while in Vienna a tendency toward darkness dominated the scene.

He allowed us great freedom in our acting performances. Occasionally he had remarkably good ideas and highly practical suggestions, even for the "old pros" on the operatic scene. As he concentrated his attention on everything theatrical on the stage, his musical interpretation was often somewhat neglected. But as far as that element was concerned, all of us had already enjoyed the solid grounding from a Clemens Krauss or a Hans Knappertsbusch. There were no difficulties in the theater, in the scheduling of rehearsals, no jealous disputes with other conductors, as Karajan had the final say on everything that happened in the theater. In similar unsullied harmony, I later experienced the subsequent *Rheingold* and *Siegfried* productions.

Since the beginning of this new era, the theater's director had always kept a watchful eye on operatic events in neighboring Italy, especially at La Scala Milan. Guest performances by Italian singers at the Vienna State Opera began stacking up, somewhat to the distaste of the colleagues on the home team. But, in return, many members of the Vienna ensemble also traveled southward, sometimes in complete guest productions, which also included the Viennese sets and costumes such as the new Vienna 1958 *Walküre*. The previous season, the Scala had presented a world premiere, to the libretto of T. S. Eliot's play *Murder in the Cathedral,* and set to music by Italian composer Ildebrando Pizzetti, a friend of Pope Pius XII.

During the week of our *Walküre* rehearsals in Milan, there were some repeat performances of *Assassino nella catedrale.* Karajan seemed interested in bringing out this work in its first German-language production in Vienna. He suggested that I attend a performance, hoping to arouse my interest in the role of Archbishop Thomas à Becket.

In the opera, with its somewhat derivative musical score, I was singularly impressed by the character of the Archbishop, virtually the only major role in the piece, not least because of the captivating interpretation by the prominent basso Nicola Rossi-Lemeni, whom I had previously seen as a brilliant Boris Godunov. Karajan had made a correct assumption and reached his goal.

In the intervening two years before we put the work on the Vienna stage in 1960, I participated in a number of Vienna productions in Milan, such as *Rheingold* (Wotan), *Tristan und Isolde* (Marke), *Fidelio* (Pizarro), and *Salome* (Jochanaan), under Karajan's baton.

Especially for these Scala performances, he seemed to muster a very special eagerness to reveal the full brilliance of his radiant personality time and again. My friend Walter Legge once very accurately characterized the special quality of this musical collaborator of many years' standing with the words: "Whether you like his music-making or not, one thing is for certain: everything he does always sounds beautiful, quite simply beautiful."

It was a known fact that the famous Salzburger had been highly athletic throughout his life. Even back in his early youth, speed fascinated him. Fast cars were his life. Whenever the opportunity presented itself, he put on his skis. Later he passed his pilot's examination and was also a speed freak up in the skies.

I was once sitting directly beside him in the dark auditorium at a Vienna opera rehearsal. He had three telephones next to him, into which, one after the other, he rapidly rasped all kinds of instructions. All around him was a veritable army of assistants, musical and scenic, technical advisers, sound technicians, and lighting specialists. A microphone to the stage conveyed his commands in a calm but very decisive voice to the soloists, or the chorus, extras, and stagehands. In the meantime, deputations from the various theater departments kept on arriving. I took advantage of one moment's silence to ask him amusedly behind my raised hand if all this hurly-burly wasn't torturous for him. He emitted a quick chuckle and then, in his typical manner, fell silent for a moment, following which he said in his raspy voice, sort of mumbling to himself without glancing over at me, "Do you know when I feel my best?" Then he pointed one finger up at the sky, "Up there, in a plane, when I'm sitting at the stick and somebody yells at me: 'No, wrong! Not now, later, now the other lever, push it all the way down, then let go—not so fast.' When I have nothing to say and have to keep my mouth shut, while somebody else gives me the orders, my flight instructor—then I feel just fine and under no pressure!"

It was a rare occasion indeed when Karajan abandoned his aloof posture toward his fellow musicians, but those events could be extremely moving. It must have been back in the fifties when I attended a concert at London's Royal Festival Hall, at which the unforgettable Clara Haskil played a Mozart concerto (I believe it was the A major) accompanied by the orchestra under Karajan's direction. When I went backstage afterward with Walter Legge to thank the artists, I found no less an immortal than the great Sir Charles Chaplin along with his wife Oona also waiting to congratulate the musicians. Chaplin stormed into the green room toward Karajan and Haskil and called out enthusiastically, "I felt like I was in heaven." Thereupon Karajan walked over to Clara, put his arm lovingly and almost paternally around her shoulders, and said softly, "And she was the angel," to which the pianist responded with a shy, almost embarrassed smile.

Shortly afterward, I was alone, and I decided to take a little walk along the Thames and let the last few hours pass in review before my mind's eye. An agreeably relaxed, carefree sensation coursed through me, and I asked myself what had brought this on. Was it the afterglow of this happy musical experience? Or was it the words that had been spoken in the green room, that now seemed to be floating in midair before me? Another listener, a more matter-of-fact, realistic individual than myself, might have perceived these remarks as somewhat high-flown and overcharged with emotion. For me, however, these were people who had just witnessed a major artistic event, and only someone who had shared this experience with us could have understood what was so special about the language that was being spoken.

After Karajan had happily completed his new *Ring* in the years between 1957 and 1960, on April 2, Easter Saturday in the year 1961, on the eve of his fifty-third birthday, he presented the Viennese and himself, who had waited a full seventeen years for it, with a generally applauded *Parsifal* production—which was nevertheless attacked by some critics for the occasionally predominant darkness on stage. One Viennese reviewer headlined his write-up with the mischievous comment: "Through Darkness to Enlightenment."

We singers and musicians were highly impressed by the collaboration with the maestro and didn't allow these critical opinions in the least to diminish our satisfaction with the harmonious atmosphere (so rarely found elsewhere) that prevailed during the preparation period. We had our own private joke when we gave the stage director a black spotlight for his birthday, with the loudest laughs coming from him.

For all of us, Christa Ludwig, Eberhard Wächter, Fritz Uhl, and myself, it had not been an everyday event to work together with a creative artist in such harmonious unity, recognizing at every phase of our collaboration the joy he derived from making new ideas and new approaches become reality.

I was now able to allow the role of Gurnemanz, which I had sung virtually without rehearsals one time each in individual performances during the Wagner Festival in Bayreuth and the Met Easter season, to mature gradually during an extended rehearsal period. Friends, colleagues, and audiences reacted differently to this new role of mine, for which the first impulses had come from Wieland Wagner. As I mentioned before, many initially felt that there was a lot of Wotan in my Gurnemanz. I myself can only say that there was hardly a role in my repertoire that was so made to measure for me vocally as was that of the wise mentor in the realm of the Grail.

In the spring of 1960, in other words a year before the new *Parsifal*, Karajan finally implemented what he had planned back in 1958 during the guest performances in Milan. He brought out Eliot's *Murder in the Cathedral* in Pizzetti's musical setting in Vienna. The stage production was in the com-

16.1.   Herbert von Karajan lured me into a La Scala performance of Ildebrando Pizzetti's *Murder in the Cathedral,* based
on the play by T. S. Eliot, in hopes of arousing my interest in
singing the leading role with him in Vienna. As you can see,
he succeeded. Photo, ©Photo Fayer, Vienna.

petent hands of the once well known choreographer Margherita Wallmann,
who—if memory serves—had, back in my student days, done the staging
of Gluck's *Orfeo* in a Salzburg production conducted by Bruno Walter. I
recall with great pleasure the way she acquainted me with the role of
Thomas à Becket, which was primarily interesting from an acting point of
view. Back then, the wags of Vienna quipped: "Hotter, a specialist in
princes of the church (Cardinal Borromeo in *Palestrina* and the Grand Inquisitor in *Don Carlo*), has donned yet another bishop's miter—his third to
date!" And on the podium, Herbert von Karajan conducted and reigned, in
one of his very rare excursions into the mid-twentieth-century repertoire.

16.2. *Murder in the Cathedral* was one of Karajan's infrequent excursions into contemporary opera, and after the dress rehearsal, he displayed a rare burst of enthusiasm backstage. Photo, ©Photo Fayer, Vienna.

Much to the detriment of artistic life in the house on the Opernring, soon relations became strained between the master and the Viennese cultural establishment. The restless conductor then sought a task in the city of his birth, Salzburg, one that might perhaps satisfy his ambitions even more. Only shortly before this, after all the successful mutual Wagner productions and the eminently rewarding Eliot-Pizzetti *Murder in the Cathedral,* relations between the two of us had reached an absolute high point, which went so far that he, impressed by my directorial work with younger singers, offered me in all seriousness a chance to stage future productions that he would be conducting.

Shortly before his death, somebody proposed that I participate as a lecturer in a seminar Karajan would be chairing. I traveled to the episcopal city and ran across the maestro by chance in the Festival office. When he saw me, he spontaneously walked over to me, laid his head on my chest and embraced me firmly with both arms. This kind of physical closeness was something completely new in our relationship. Without looking in my face—he hardly ever looked his opposite number in the face—he allowed the words to escape his lips, as if they had suddenly drifted into his consciousness, "How wonderful of you to come to us. Please choose for yourself how you would like to participate in the program here."

Those were the last words he ever spoke to me. While he stood so close to me for so long, I recalled how skillfully he had previously avoided any close contact with me when he went out in front of the curtain after a performance. I believe he suffered greatly from the fact that he had never grown any taller.

Chapter 17

Now I'd like to say a little more about my experience as a lieder singer, the recitals I've given all over the world, and some of the things I've learned as I stood alone on the concert platform.

As a rule, a concert hall is too large for the intimate atmosphere of a song recital, and it may happen that a singer will feel very lonely and downright forlorn standing up there. Nevertheless there are houses with very familiar stages that one always looks forward to. I'm thinking of the Brahmssaal in Vienna and the small chamber music hall in Amsterdam's Concertgebouw.

Interpreting the song repertoire also means capturing moods. You take a little song and build a whole world with it. Yet shortly afterward you have to be able to exchange it all for a new setting with a completely different background color.

The most important and helpful element for a recitalist, apart from the voice, of course, is the accompanist, the partner at the keyboard. And this person must be a real partner as he or she has more than just the task of rolling out a sonic carpet on which the singer can self-confidently stride. The accompanist must assume an incredible responsibility: not only is he expected to have an abundance of skill, improvisational talent, and flexibility, he also has to breathe with the singer; he has to stay with him if he decides to dwell on a given phrase. He also has to be able to hit the brakes and guide the singer back to the original tempo whenever necessary. This calls for a high level of harmoniousness between singer and accompanist so that a symbiotic music-making can come about. I always advise my students to check out several accompanists, whenever possible, rehearse with them, and try to get accustomed to one another. My advice has always been to work with an accompanist who is critical and will tell the truth. It is so important to have an honest partner you can completely count on.

Among the many partners with whom fate and fortune have brought me together, I would like to mention one outstanding artist I worked with right from the outset of my career: Michael Raucheisen. He figured very importantly in my life because he was the first major chamber musician who believed in me, and our work together was marked by a very special harmony. A fellow Bavarian, born in 1889 in the small town of Rain am Lech, he began his career in Munich, where I often heard him during my student days as piano accompanist of such great singers as Heinrich Rehkemper, Luise Willer, and Paul Bender (to mention just three of the biggest names at the Bavarian State Opera in those days). Raucheisen then moved on to Berlin, where he headed the chamber music division of German Radio in addition to serving as recital accompanist to scores of singers and instrumentalists, including such luminaries as violinist Fritz Kreisler, whose piano partner he was for many years, and singers like Peter Anders, Maria Müller, Erna Berger, Rudolf Bockelmann, Elisabeth Schwarzkopf, Julius Patzak, and Maria Ivogün, who had been the voice teacher of both Berger and Schwarzkopf, and who became his wife in 1933. Our initial direct contact came about when he invited me to do radio recordings with him in Berlin. It has been suggested that he acquired his position at the radio station, one of the most prestigious in Central European musical life at the time, because of Nazi connections; I can personally attest that this is totally untrue. With our origins in the southern part of Germany and our very similar attitudes toward music-making, we soon became good friends, and in many a private conversation we both openly expressed our revulsion toward one event after another promulgated by the regime that had taken over our country. So I know for a fact that the position at Berlin Radio was offered to him exclusively because of his enormous musical expertise.

In the course of time, we appeared frequently in recital as well as making a number of recordings for the radio station under his supervision. Every time I had an opportunity to work with this consummate musician over the years it was invariably a great learning experience for me. Not only could he sight-read just about anything that was put in front of him, he also had a phenomenal ability to transpose music at sight, placing it in just the right key for the singer he accompanied, a talent I seldom experienced at that quality level in any of the other great accompanists I had the honor to work with.

He once told me he had actually aspired to a career as a concert pianist, but had to abandon that ambition because of his inability to commit music to memory. I cannot but believe this was a case of his hiding his radiant light under a bushel, because his knowledge of the literature was voluminous. But that was the story he told, and certainly the loss of Raucheisen as soloist from the concert stage was an incalculable gain for the recital platform.

In many ways, Raucheisen defined for me the qualities of a really good accompanist. Now, just exactly what are those qualities? As I see it, a good accompanist must be able to tell a singer, no matter how famous that singer might happen to be, where his or her weaknesses lie, and where he or she is doing something right or wrong and make the singer aware of quirks and idiosyncrasies that get in the way of the music and its interpretation. This candor is an absolute necessity, and no singer who has the privilege of working with someone with that kind of perception should ignore the partner's good advice. In many ways, singer and accompanist must be a unified team in a relationship that has some similarity to a good marriage, where one party complements the other, and each steps in to help the other whenever necessary. With his vast knowledge of style and tradition, Raucheisen could set the musical stage for the song that was to come; he always knew when something needed to be taken faster or slower, louder or softer, in which cases he adroitly brought the music back to where it had to be without ever interrupting the flow. He was also an incredible troubleshooter and knew exactly how to adjust when a singer made a mistake, thus restoring an almost seamless continuity to the performance.

He died not very long ago—in 1984—at the ripe old age of ninety-five.

And of course I am also eternally grateful to the incomparable Gerald Moore, who supplied me with the most valuable counsel as well as vigorous assistance in his accompaniments. Like Michael Raucheisen, he was a past master of adjusting to whatever situation came about in the course of our joint performance. Yet, in one respect, while Raucheisen was the child of his time, and often had to adapt himself, whether he liked it or not, to the theatricality that was often part of a recital performance by a major opera star back then, Gerald Moore was one of the fathers of today's generation of accompanists, who knew, and insisted on, the fundamental difference between theater and concert. What would have become of me without him—and also without his captivating sense of humor?

Many of my readers will be familiar with Gerald's rapier wit from some of his own solo performances and in his delightful books, which are also not without a goodly portion of musical wisdom. Of course, those of us who enjoyed collaborations with him were also able to note how quickly and spontaneously he could make a point with a spontaneous quip and resolve a situation that, in another case, could easily have turned into a horrible snag. I remember one session in which we were recording a very delicate Schubert song together, and every time I came to a certain phrase, my voice would get a little raspy. As fate would have it, after four or five attempts, I finally managed to clear the frog out of my throat and sing the phrase with the requisite smoothness, whereupon (perhaps because he was so flabbergasted that it finally worked) his finger slipped off a black key, and he hit a real clinker. Finally we managed to get the recording flawlessly in the can, upon which he rose from his seat at the keyboard and walked somewhat sheepishly over to me at my music stand, where he smiled self-effacingly and said, "This time *I* had a little frog."

Gerald Moore's wit could also be a very useful weapon when recording producers, perhaps frustrated by their inability to do it themselves, felt an urge to be dictatorial in their musical demands. More than once, a bit of badinage from Gerald could pare a self-styled tin god right down to size, and then we were able to proceed in a far more cooperative spirit than had been feasible before. I remember one rehearsal for a joint recital in which Gerald made a perfectly reasonable suggestion to my soprano colleague on how to interpret a certain phrase, telling her not to overdo something in her interpretation, to which my colleague replied that she had already been advised by the gentleman who would produce the recording of our recital that he wanted it the way she had just done it. To which Gerald remarked laconically, "Well, who's singing, him or you?"

Interestingly enough, many of the best conductors were also magnificent piano accompanists, and I had the pleasure of working with several of the best, starting with the pianist in my very first public recital, Meinhard von Zallinger, and moving on to the likes of Georg Solti, Wolfgang Sawallisch, and one of the very best recital accompanists I ever had the joy to work with, Richard Strauss (and not just in his own compositions).

Before moving on to some of my experiences on the concert stage, I would like to indulge in a bit of general theoretical comment on the art of recital singing. Even though my teacher, and with him a goodly number of well-meaning advisers, told me time and again how important it is for an opera singer to amplify his or her operatic repertoire with recital singing, it took several years for me to understand and appreciate the importance of this advice. Earlier in this book I told the story of Richard Strauss, who, late in his own life, during an unforgettable session in which he gave me invaluable advice on the interpretation of his own song literature, suddenly exclaimed, "of all I have written, my favorite pieces are my lieder." That not only left a profound impression on me; it was also an enormous source of personal satisfaction. It was clear that anyone with the good fortune to have known Strauss as well I did would be aware that this exclamation was the product of a momentary enthusiasm and did not represent a value judgment for all times. But that moment deserves being preserved on paper, especially as it made me the ear-witness of a remarkable statement from the mouth of a great master.

Much has been written on the difference between operatic interpretation and song performance. I was always convinced, and share this view with many experts on singing, that from a purely vocal point of view a song is given audible expression exactly the same way as an operatic aria. The difference lies more in the form of the personal attitude toward the respective medium than in the use of a different vocal technique. Let me try to clarify one or two points without the observance of which both singing and interpreting the song literature seem impossible to me.

First, even more than in opera, a recital singer must use his voice like an instrument with which, because it is a living instrument, he must be able to make living music and form it artistically. This means that recital singing calls for above-average musicality and artistic expressiveness.

Second, even more than in opera, the words—in most cases the words of a great poet—are equal in importance to the music. Good diction and unobtrusive comprehensibility are decisive. In a long period of development I have learned how important equal treatment of the words is to the flow of the music. But only now that my active performing career has come to an end am I really aware of how much the singing of lieder contributed to the growth of my understanding and great love for the precious gems of German lyric and romantic poetry as manifested in the words of Johann Wolfgang von Goethe, Heinrich Heine, Eduard Mörike, and Friedrich Rückert, to mention but a few. I do not consider it sufficient for a recitalist merely to feel an obligation toward the musical composition of a song. The rhymed words, with the aid of which he or she interprets a song, must mean just as much as the music; it was they that inspired the composer to devise the suitable music in the first place.

Third, and finally, it is important for a recitalist to learn that the interpretation of a dramatic musical sequence is not limited solely to the operatic stage. Dramatic interpretation also takes place on the concert platform, albeit with different means than are used on stage. Here, too, language becomes indispensable.

One of the most tempting, and also the most daunting challenges of recital singing is that, unlike in opera, where you are bound to a certain musical score, *you* are the one who creates the program for your performance, selecting from the vast array of literature available for this art form. It is fascinating to note that almost every major operatic and symphonic composer at one time or another in his career has written magnificent works for the recital repertoire: Mozart, Rossini, Verdi, Wagner, Puccini, Beethoven, Schubert, Schumann, Brahms, Bizet, Tchaikovsky and Rimsky-Korsakov, are just a few of the most important ones, along with any number of contemporary composers. All of them have left gems of concert songs for us and our audiences. And of course many of our greatest poets have achieved additional immortality through musical settings of their finest words, and this treasure trove is ours to choose from. But what a job it is making those choices!

Putting together a recital program is really a subject for a separate book, and many fine singers and other musicians have done just that. For this volume of memories, let me just add one or two hints from my own experience. Needless to say, there are many people who advise us on program building: our accompanist, of course; our vocal teacher, who knows our assets and limitations, and other counselors familiar with our vocal resources and the suitable literature. Nevertheless, in the final analysis, it is always the singer who must make the crucial decision; as Gerald Moore so wisely said, "Who's singing?" And so, recital planning becomes a voyage into ourselves and our artistic inclinations; as such, it represents a useful yardstick for much of what we do in other musical disciplines.

There are a number of different systems for building a program, but all of them must be based on the singer's familiarity with the available literature, both in terms of poetry and music. In this context, it would be a good idea to recall to mind an intriguing story I read many years ago in a biography of young Hugo Wolf, who, as a young man, used to get together with friends in Vienna to recite poems and test their reaction to them. While other young composers enjoyed performing their own music for their friends, almost driving those friends to distraction with their enthusiasm for their own creativity, the more self-effacing Wolf was particularly interested in people's response to the verses that appealed to him—doubtless the case with many of the other great song composers. Many of the finest poets were keenly interested in music and its possibilities of enhancing their words—although Goethe, it must be said, certainly missed the boat when the young Schubert sent him some settings of his poems and he chose to ignore them in favor of Carl Friedrich Zelter, his "house composer" in Weimar. But this was an exception rather than the rule, and, in defense of Goethe, we should also point out his love of Mozart and Beethoven's music and his championship of the young Mendelssohn. In this sense, we, as singers, cannot afford to neglect the content of the literary component in our recital programs. With those ground rules as given quantities, either we can create a historical sequence in strict chronological order, or we can relate the songs to one another in terms of the moods they evoke and how those moods relate or contrast with one another. Both close relationships and sharp contrasts can make for fascinating programs. In earlier times, almost every vocal recital concentrated on a single language, invariably the native language of the singer, and often focused on one composer. After all, a song cycle is always the work of a single composer, and many of the best cycles fill an entire evening. In more recent times, singers have used recitals to emphasize their versatility and perform in several languages and musical styles in a single program. There is certainly no reason why an artist should not put together this kind of program, but here, too, this selection presupposes a real familiarity with the various languages and styles; the program must have some overall unifying theme, otherwise the variety is just a kind of virtuosic circus act without much artistic depth. Sometimes an interesting guideline for recital programming can be found in the kinds of programs knowledgeable symphony conductors put together for an orchestral concert, stressing variety, contrast, or striking similarities. The whole scope of program planning also points up the importance of regular collaboration with a keyboard partner, who also has a fund of experience to draw from out of his work with other singers. The better the accompanist knows the singer, the more meaningful will be the advice the singer receives on what songs best suit his talents.

Not every gifted opera singer is suited for recital singing. Nevertheless, even these pure stage talents should never completely neglect delving into the song repertoire, if only for their own private satisfaction and development. The day will come when their voices will thank them for having done so.

Having said that, now I'd like to turn to one of my recital tours in a very distant land. Everything had started off splendidly; the concert audiences may have comported themselves somewhat distantly, but the hearty round of applause I received when I came out onstage gave me that soaring feeling one needs to launch into the correct musical-interpretive mood for singing a recital program. I had again determined to pay special attention to the clarity of word articulation. Clear diction is even more important when you are not singing in the audience's native tongue.

There were still a couple of bars of piano accompaniment before my first vocal entrance. I voluntarily allowed the sound of the piano to transport me into the first notes and words, and then something unexpected happened, something that almost robbed me of the evenness of my breathing. My glance was still directed at the virtually motionless listeners in the first row when I suddenly noticed that their lips were moving, forming words, as if they were starting to talk without making a sound. "This can't be happening!" I suddenly thought to myself. "They are at one with you, making the same lip movements, they are actually speaking the German words of the *Winterreise* in synch with you—in what, for them, is a foreign language!" I had to force myself to look away from the faces in front of me; I couldn't afford to become distracted. Slowly I adjusted to this unusual happening and regained the necessary calm to guide everything back onto the right track.

The first song in the cycle came to a happy conclusion, and twelve more were still waiting to brought to life for the audience until intermission gave me an opportunity to find my way back to my inner balance. In contrast to today's classic attitude that the *Winterreise* must be sung without an intermission, I always followed the example of my great role models and took a pause, agreeing with them that a little break is agreeable and beneficial for both the listeners and the performer.

The story I just told took place during my first appearance in Tokyo during a concert tour of Japan in 1962. Many travels of this kind would follow this first one in the course of the next twenty years, and this first one pointed the way toward a number of new experiences for me. This distant land in the east was still in a state of development as far as interest in classical music was concerned. Today, with the Japanese not only firmly established as the market leaders in the manufacture of radios and televisions but also spearheading the recording industry, as well as producing the latest state-of-the-art sound reproduction equipment, having invented both the cassette and the CD, hardly anyone still remembers that although the history of Western classical music in Japan goes back to the early 1930s, these people only developed a truly widespread knowledge and understanding of that music around the time the long-playing record was invented back in the 1950s. Before that time musical life in the classical sector was fairly sparse. In other words it took only a scant twenty years for an entire new generation of instrumentalists, conductors, and singers to come along, many of whom are active in today's music field far beyond the borders of their own country, indeed, throughout the entire world.

In the course of thirty years, I personally witnessed this rapid development, taking note of its advancement from one visit to the next. One orchestra after another, radio and television stations, as well as a flourishing recording and sound reproduction equipment industry, have fostered the education of an enthusiastic audience, supported by any number of first-class public and private music schools all over the country, which have assumed responsibility for the expert training of a young generation of top-ranking musicians.

The Japanese capacity for enthusiasm was a source of constant surprise to me. At my initial contacts I got the impression that the people there, despite their amiability, tended to be somewhat diffident and seemingly inhibited in their expression of emotions, especially toward strangers. I soon discovered that the constant smiles we Europeans found somewhat artificial had given me a false impression. It was explained to me that people in this country were taught at a very early age, both at home and school, not to display their feelings, whatever their nature, too spontaneously and uncontrolledly to others. The smile is then the means of concealing a lack of control, and also finding the way to a certain relaxation and ease.

I have seen how the generally stiff, unemotional, and all too buttoned-up Japanese can become very fiery when someone succeeds in arousing their enthusiasm for music. What was new to me was the way numbers of thrilled listeners sought out the artists with great endurance, especially at the end of concerts, in quest of an autograph and a chance to exchange a few words (many of them speaking German), after which they pull out the inevitable camera. There were concerts after which giving autographs took more time than the whole program.

The Japanese music lover is almost always a lover of classical German

17.1. My concert appearances in Japan brought me together with some of the most knowledgeable and appreciative audiences I ever encountered. This photo is of a 1969 recital in Tokyo.

lieder and often has a remarkably comprehensive knowledge of the song texts, as I experienced as far back as 1962. Schubert's *Winterreise* was a particular favorite among the recital programs. This fondness is not all that surprising when one takes into consideration the great closeness and affection the Japanese have for nature. Just think of the role of the cherry blossom in painting and poetry. In addition, they share a common trait with Germans: a certain inclination toward sentimentality and melancholy.

Schubert's *Winterreise* has exerted its uniquely powerful, eternal attraction on both the empathic listener and the interpretive artist for almost 180 years. Exactly why this most brilliant, heartrending music of all times is so effective will certainly remain a mystery forever. And it is this mystery that makes this artwork so special. With his subtle capacity to plumb emotional truth, the composer invented a form of musical expression that perfectly fits the sorrow of the rhymed poetic lyrics and, in a fortunate unity of music and words, gives the language an added ennoblement.

This conjoining of language and music points up the most pressing questions an interpreter of this cycle, one with a deep loyalty to the work, has to cope with. Should the musical line be given greater stress at those places when the music is more ingenious than the text, possibly at the cost of declamation and dramatic expression? How do we confront the peril of monotony in view of the primarily depressive fundamental character of the work? Would the listener rather be witness to a subjective interpretation in which the interpreter himself wanders suffering through the various stages of emotional experience? Or would he prefer a more objective performance in which interpretation is built on an interaction of emotional involvement and interpretation, eliminating the element of self-pity?

Fortunately, a friend of Schubert's, the lawyer Dr. Leopold Sonnleithner, has passed down to us some hints from the great genius himself who created these "gruesome songs" (as he himself described his *Winterreise*). In these hints, Schubert gives us what can certainly be regarded as authoritative answers to the aforementioned questions. Schubert's friend reports, "I heard Schubert coach and accompany his songs more than a hundred times. He never tolerated violent expression in the performance of lieder. He always kept strictly in tempo except for those few passages where he himself had specifically marked a tempo change in writing. The lieder singer should as a rule only relate the experiences and sensations of another person; he does not assume the role of the person whose feelings he is describing. Poet, composer, and singer must approach the song lyrically and not dramatically. Particularly in the case of Schubert the true expression, the most profound sensitivity has already been placed in the melody as such and is splendidly enhanced by the accompaniment."

When I first read such revealing words in these notes from the pen of a true authority I was more than satisfied. I remembered any number of pointless arguments, critical reviews, and opinions of all kinds—but here, in black and white, we have what the composer himself had to say on the subject. This being the case, today's approach of avoiding exaggerated pathos because it distorts the work all out of shape isn't all that "new." On the contrary, it is thoroughly in keeping with the composer's original intentions. I personally believe we can adopt these stipulations from the musician who doubtless ranks as the father of the German lied for the interpretation of the entire song literature, regardless of the composer or his period. This interpretation should never degenerate into an evening of grimaces and gesticulations but remain focused on the values of the words and music. If you don't believe me, just imagine your annoyance if a violinist or an entire orchestra were to start performing in line with some kind of tangential choreography!

It would be wrong to try to distill the experiences garnered over the course of fifty years in more than one hundred twenty concerts, some twenty broadcast transcriptions, and four commercial recordings of this cycle down to some kind of common denominator of generally applicable formulas. Knowledge like this is generally acquired in actual practice, and it is this knowledge that has the greatest value for the individual who has experienced it him- or herself. But perhaps the following points may give rise to revealing discussions. The more brilliantly conceived and "popular" an artwork is, the more loyalty to the letter of the score is called for in its interpretation. The almost folk song–like basic quality of the *Winterreise* can only be retained if it is approached with simplicity and with no self-indulgent superimposition of an alien interpretation on the part of the singer. The true personality of the interpretive artist comes out most effectively when he subjects himself to the will of the author.

As dark moods predominate, it makes sense to point up the contrast with positive elements such as the constantly recurring descriptions of nature. Anyone with sufficient imagination will be able to discern from the *Winterreise* music how the composer, with his own profound closeness to nature, must have yearned to capture all the different moods evoked by the winter landscape, the dream of green meadows and blossoming flowers, the diverse forms of water (one of Schubert's favorite themes in any case) in the clear brooklet, in the icy stream, in the frozen dewdrops or tears. All of these are bright, pleasing thoughts. When they are consciously stressed, the singer may succeed in distracting the listener from the incessant lamentation of the unhappy lover, who—basically quite an egotist—never stops thinking about himself and misses no opportunity to bewail and bemoan his sorry lot. I first began thinking about the necessity of brightening up the rather gloom-ridden basic mood of these "gruesome songs" when I began performing them outside my own country, where I discovered that while audiences and critics may love the music, they still found the basic tone of the poetry unremittingly oppressive and sorrowful. Occasionally I was even told that that the restless, unhappy wanderer—like Goethe's suffering Werther—reflects nothing quite so much as that self-pity so typical of the Germans.

The choice of the right tempo is prerequisite for a successful performance, especially of this work. This problem can only be solved when, while paying attention to the tempi marked in the score, we find a basic time signature, with which the spiritual continuity of the lieder can be brought into a common musical relationship. Just think of the recurring rhythmic structure of "Gute Nacht," "Gefrorene Tränen," "Auf dem Flusse," "Die Krähe," and "Der Wegweiser." The steady, virtually relentless, forward motion becomes all the more meaningful the more clearly it is repeated in the individual songs.

Under no circumstances should the importance of the differing lengths of pauses between the various individual songs be underestimated. An intentional variation, for both musical and mood-determining reasons, also heightens the tension and furthers the cohesiveness of the whole.

Can one sing an encore after the *Winterreise?* Does anyone know a song that can be sung after the "Leiermann"? I can't imagine any. A good audience will understand that.

Chapter 18

Just as in Australia, I was also pampered on my Japanese tours by the perfect organization of the local agency. The head of the agency, Yoshikazu Nishioka, who knew just a little English, was an enthusiastic music lover. Right at the beginning of my first visit to Tokyo, he offered me a typical example of legendary Japanese courtesy. My very first morning, he surprised me at eight A.M. with a telephone call from the lobby, asking if it would be possible to come up and welcome me in my room. I had just made myself decent to receive visitors when he walked into the room with a bow, paused for a moment, then with his head lowered took another couple of steps forward, bowed again, the way we have seen people do in many an old Japanese film, paused again, his eyes still riveted to the floor, then uttered the words, "Good morning. Today, no sun—excuse me." I was impressed.

For three weeks, my friend Nishioka or one of his staffers looked after me on the concert tour to such cities as Osaka, Kobe, Nagoya, Kyoto, and Sapporo. And this was repeated several more times every two years on new trips to Japan: everywhere the same hotels, similar concert halls, time and again enthusiastic concert audiences, disciplined, courteous, and always many autograph seekers after each appearance.

There was a young agency staff member, who emerged from his reserve a little more with every day of the tour. He spoke quite good English, was very witty, and had a special fondness for the *Winterreise*. Once he told us with great pride that he was planning to get married. Two years later, when I returned to Tokyo, he glowingly reported that he had meanwhile become the proud father of a son. He also told me the name he had given the baby: Toroyo. It sounded almost ceremonious. And then, as if revealing a secret, he added, "That's the Japanese word for *Winterreise*." I was deeply moved. I'm quite sure Schubert would have been, too.

Another rather poignant event also took place there. About a year before my first visit to Japan, I had received a letter from a Japanese student asking for an autograph. I sent her a photo and received by return mail an effervescent thank-you letter with a series of questions about my operatic repertoire and my lieder recordings, phrased in excellent German. As this correspondence was fun for me, a lively exchange of letters evolved between us, especially after I had told her that I was planning to visit Japan to give concerts in the foreseeable future. After making a date to meet her in Tokyo, I was startled and a bit disappointed when one month before my departure our connection suddenly broke off, and I finally got on the plane without hearing from her again.

Soon after my arrival in Tokyo I found a Japanese gentleman in the lobby of my hotel, who introduced himself as a professor of German at the Tokyo University and asked for a brief meeting with me. In flawless German he asked if I could remember corresponding with a college student from Tokyo, and told me her name. I answered in the affirmative and expressed my astonishment over the abrupt interruption in our correspondence. Thereupon he removed a sealed letter from his pocket and said calmly, "I was asked to give you this letter. The girl who was corresponding with you is . . . that is to say *was* my daughter. She had suffered from leukemia for a long time, and two weeks before your arrival she passed away." To my horror, he accompanied the last three words with a sudden loud laugh. Bewildered and shocked I listened, as if from a distance and half benumbed, as he said calmly and totally under control, "Shortly before she left this world, she listened to your *Winterreise,* which she loved very much. She was so looking forward to meeting you. She wanted me to give you this letter and apologize for her that she was no longer able to write you in Munich."

I was seriously thinking of sending for the porter because I was afraid I might be sitting opposite an insane person, as he rose to his feet, bowed and, with his head held high, wordlessly left the lobby. When I later told this story to Mr. Nishioka, I was very curious how he would react to the event. He listened silently to the whole story without once interrupting me. When I finished it, he looked very earnestly over at me and said, "To be able to laugh in moment of deepest sadness is in Japan sign of greatest self-control." This encounter moved me deeply and once again showed me how very different people can be.

My final visit to the land of Nippon is now almost twenty years in the past. Some forty years have passed since my first stay in that country, but the many impressions I brought back home with me are still clear and present in my mind. Fortunately there are many Japanese artists, former pupils, who help keep the contact alive.

At the end of my short flashback to experiences with the people in the Land of the Rising Sun, I would like to place, as a representative of many others, the name of a highly successful Japanese gentleman, who saw to it during all of my visits that my time in Japan passed as pleasantly as could be made possible: Norio Ohga, the brilliant head of Sony (who had originally been a concert singer with a glorious Vienna-trained baritone voice). It was fascinating for me to observe, from one visit to the next, the way the one-time university student, diligently gaining practical experience in the plant, slowly but surely worked his way up the corporate ladder until he stood at the top of the firm as president and chief executive officer, making major contributions to the development and growth of the company. To him, who always took a personal interest in up-and-coming young musicians, I extend my deepest gratitude and admiration.

❧ Chapter 19 ❧

When, in 1970, I received an offer from the Grand Opéra de Paris to direct a revival of a Wieland Wagner production (originally created in 1965) for the 1971–72 season, I initially turned it down, remembering how I had frequently been forced to experience what a thankless task it is to "warm up" another director's work, especially when that other director is an eminent personality. But the general manager of the Grand Opéra at the time, Bernard Lefort, wouldn't let up on me, mentioning how I had successfully collaborated for so many years with the composer's grandson and, after his untimely death in 1966, had looked after his orphaned *Ring* in the summer of 1968 in Bayreuth. So, for Wieland's sake, I agreed to take it on.

The job I did seemed quite successful. I had managed to garner a fair amount of experience over the previous ten years in the "role" of stage director. I remember we had an endless number of rehearsals for the scene with the Valkyries in act three. At one of them, Lefort asked me if I didn't want to sing Wotan on one of the coming evenings to take my leave from the operatic stage in a farewell performance. I was sixty-three years old and had put in some forty-two years on the opera stage. This suggestion didn't please me one bit. I have never been particularly fond of the institution of farewell performances. Besides this, at that point in time I didn't consider myself young enough for the demanding role. Then Lefort tried another tack. He suggested that I sing the third act. Franz Mazura, who sang Wotan in this production, would certainly waive his right to the third act for my sake and just do the second act. Well, my friend Franz, not only a great singing personality but also a good colleague, immediately declared his readiness to do me the favor. Finally I relented under the condition that this would not be called my final departure from the stage but simply my farewell from the part of Wotan. So I interrupted a lieder class in the Netherlands for two days, traveled to Paris and sang on June 29, 1972, "zum letzten Mal letz' es mich heut mit des Lebewohles letztem Kuss," where Wotan gives his daughter a final kiss, a moment in the opera where we frequently have to fight back the tears. On this evening, the pain of parting was not only related to my beloved Brünnhilde.

When I returned to Munich, Günther Rennert, one of the greatest stage directors of our time, and later a general manager of the Munich Opera (everyone in the house adored him), surprised me with the question of whether I might like to take over the role of Schigolch in a new production of Alban Berg's *Lulu* he had planned for that theater. I was so flabbergasted that I initially didn't want to say yes or no. This part, I felt, did not fit into my previous repertoire in any way. In all the *Lulu* productions I had seen up until that point, this character was always cast with a basso buffo. Calmly but firmly I tried to convince Rennert that I was totally unsuited for the assignment, but I should have known that a man like him could not be shaken from a decision he had once taken. For my part, I had no desire to listen to any more of his arguments and asked him, in an almost unfriendly tone, why this role, which wasn't all that interesting to the performer, was so important for him. He then looked at me pleasantly and said in a calm voice, stressing every syllable, slowly and softly, "That's exactly what I find so fascinating about that bizarre *clochard* character: I want to prove that this Schigolch can be made into an incredibly interesting figure if somebody like you takes it on."

"Thanks. I guess that was a compliment," I said, somewhat facetiously.

"Now listen carefully to me. Do me the kindness of reading carefully through both of Wedekind's plays again. Then you'll notice that, of all the men who get caught up in Lulu's sphere of influence, Schigolch is the only one who survives unscathed. Let me make you a suggestion: come to my rehearsal. You don't have to know the text and the music by heart. We'll work on a scene. No obligation. And then the next day we'll talk again."

Of course, at this "noncommittal" rehearsal, he put all his considerable charm and deftness into play, handled me like a raw egg and did everything in his power to present the role as appetizingly as possible. Of course, he won me over, and today I must confess: Thank God! Over the succeeding twenty years I've worked on this role in eight further productions and savored the way it has developed with other great directors like Otto Schenk in Vienna and Jean-Pierre Ponnelle in Munich (my only collaboration with that colossally imaginative French theater professional), making my final appearances in Paris at the Châtelet at the age of eighty-three, plus two recordings.

After the first performances the audience reaction was largely positive, even though many of the older ones in the auditorium had seen me not too long ago as Gurnemanz, the Dutchman, and Wotan, and the readjustment didn't work for all of them. At the beginning, some people told me I had made "a big mistake." Still, it was fun for me to be known by a younger generation not as the elegant Scarpia but rather as the down-and-out Schigolch.

19.1.   The role of Schigolch in Alban Berg's *Lulu* extended my career well into my eighties. One element I found particularly appealing is that Schigolch is the only man in Lulu's life who is still around at the end of the opera—a factor made doubly appealing when Lulu is sung by someone as lovely as American soprano Patricia Wise. Photo, © Jaie-Noëlle ROBERT, Paris.

On an April evening in 1977, the phone rang in my Munich home. "This is Zubin Mehta from Los Angeles. Do you know the *Gurre-Lieder* by Schoenberg? No? It's one of my favorite works, and I'm in the middle of preparations for it. Unfortunately George London, who had been engaged as the narrator, has had to cancel. Could you step in for him? It's a wonderful speaking part."

"I'd have to take a look at it first. When is the concert? I beg your pardon? In four days!? But that's . . ."

"Why don't you get a score right away and check it out? I'll call you tomorrow at the same time. Then we can discuss it again. It would be lovely if you could say yes. Until tomorrow then."

When he called back, I agreed to do it. He was thrilled and, frankly, so was I. Twelve hours later, I was on a plane to Los Angeles. The next day was an orchestra rehearsal. When I walked out on stage, the brass players greeted me by playing Wotan's spear motive from the *Ring*. The last time I had sung there was in 1956. The older members of the orchestra could still remember it.

My short appearance, quite effectively placed by Schoenberg at the end of the work shortly before the final apotheosis, pleased the audience more than I had expected. One critic called my short, emotionally charged, dramatic spoken scene as "Wotan of his old age." I was feted like a prodigal son; there were happy reunions with friends and acquaintances from earlier times. I could hardly suspect that this extemporaneous replacement would develop into an assignment I would continue to carry out for years to come as an unexpectedly successful new role in concerts all over the world.

19.2.   My later career took me into the world of 12-tone opera. This scene is from a Frankfurt production of Arnold Schoenberg's only opera, *Moses und Aron,* directed by Vaclav Kašlik and conducted by Christoph von Dohnányi in which I performed the role of Moses in "Sprechgesang." Photo, ©Günter Englert, Frankfurt am Main.

I had first met Zubin Mehta during his student days in Vienna, where he was learning the art of conducting from Maestro Hans Swarowsky. Shortly after the reopening of the Vienna Opera in 1955, he visited me, when he was all of nineteen, in my dressing room to ask for an autograph.

After our collaboration in Los Angeles in 1977, Mehta brought me back for three more *Gurre-Lieder* performances: in 1983 and 1991 in New York; the latter presentation, on May 23, 24 and 28, of that year, his farewell performances as music director of the Philharmonic-Symphony Society of New York.

At our first rehearsal for this prestigious farewell, I enjoyed one of those delightful encounters that makes performing in New York such a refreshingly down-to-earth experience. While great respect for the arts dominates everyone's approach, there is seldom any bogus reverence for its practitioners. We are all colleagues, and that's that. In this case, however, I guess some of my reputation had gone on before me, because I was initially accorded so much deference, all of it quite sincere, that I was beginning to feel a little like a visiting monsignor—until a well-placed one-liner from a fellow soloist quickly put the capper on that. For his farewell concerts, Zubin had chosen a lineup of first-rate American singers to perform this daunting work, including Gary Lakes as Waldemar, Susan Dunn as Tove, John Cheek and Jon Garrison in the other two solo parts, and, singing the poignant song of the wood dove, mezzo-soprano Florence Quivar, a lady with both a gloriously lush voice and an equally refulgent sense of humor, which she proved by greeting me at one rehearsal, "Now, honey, if you need any help with your German diction, I'm right here for you!" That remark certainly cleared the air and consigned whatever sacred cows that might have been lurking about the musical pastures to the safe confines of a hamburger bun.

I did another performance of the *Gurre-Lieder* with Zubin in 1988 in Munich, where, to the great joy of the local audience, including yours truly, he would subsequently become general music director of the Bavarian State Opera. I have participated twice in recordings of this early Schoenberg work: in 1986 in Berlin with Riccardo Chailly on the Decca label, and in 1991 in New York with Mehta for Sony. Finally, I was reengaged to perform it in Salzburg, when Claudio Abbado brought out the work for the 1996 festival there.

Anyone publishing his reminiscences needs a good memory. Fortunately my dear mother handed down a goodly portion of hers to me, so that today I continue to enjoy that precious legacy. But how would I have managed if my darling wife had not carefully saved my reviews throughout the sixty-plus years of our marriage, pasting them carefully into a whole shelf-ful of albums? Thanks to her efforts, I can not only mention the year, but also often the actual month and day something happened.

Today's opera singers, unlike their predecessors in earlier generations, have learned to live with the media, whether they want to or not. In this sense, it has come about that the presence of a television camera while we work is not all that unusual. In former times, when this was not possible, not only actors but also singers were happy to take part in the making of a film whenever they had the chance. When I was asked to perform in motion pictures, of course I was curious as to what it would be like and thus more than eager to accept the offer. Unfortunately my introduction into this medium came about concurrently with the outbreak of the war, which limited my options to begin something new in my career.

I briefly mentioned my first film appearance in an earlier chapter. It was in a movie entitled *Mutterliebe* (mother love) produced in 1939. Besides such motion picture celebrities as Käthe Dorsch and Paul Hörbiger, I appeared mainly as an opera singer, gratefully playing a small role. Five highly trained actors also made their film debuts in this picture, later to go on to stage and screen prominence in our part of the world: Winnie Markus, Susi Nicoletti, Siegfried Breuer, Hans Holt, and Rudolf Prack.

In my next film—two years later—I was again, as in *Mutterliebe,* cast in a small acting role. In *Brüderlein fein,* the film biography of the Austrian playwright Ferdinand Raimund, I was entrusted with the role of the poet Nikolaus Lenau. Again this represented a get-together with some of the top Austrian acting stars, primarily some celebrated comics. No wonder I think back with great pleasure on shooting that picture. In my third film, *Lache Bajazzo* (Laugh, Clown, Laugh), based on the life of the composer Leoncavallo, I simply sang the prologue from the opera *Pagliacci.*

There then followed two films based on the lives of singers—proper opera films, in other words—in which I played the leading parts. For the first of the two, *Seine beste Rolle* (His Best Role), made in 1943, they had acquired two major stars, Camilla Horn and Paul Dahlke. My partner was the enchanting Marina von Dittmar. The last of the five films was shot after the war in 1950 and was unfortunately a flop.

For *Seine beste Rolle,* by the way, the well-known film composer Lothar Brühne contributed some truly charming melodies. In a little operatic scene, composed especially for this picture, he came up with a delightful tune for the arietta: "Schöne Nina" (Lovely Nina). Many autograph letters asked me what opera this pretty little aria had been taken from. In one scene in the film, in which Lothar made a brief appearance as a rehearsal pianist, he erected his own monument as a well-versed, witty performer. From then on, we were good friends until his untimely death only a short time afterward.

My film work offered me a highly educational and interesting, as well as most enjoyable, insight into a new milieu. I took full advantage of the opportunity to gain a lot of new experience that I could then apply in my work on the operatic stage. The precision with which motion picture actors must maintain the predetermined distance from the camera, especially in close-ups, proved a highly informative lesson for the discipline of an operatic performer. Of course, working with a good operatic stage director also calls for a positive attitude and a high level of adaptability. But you only realize how much tranquillity, patience, and endurance you need for filming when you've actually been seriously initiated into this world. The brutal combination of artistic romanticism, sober reality, and the hard-boiled business practices of a dog-eat-dog industry is also not everyone's cup of tea. All in all, the knowledge I gained at the film studios had practical application in both professional and private life.

Chapter 20

If, during my fledgling years on the operatic stage, someone had predicted that I would once get a serious offer to stage opera productions, I probably would have laughed in his face. And yet thirty years later, it happened. This is how it came about: in the late 1950s, after the Royal Opera House, Covent Garden, in London had reverted to the practice of giving German opera in the original language, there was plenty of opportunity for me occasionally to help my British colleagues with their German pronunciation and show them that German, which the Italians like referring to as "la brutta lingua" (the ugly language) is quite compatible with Italian bel canto vocal style, and should not, as often happens outside Germany, be sung in a hard, choppy, "machine-gun" legato.

The English were already aware of my collaboration with Wieland Wagner, which had led to my having been, so to speak, anointed into the lower orders of the New Bayreuth acting style. I had told them that there we tried to replace the often meaningless, phony gestures of yesteryear with natural action or simply do nothing and let our eyes or our facial expressions and physical stance do the acting for us. At the same time, Karajan was also trying to capture a touch of New Bayreuth in Vienna for the benefit of the fairly conservative Viennese public.

In those days, the Royal Opera in London was under the benevolent rule of Sir David Webster, an English business executive with a big heart and a brilliant nose for anything that had anything to do with art. By his side stood the ultrasensitive Lord Harewood, a cousin of the young Queen Elizabeth. At the time, Harewood was still married to a brilliant pianist named Marion (née Stein, who had emmigrated from Vienna) and gathering experience in operatic management, eager to endow London's operatic temple, set amid the fruit and vegetable stands on the Covent Garden street market, with something of the flair of Britain's high aristocracy.

I had a special fondness for the musical lord and admired his highly developed artistic sensitivity as well as his delectable British sense of humor. He, for his part, treated me, the foreign interloper, in both our artistic and human relations as a good friend. Stories of my linguistic and scenic

"brush-up instruction" had made their way to the upper echelons of the
theater's management. It was George Harewood who first asked me if I
might like to direct a new production of Wagner's *Ring* to be conducted
by Georg Solti. The proposal pleased me no end. Nevertheless I exercised
proper British reserve and asked for some time to think it over. Back in Munich I consulted some people in the field. Finally it was Wieland Wagner
who told me I should accept the offer by all means. It was his advice that ultimately tipped the scales in favor of accepting the job.

The productions of the four *Ring* operas, created over the course of four
years, were under the care of a lucky star right from the beginning. Georg
Solti was a perfect musical director for the undertaking. With his high-
strung intensity, always investing the fullest measure of his seemingly
boundless energy, he gave the Wagnerian score his almost autarchic imprint
with his paramount level of musical understanding. This self-assurance
might very well have led to tensions on stage had we not known one another so well from Munich; fortunately, having acquired such a high regard
for one another, we were able to nip any possible disharmony in the bud.
From my long practical experience as a singer I had often experienced how
fundamental misunderstandings among the triumvirate of conductor, stage
director, and production designer can lead to paralyzing conflicts, much to
the detriment of an entire ensemble's ability to work together. I can thank
yet another lucky star, that the greenhorn at the stage director's desk was
spared any unpleasant experiences while taking his first steps.

Last but not least, I had a top-ranking professional working with me as
set designer in my friend Günther Schneider-Siemssen. I had met this fellow Bavarian and native-born *Münchner* toward the end of the Second
World War when he was still an assistant to the designer Professor Helmut
Jürgens at the Bavarian State Opera. At the time he very touchingly helped
the entire Hotter family out of a dire predicament. Christmas was just
around the corner, and there were almost no toys for us to put under the
Christmas tree for our children. Then Günther came up with the bright idea
of hand-crafting a puppet playhouse with all the appropriate appurtenances
for us. Our children were tickled pink when they saw the theater, which
practically took up the entire front parlor. For a number of years it remained
the main attraction in the children's room.

Günther and I met again in 1962 during the *Ring* in London, beginning
our extremely successful artistic collaboration. There then came possibly
our finest joint effort, a *Holländer* at the Munich Opera in 1964; it was initially to have been conducted by Hans Knappertsbusch, but by then he was
already terminally ill. That same year, in another happy collaboration, Günther and I joined forces on a new production of *Palestrina* at the Vienna
State Opera, which we still remember with special fondness.

I am convinced we might have created a large number of joint projects had I not decided to discontinue my activities as an opera director. I remember our cooperative "deeds" with joy and satisfaction. We complemented one another wonderfully; there were never any of the disharmonies or petty disputes that so often trouble the waters between director and designer. Instead, we always had fun; for all the earnestness we brought to the task, there was invariably plenty of kidding around, as well. Perhaps I should relate one amusing episode that took place during the *Ring* rehearsals at the Royal Opera House in London.

Many opera lovers would give anything to catch a glimpse of activities behind the scenes during the rehearsal period, but they would be amazed if not downright disappointed by things that sometimes happen there. There is, for example, the "lighting rehearsal": on this occasion, the head of the lighting department gets together with the scenic designer and the stage director in the auditorium to establish the various light settings to run in the course of the action, one after another. There are several high-grade expert technicians on stage—called simply the "electricians"—at various points on the set, where they receive instructions from the head of lighting in the auditorium.

As the stage in London was in use every day during the week, we were told our lighting rehearsal would have to take place on a Sunday. This was really an emergency measure: Sunday in Great Britain is kept absolutely sacred. Because he had been burned by so many unpleasant experiences at Sunday rehearsals, Günther Schneider-Siemssen promptly registered his most serious misgivings at having to do his lighting on the holy day, particularly as the British trade unions are tougher than anywhere else. His concern that we would not have enough electricians on stage seemed thoroughly justified. But we were placated in the usual subdued British fashion; everything would work out just splendidly, we were told.

The rehearsal began. Schneider-Siemssen, whose English at the time was not very fluent, spoke German, or rather a strong Munich dialect, and I attempted to translate everything into understandable English, while the head of lighting gave his instructions over a loudspeaker in Anglo-Electricianese to his minions on stage. Inquiries from them came back over the same route. Our head of lighting looked like an old county family member of the House of Lords, had a Scottish *Mac* in front of his surname, and in classic British manner, his tone was graciously genteel and soft-spoken—a style that made him even harder for us rough-hewn Bavarians to understand.

Consequently there was a fair bit of tension in the auditorium, further compounded by "Mac's" addressing all his cohorts on stage as "Johnny." A horrible suspicion arose in Schneider-Siemssen's mind, and he said to me disconsolately, "Now these rotten Limeys have only got one man up there on the stage. This will never do. And they swore to us there would be at least five electricians up there."

We looked accusingly over at our "electrolord," who clearly was more than used to manifestations of distress from irascible Continentals. In all my life I have never seen a more self-satisfied smile festoon anyone's face than the Cheshire cat grin he flashed at us as he said, "We just happen to have five Johnnies on our crew." The heavy weather was suddenly dispelled in a gust of liberating laughter, and then one of the assistant directors took advantage of the pause to inquire with a superior smile, "How about a nice cup of tea, luvs?"

Of course there were plenty of other comical occurrences during our regular rehearsals and performances as well. When the curtain rises on the final scene of the third act in *Siegfried,* we see Brünnhilde, her body covered with her shield, sleeping on the rock where Wotan had left her at the end of *Die Walküre.* Shortly thereafter, the young Siegfried appears, releases her from the constriction of the shield, and then kisses her into wakefulness. In the London production, the young Birgit Nilsson sang Brünnhilde while the now legendary Wolfgang Windgassen appeared as Siegfried. In one of the performances, we had just reached the scene where Siegfried makes ready to liberate Brünnhilde from her armor. I happened to be backstage at the time and watched Wolfgang as he lifted the breastplate. As his glance fell on Brünnhilde's torso, a shocked expression crossed his face, and it was clear he was struggling valiantly to keep from totally cracking up. What had happened? Birgit had removed the little sign from the door of her hotel room and placed it strategically on her thorax, where poor Windgassen could see, spelled out in large golden letters: Do not disturb.

Georg Solti, when he spoke to the orchestra during rehearsals, often had a gruff tone that was not at all to the liking of some of the musicians. Once, in a *Götterdämmerung* rehearsal with the orchestra alone, he delivered such a vituperative harangue that the players manifested their disapproval by scraping their shoes on the floor. Solti realized he had gone a little too far; to restore a little sunshine to the scene, he suddenly changed his tune and called out in a loud, chummy voice to the musicians, "Now, ladies and gentlemen, let's all have a jolly good *Rheinfahrt!*" The whole orchestra roared with laughter.

The cast was a healthy mixture taken partly from the circle of experienced, well-known international opera stars, all friends and colleagues from Bayreuth and Vienna, first-rankers on the level of Birgit Nilsson, Gustav Neidlinger, Anita Välkki, Wolfgang Windgassen, Gerhard Stolze, Gottlob Frick, and Rita Gorr, with a contingent of singers from the theater's regular roster, many of them with equally fine voices and, in several cases, with

20.1.   My work as a stage director was pure delight when I was able to work with practiced veterans like my longtime basso colleague, Gottlob Frick. Photo, ©Rudolf Betz, Munich, and the Bavarian State Opera.

international reputations on a par with those of their Continental colleagues. One classic example of this quality was the hardy Yorkshireman Peter Glossop, who had skyrocketed from the Sadler's Wells chorus to become one of the stars of the Covent Garden house, as well as singing leading baritone roles, largely in the Italian repertoire, all over the world. Yet Peter gladly joined our *Rheingold* production in the relatively small, but important part of Donner. In that same production, two of the top singers in Great Britain, Forbes Robinson and Michael Langdon, sang the two giants, while I shared the role of Wotan with Scottish baritone David Ward, who also appeared in leading heroic baritone roles on more than one continent. In *Die Walküre*, two popular international stars from across the Atlantic, American Claire Watson and Canadian Jon Vickers joined the cast as Siegmund and Sieglinde with fellow North Americans Thomas Stewart from Texas as Gunther in *Götterdämmerung* and Joseph Rouleau from Quebec as Fafner in *Siegfried*. Covent Garden also drew from the company's sizable

contingent of wonderful Antipodean singers to grace our cast with the likes
of Margreta Elkins, Marie Collier, and Yvonne Minton from Australia,
along with New Zealander Donald McIntyre. Sharing the role of Alberich
with Frans Andersson and Gustav Neidlinger was a regular member of the
Covent Garden ensemble who had already sung the role in Bayreuth and
many other international venues, Prague-born Otakar Kraus, who did double duty at Covent Garden as translator of the English performance texts for
operas originally written in Czech: the libretto of Leoš Janáček's *Jenůfa* on
which he collaborated with conductor Edward Downes, who also led some
of our *Ring* performances, is still the standard text used for English-language productions to this day. The second Rhine maiden, Wellgunde, in
both *Rheingold* and *Götterdämmerung* was an attractive young Welsh girl
with a glorious sound. She impressed me with her excellent unaccented
German, not only when she sang but also in conversation. Her name was
Gwyneth Jones. I've already told about her path to Bayreuth, which I was
able to smooth somewhat for her.

The production ran from the early 1960s to the seventies, some ten years
in all, and the cast was swelled in the course of those repeat performances
with the likes of Helga Dernesch, James King, Ludmila Dvořáková, Zoltán
Kelemen, Grace Hoffman, Kurt Böhme, Ingrid Bjoner, Martti Talvela,
Heather Harper, and a local London dramatic soprano named Amy Shuard,
who scored a major success as Brünnhilde. After switching from mezzo-
soprano to dramatic soprano, Gwyneth Jones returned to the cast making a
sensational role debut as Sieglinde.

One of the members of the London home team proved to be a problem
for us, not because of her singing and acting talent, which was considerable,
or because she was in any way uncooperative, which she most certainly
wasn't; put simply, Josephine Veasey, our Fricka, was a good bit shorter
than both David Ward and myself. Our ultra-imaginative designer, Günther Schneider-Siemssen, however, came up with a brilliant solution for
that problem: he gave her a garment that was slightly longer than she was
and then placed her on a raised mound of turf for her confrontation with
Wotan, bringing her closer together with us and balancing out the height
difference without the audience catching on.

The agreeable circumstances during rehearsals and performances satisfied the prerequisites for a successful collaboration, a doubly beneficial
blessing for a relative newcomer on the directorial scene like myself. I am
eternally grateful to all my friends and colleagues among the soloists, whose
great cooperative spirit made this unfamiliar job so easy for me, and the
same goes for the English and Commonwealth artists who took part in the
whole undertaking with exemplary discipline and great joy.

Prompted by good reports from my London *Ring,* Munich's general manager, Rudolf Hartmann, made the courageous decision to invite me to direct an opera in my hometown. I was asked to create a new staging for Wagner's *Der fliegende Holländer*. To my great joy, Hans Knappertsbusch, a conductor whom I boundlessly admired, agreed to assume the musical direction, prompting me to accept this assignment. The decision was cemented when the management spontaneously concurred with my request to have the production designed by Günther Schneider-Siemssen.

For all of this, it was still clear to me from the outset that in my hometown I would have to contend with a certain reticence to accept a "singer-director," leaving me a prophet in his own country. With two native sons like Günther and myself on the job, we were soon joined (when it became clear that Knappertsbusch's illness would not allow him to conduct) by yet another local boy, one-time Clemens Krauss pupil Hans Gierster, on the conductor's podium.

For the solo roles, we were offered the first-class selection of singers then on the roster of this prestigious house, supplemented by the excellent artistry and agreeable, cooperative attitude of the lovely Czech soprano Ludmila Dvořáková, with whom I had worked in the London *Ring,* as Senta. Another highlight was the participation of an artist at the start of his ascent to international greatness: the unforgotten Fritz Wunderlich in the relatively small part of the helmsman.

I had known Fritz from the 1959 Salzburg Festival, where he made his first appearance before an international festival audience as Henry in Strauss's *Die schweigsame Frau*. Karl Böhm conducted majestically, and Günther Rennert was the highly imaginative stage director. On the stage, the iridescent Hilde Gueden in the title role vied for top honors with the electrifying vocal and dramatic performance of Hermann Prey and the captivatingly comic antics of Georgine von Milinkovič.

Back to the 1964 Munich *Holländer,* for which my friend Günther had resolutely used modern means to create a classic-realistic setting, thus satisfying my own wish to observe the author's intentions and give honest expression to his music. In all modesty, yet with a touch of pardonable pride, let me state that our *Holländer* with a grand total of no less than one hundred and fourteen performances, remained in the repertoire of the Munich Opera for seventeen years, truly a Methuselah lifespan compared to some of the here-today-gone-tomorrow, contemporary productions.

One of my most satisfying staging assignments was offered to me in 1964 by Vienna's influential theater enthusiast at the time, Dr. Egon Hilbert (who, let us recall to mind, heaped the full measure of his wrath on my head in Salzburg back in 1945 because I had allegedly trampled the honor of a Wagner singer underfoot clowning around with my Carmen parody in a U.S. soldier show). The statute of limitations had since run out on that past

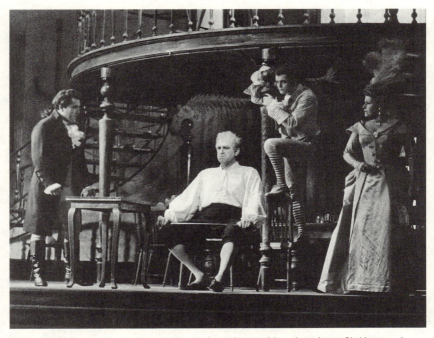

20.2.   Another senior-citizen characterization I thoroughly enjoyed was Sir Morosus in
Richard Strauss's *Die schweigsame Frau,* with its sparkling libretto by Stefan Zweig. I sang
at the Salzburg Festival with three genuine all-stars as colleagues: Fritz Wunderlich as
Henry, Hermann Prey as the barber, and Hilde Güden as Aminta. Photo, ©Max Reinhardt
Institute, Salzburg.

malfeasance; otherwise he would hardly have asked me if I would like to
stage Hans Pfitzner's solemn *Palestrina* at the Vienna Opera. This request
really represented the fulfillment of a heart's desire for me. Highly honored,
if I may put it that way, by an artistic friendship with the significant composer of the work, I was totally familiar with his opera through his often
acerbic but always wise comments. I promptly made sure I would again be
collaborating again with Schneider-Siemssen, who created settings true to
the work: the council chamber, with its imposing Renaissance ceiling,
based on historical models, profoundly impressed me.

    I was very lucky, as I had been a couple of months previously in Munich,
with an all-star cast in the principal roles. Just one look at the cast list for the
premiere in those days gives you an idea how blessed the Vienna Opera was
with beautiful voices and spellbinding stage personalities. There were
names like Sena Jurinac, Christa Ludwig, Walter Berry, Otto Wiener, Gottlob Frick, and Peter Klein. The baroque music fan and passionate lover of

organ music Anton Dermota seemed to be the ideal casting for the title role of Palestrina, but I had set my sights on bringing in the wonderful oratorio and lieder singer Fritz Wunderlich, and needed all the persuasiveness at my command to convince him that he was right for the role. Fortunately a recording of this inspired German tenor with the Italian timbre has captured his performance of this part for the gratification and delight of posterity.

Of course Dermota, and all his Viennese fans, were disappointed and cross with me, but Dermota had several later opportunities to perform this role, which he loved so much, and which truly suited him to a T. He had lived a satisfying singer's life, but I'm afraid he never forgave me for having disabused him of the expectation he would take part in the first performance. In the course of our careers, though, we all have to learn that we must occasionally forego some of our secret hopes and dreams. On the podium for all the performances was the thoroughbred musician Josef Krips, who saw to it that Pfitzner's true spirit was reverently preserved.

The chronicle of my directorial activity includes another four operas staged for the Municipal Theater in Dortmund. Along with that house's general music director, Wilhelm Schüchter, a conductor highly regarded by Herbert von Karajan among others, I was able to work truly hand in hand on the Wagner operas *Der fliegende Holländer, Lohengrin,* and *Tristan und Isolde.*

The remembrance of another opera produced for this house, Werner Egk's *Die Zaubergeige* (The Magic Fiddle), holds even greater significance for me because of the participation of the composer as conductor of that production. He was no stranger to me, as I had worked with him on the world premiere of the piece back in 1935, when it was conducted by Hans Schmidt-Isserstedt with yours truly on the stage of the Hamburg State Opera in the role of Kaspar.

I have retained a very positive remembrance of this entire Dortmund period, marked by an ideal working climate. With just a few exceptions, all the solo roles were cast with members of the regular ensemble, which guaranteed us an excellent continuity for our work. This directorial phase was followed by Vienna productions of the Strauss operas *Arabella* and *Die schweigsame Frau,* in which I had the somewhat less thankful task of warming up productions originally conceived by Rudolf Hartmann.

Two more Wagner stagings—*Tannhäuser* in Zurich and *Parsifal* in Hamburg—were regrettably failures because of lack of experience on my part. Spoiled by the wonderful partnership with Schneider-Siemssen, I unfortunately underestimated the effect that differences of opinion between designer and director can have on a production and neglected making the effort I should have exerted to set forth my own artistic point of view. The consequence was that in both cases the success of the productions knew bounds (to put it mildly).

To the oft-asked question of why my satisfyingly launched directing career came to such an abrupt halt, I have no real answer. I believe the main reason was the development of a new form of operatic production, which is an acquired taste I never acquired—nor did I wish to. Yet anyone who knows how little I thought of what was happening on stage during my early years as a singer will have no trouble believing that I am keenly interested in the principle of innovation. I am anything but hardheadedly determined to praise everything in the past and condemn anything new and forward-looking. I still cherish the memory of Wieland Wagner's statement, "I'm not so stubborn as to believe every innovation I want to carry out is necessarily the be-all and end-all, but perhaps some of the things I want to do now may lead us to a newer, even better way in the future." I can only agree. In other words, I don't reject many of the things I cannot accept out of hand. I look with an open heart, but not with totally blind faith, toward a future I am not too old to understand or appreciate, even though I am no longer all that young in years.

I only ask myself occasionally why a Wieland Wagner lived and spent an entire lifetime trying to expunge old-fashioned, artificial posturing on the operatic stage from our performances when often today, in glaring contrast to the truly modern concept of new stagings, the whole business of directing the individual soloist is so sadly neglected. Why do stage directors accept the way so many lyric artists pay homage to an ancient, antedated acting style, which would have better suited some of the singers that came along before the First World War? Nowadays, how much we miss the cleansing influence of a genius like Jean-Pierre Ponnelle!

❧ Chapter 21 ❧

Having spent my childhood and student days in Munich, I received my first musical impressions from that city's artistic life. It was in the 1920s, in other words more than eighty years ago, that I began attending concerts and performances of opera and drama there. This was the time when, like many another youngster my age, I began thinking about my future occupation. I have already described how I may have set my sights on doing something in the music field but certainly had no intention of embarking on a singing career.

I should mention that musical life in a big city like Munich, Dresden, Berlin, and Vienna back then was certainly very different than it is today. Audiences then differed greatly from today's audience in their attitude toward recital singing. As radio and recordings were still in their infancy, the only way to communicate music effectively was directly from the concert platform. Concert audiences had a rich selection of recitals, most of them featuring the local stars of the operatic stage. Thus it was understandable that people primarily wanted to see and hear their favorite operatic celebrities in a different guise, a bit more as they really were without costumes or character makeup. It made no difference to them if the celebrated opera star was a real lieder singer, had sufficient sensitivity for this style of music, or possessed the necessary understanding for the importance of the poetic word—criteria that go without saying for today's audiences.

Anyone who takes the trouble to listen to art song recordings from those days, despite their technical drawbacks, can clearly see what little value people then placed on loyalty to the work, the style, and the composer's specific musical instructions. Of course, every era had artists who were born to sing lieder, vocalists with an innate instinct for the demands of recital singing.

The love of songs and the joy of presenting them are emotions that have been with me throughout my entire life. This fact was corroborated and supported by experiencing in actual practice the way an ongoing healthy changeover between the drama of opera and the lyricism of recital singing gave me a much longer singing career than I might otherwise have enjoyed; my vocal resources were never one-sidedly stressed. It is most certainly not my intention to accord the lied a higher value than the operatic aria; I am quite aware that I would never have been able to mount the concert platform had the path to it not been smoothed for me by my operatic career. For all of this, I make no secret of the fact that I had a long struggle to quash the bias against me as a recitalist. At the beginning, people were totally unwilling to accept the dramatic Wagner interpreter in the gentle lyricism of a Franz Schubert or the fine-grained humor of Eduard Mörike as set to music by Hugo Wolf. But my battle against this prejudice also had its good side: it mobilized my ambition and released new, unforeseen energies.

Certainly not every operatic voice is suited for the gentle art song any more than a master of lyrical tones is invariably fit to take arms against the surge of a voluminous Wagnerian orchestra. I think every lieder specialist should likewise face the challenge of an operatic aria once in a while, just as every true opera star delectates in the concentrated tension contained in the subtle phrasing of an art song.

My personal worry in the area of vocal culture, and especially as a teacher, is the troubling, steadily increasing neglect of language in singing. Unfortunately I really can't help believing that much of this linguistic distortion is quite conscious and intentional. I am happy to be able to say that everyone who instructed me, starting with my own singing teacher, always insisted on my paying attention to language in singing. How can any listener be able to draw full satisfaction from a poem if it is not presented in the garb of proper declamation?

Today, in the late autumn of my life, when, in the words of Friedrich Rückert in his poem "Mit vierzig Jahren" (At the age of forty) "on the way to the port, the path has begun to slope imperceptibly downward," the heart has nonetheless remained sufficiently young to "enjoy and be glad." I have become truly aware that a life with these songs have opened up the full glory of the rhymed language of a Johann Wolfgang von Goethe, Heinrich Heine, Eduard Mörike, and Friedrich Rückert for me far more than would have been the case without the medium of song.

I believe the most precious legacy my beloved, oft-mentioned teacher Römer passed on to me in all the years of our work together was the insistence he manifested in his wish to awaken and develop in me the joy and interest in teaching, a gift that he possessed in the fullest measure. At a very early stage of my vocal training, he convinced me that people are better able to hear and control their own singing the more they have learned to hear and control a pupil.

One of the main difficulties in "learning" how to sing is that, in contrast to learning to play an instrument, most of the tone-producing functions cannot be seen, they take place, so to speak, "inside" us. The only "organ of control" that remains is the ear. This is why it is so important to learn how to "listen to ourselves." I have always noted that very few singers, even among the most prominent, have ever really learned to listen to themselves.

And few of them are aware that someone singing is going to hear a totally different sound from the one heard by the listener. Here's the proof: there is nobody who, when first hearing his singing or speaking voice recorded, has not said, "What? Was *that* my voice?"

I took my first steps as a teacher while still under the aegis of Matthäus Römer. He simply let me take his seat at the piano, and my poor victims— all pupils of my teacher's—were consigned to my tender mercies. As time went on, I began observing Römer in his teaching function. Gradually I became accustomed to making his way of saying things and his terms of the trade my own. In fact, I still find myself using them today.

The study of singing, as far as the student is concerned, begins with the selection of the right teacher. For a number of obvious reasons, this decision is paramount yet, for most people, not very easy. Normally, a still inexperienced young person is hardly in a position to take this decision alone, but should seek the advice and assistance of a suitable professional; it goes without saying that a good teacher-student relationship must be built on the firm foundation of mutual trust, the suitability of the two people to work together and develop a certain rapport with one another. This is why it's always a good idea for both sides to agree on a trial period. In the final analysis it is and always will be a question of luck whether or not we find the teacher who teaches us what we need.

Another significant element is the time a learner needs until he has reached his goal. The careers that develop slowly are not always the worst ones—quite the contrary. My teacher always used to say, "There are no good teachers, there are only good pupils."

It is really no secret that a successful career does not automatically qualify even an excellent singer to be a good teacher. Teaching calls for a few anything-but-everyday qualities: certainly an abundance of patience and endurance, the capacity to regard and treat each learner as an individual, and never to operate in line with some catchall system or scheme. If the only reason singers, no matter how successful they may once have been, want to engage in this activity is because the spotlight on their already dimmed halo has totally gone out, or life in retirement is dull, then they really should stay assiduously away from teaching.

I would now like to say a little about a form of study that didn't exist back in my own years of training and to which I have devoted more time after I discontinued giving private instruction: master classes. I think very highly of this institution, provided that the right people are taking part. I personally prefer lieder classes to opera classes, simply because they arouse a common interest on the part of singers in all the various voice categories. Also, in recital singing, considerations of vocal technique take a back seat to interpretive requirements, in other words, style and musicality.

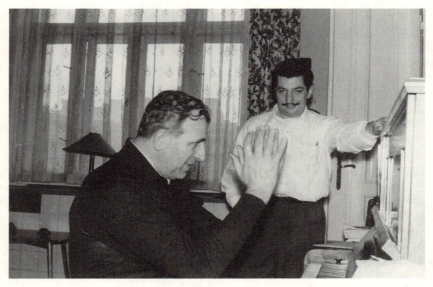

21.1.   Teaching voice has always been a source of enormous satisfaction to me even when the students do not pursue singing careers. I taught Donald Arthur in a master class in Aspen, Colorado, then later in Europe. Years later, when he moved on to acting and writing, we reunited to collaborate on this book.

As often mentioned, I find every aspect of language extremely interesting. The quality of the rhymed poetic word and its preferential treatment have always been very near to my heart. The prerequisite for participation in a master class should be an advanced level of vocal and artistic development. The objective and the success of such a class depend on the degree to which the participants are in a position to form an opinion of their own on matters of interpretation, style, and all other artistic-musical matters. This is why I like to call this kind of institution a seminar.

Most of my comments have their origin in impressions and experiences I received in the time during and following my studies with Matthäus Römer. Many considerations only came into my full awareness and understanding after years of maturation. Perhaps this is the appropriate moment to pay a closing homage to him. Throughout his own life he made it very hard for me to find out anything interesting about him, because he was so modest that he always simply pooh-poohed anything to do with himself as unimportant. He did all he could to avoid any discussion of his artistic development. The little I know about him comes either from occasional conversations with his wife or incomplete reports from friends and acquaintances, the reliability of which I couldn't swear to.

Matthäus Römer was born in 1875 near Bamberg in Central Franconia and completed a doctorate in modern languages. At a relatively early age he also concurrently took singing lessons from the highly renowned Viennese operatic and concert basso, Dr. Felix von Kraus, who had studied harmony in his own youth with no less an authority than Anton Bruckner, and who had been engaged by Cosima Wagner for the Bayreuth Festival, where for several years he sang all the major bass roles in Wagner's operas. I've already mentioned his studies with the great Polish tenor Jean de Reszke at the instigation of his wife, who had also been a singer. During my own lessons, he often quoted from de Reszke when making vocal and musical points.

In the summer of 1909, teacher Felix von Kraus and his former student Matthäus Römer joined forces on the stage of the Bayreuth Festival in a *Parsifal* production conducted by Karl Muck. This festival summer also marked the beginning of my teacher's friendship with Siegfried Wagner, from which I subsequently profited when, as previously reported, I was allowed to audition for the head of the festival shortly before his death in 1930.

I've already mentioned his connection with the Royal Bavarian Court and his acquisition of the hunting lodge where I took many of my singing lessons during my vacations from the academy, making the trip from Munich to the lodge, near the town of Kreuth on Tegernsee Lake in the Alpine foothills by bicycle.

Since then, as my own singing career gradually slowed down, and I made it the task of my later life to concentrate more on vocal instruction, I have tried to institute a kind of apostolic succession, passing along the ideas and inspiration I received from my teacher, and thus indirectly from Jean de Reszke, Felix von Kraus, and their teachers, combined with some experience of my own, to my students. This way I was able to go through the slow decline of my own career without a trace of bitterness, such as I have often observed in the lives of colleagues, who view this decline as the tragic end of everything meaningful in life.

The little hunting lodge near Kreuth has become the site for a precious memory of a great human being I last saw there before he left us in the year of Our Lord 1954—the same year two other great musicians departed this earth forever: Clemens Krauss and Wilhelm Furtwängler.

My attempt to purchase his grave and retain it as a memorial to him came to naught. The parish priest in Kreuth rejected my request: he said the village of Kreuth was becoming overpopulated, and the cemetery there needed the land for new graves.

For here we have no continuing city
— HEBREWS 13

Discography

Not all of Hans Hotter's vast collection of recordings are still available, but, as much superb music returns to the market on re-releases, of course catalogue numbers change, and labels often vary from country to country. While we have researched this discography to the best of our ability, readers are kindly advised to check with retailers, the Internet, or other sources on availability and current labels in their territory.

Johann Sebastian Bach
"Ich habe genug," Cantata BWV 82, Philharmonia Orchestra London, conducted by Anthony Bernard, recorded March 22 and 24, 1950 in Kingsway Hall, London (EMI 555–763 198–2).

Ludwig van Beethoven
Lieder "Abendlied unterm gestirnten Himmel," "Des Kriegers Abschied" with Michael Raucheisen, piano, recorded between 1942 and 1944 in Berlin (Acanta CD 43 126).

Symphony No. 9 in D minor, Opus 125:
   1. Elisabeth Schwarzkopf, soprano; Elisabeth Höngen, mezzo-soprano; Julius Patzak, tenor; Wiener Singverein and Vienna Philharmonic Orchestra conducted by Herbert von Karajan, recorded on December 10, 12 and 14, 1947, in the Musikvereinssaal, Vienna (EMI 555–761 076–2).
   2. Aase Nordmo-Løvberg, soprano; Christa Ludwig, mezzo-soprano; Waldemar Kmentt, tenor; Philharmonia Orchestra, London, conducted by Otto Klemperer, recorded between November 21 and 23, 1957, in Kingsway Hall, London (TESTAMENT SBT 1177).

Opera *Fidelio:* Opus 72 Sena Jurinac, soprano; Elsie Morrison, soprano; Jon Vickers, tenor; John Dobson, tenor; Joseph Ward, tenor; Gottlob Frick, bass; Forbes Robinson, bass; Victor Godfrey, bass; Chorus and Orchestra of the Royal Opera House Covent Garden, London, conducted by Otto

Klemperer, recorded on March 7, 1960, in the Royal Opera House, Covent Garden, London (TESTAMENT SBT2 1328).

Alban Berg
Opera *Lulu:*
   1. Cynthia Clarey, soprano; Catherine Estourelle, soprano; Patricia Wise, soprano; Laura Zannini, soprano; Brigitte Fassbaender, mezzo-soprano; Graham Clark, tenor, Stuart Kale, tenor; Peter Straka, tenor; Francis Dudziak, baritone; Ernst Gutstein, baritone; Wolfgang Schöne, bass; Bodo Schwanbeck, bass; Orchestra National de France, Paris conducted by Jeffrey Tate, recorded in 1987 at the Théâtre du Châtelet, Paris (EMI 667–754 622–2).
   2. Anja Silja, soprano; Brigitte Fassbaender, mezzo-soprano; Trudeliese Schmidt, mezzo-soprano; Josef Hopfenwieser, tenor; Werner Krenn, tenor; Heinz Zednik, tenor; Walter Berry, baritone; Kurt Moll, bass; Harald Pröglhöf, bass; Manfred Schenk, bass; Alfred Sramek, bass, Vienna Philharmonic Orchestra conducted by Christoph von Dohnányi, recorded in 1976 in the Sofiensaal, Vienna (Decca 430415–2).

Hector Berlioz
Opera-Oratorio *La damnation de Faust*, Opus 24 (sung in German): Elisabeth Schwarzkopf, soprano; Frans Vroons, tenor; Alois Pernerstorfer, bass, Chorus and Orchestra of the Lucerne Festival conducted by Wilhelm Furtwängler, recorded on August 26, 1950, in Lucerne (Fonit Cetra Furtwängler Edition FE 21).

Georges Bizet
Aria "Votre toast, je peux vous le rendre" (Toreador Song) from the opera *Carmen,* Orchestra of the German State Opera, Berlin conducted by Artur Rother, recorded in 1942 in Berlin (Fono Pr 90 200).

Johannes Brahms
Ein deutsches Requiem, Opus 45: Elisabeth Schwarzkopf, soprano; Singverein der Gesellschaft der Musikfreunde; Vienna Philharmonic Orchestra conducted by Herbert von Karajan, recorded October 20–22 and 27–29, 1947 in the Musikvereinssaal, Vienna (EMI EAC30109).

Quartets from *Liebeslieder Walzer*, Opus 52, nos. 6, 9, 16, 17, and 18: Irmgard Seefried, soprano; Elisabeth Höngen, mezzo-soprano; Hugo Meyer-Welfing, tenor; Friedrich Wührer, piano; Hermann von Nordberg, piano; recorded on November 16, 1947 (EMI RLS 1547003).

Lieder "Botschaft," "Heimweh," "Minnelied," "Sommerabend," "Mondenschein," "In Waldeinsamkeit," "Feldeinsamkeit," "Auf dem Kirchhofe,"

"Ständchen" song cycle *Vier ernste Gesänge,* Opus 121 with Gerald Moore, piano, recorded in EMI Studio 1A, London (EMI 555–763 198–2).

Lieder "Wie bist du, meine Königin," "Ruhe, Süssliebchen," "Treue Liebe dauert lange," "Wenn du nur zuweilen lächelst," "Dämmrung senkte sich von oben," "Dein blaues Auge," "Willst du, dass ich geh?" "Versunken," "Todessehnen," "Mit vierzig Jahren ist der Berg," "Kein Haus, keine Heimat" with Michael Raucheisen, piano, recorded on February 9 and April 29, 1944, in Berlin (Acanta 40.23.524).

Lieder "Sonntag," "Ständchen" with Michael Raucheisen, piano, recorded in September, 1950 (RIAS Berlin LW 45).

Lieder "Mit vierzig Jahren ist der Berg," "Auf dem Kirchhofe"; song cycle *Die schöne Magelone,* Opus 33, no. 9, with Geoffrey Pasons, piano, recorded in May 1973 in the Sofiensaal, Vienna (Decca SXL 6738).

Lieder "Wie Melodien zieht es mir," "Sonntag," "Komm bald," "Wir wandelten," "Wie bist du, meine Königin," "Heimkehr," "Wenn du mir nur zuweilen lächelst," "Verrat" with Gerald Moore, piano (TESTAMENT SBT 1198).

Lieder "Sonntag," "Ständchen," "Mit vierzig Jahren" with Michael Raucheisen and Gerald Moore, piano (TESTAMENT SBT 1199).

Peter Cornelius
Lied "Komm, wir wandeln zusammen im Mondenschein" with Hans Dokoupil, piano, recorded in 1968 (Fono Pr 93 390).

Gottfried von Einem
Opera *Der Besuch der alten Dame,* Opus 35: Laurence Detour, soprano; Emmy Loose, soprano; Christa Ludwig, mezzo-soprano; Ewald Aichberger, tenor; Hans Beirer, tenor; Kurt Equiluz, tenor; Karl Terkal, tenor; Heinz Zednik, tenor; Sigfried Rudolf Freese, baritone; Eberhard Wächter, baritone; Hans Braun, bass-baritone; Manfred Jungwirth, bass; Alois Pernerstorfer, bass; Harald Pröglhöf, bass; Chorus of the Vienna State Opera, Vienna Philharmonic conducted by Horst Stein, recorded on May 23, 1971, in the Vienna State Opera (world première) (DG 419 552–1).

Robert Franz
Lieder "Aus meinen grossen Schmerzen," "Für Musik," "Das macht das dunkelgrüne Land," "Es hat die Rose sich beklagt" with Hans Dokoupil, piano, recorded in 1968 or 1969 (Fono Pr 93 390).

Edvard Grieg
Song "Jeg elsker dig" (sung in German) with Michael Raucheisen, piano, recorded in September 1950 in Berlin (RIAS Berlin LW 45).

Song "Jeg elsker dig" (sung in German) with Gerald Moore, piano (TESTAMENT SBT 1199).

Georg Friedrich Händel
Aria "Aure, deh per pietà" from the opera *Giulio Cesare*; aria "Shall I in Mamre's Fertile Plain?" from the oratorio *Joshua*; aria "How Willing my Paternal Love" from the oratorio *Samson;* Philharmonia Orchestra, London conducted by George Weldon, recorded on November 10, 1951, at EMI Studios, London (EMI EX 2913213).

Franz Joseph Haydn
Oratorio *Die Schöpfung* with Irmgard Seefried, soprano; Walther Ludwig, tenor; Bavarian Radio Chorus and Orchestra conducted by Eugen Jochum, recorded in 1952 in Munich (Melodram Mel 208).

Songs from *Lieder und Canzonetten*, Hob 26a No F1 "Abschiedslied" with Michael Raucheisen, piano, recorded on November 19, 1943 (Acanta 43 126).

Ruggiero Leoncavallo
"Si può" (Prologue) (sung in German) from the opera *Pagliacci,* Orchestra of the German State Opera, Berlin, conducted by Artur Rother, recorded in Berlin in 1942 (Koch International Munich Ko 31 472–2).

Franz Liszt
Lieder from the cycle *Gesänge des Harfners,* no. 2, "Wer nie sein Brot mit Tränen ass"; and from the cycle *Wanderers Nachtlied,* no. 1, "Über allen Gipfeln ist Ruh" with Michael Raucheisen, piano, recorded on February 9, 1944 (Acanta 40 23 563).

Carl Loewe
Ballads, songs and legends
Lieder "Archibald Douglas"; "Graf Eberstein" from the cycle 5, *Heitere Gesänge und Romanzen*; "Der Nöck" with Hans Dokoupil, piano (Fono Pr 90 390).

Lieder "Der Wirtin Töchterlein," recorded on February 9, 1944; "Herr Oluf," recorded on September 24, 1943; "Der König auf dem Turme" and "Über allen Gipfeln ist Ruh" from the cycle *Sechs Nachtgesäng*, recorded on

February 7, 1944; "Graf Eberhards Weissdorn" from the cycle *Gesänge der Sehnsucht*, recorded 1943/1944; "Urgrossvaters Gesellschaft," probably recorded in 1944; "Wirkung in der Ferne," recorded on February 3, 1944; "Hinkende Jamben," recorded on February 9, 1944; "Trommelständchen," recorded on February 9, 1944, with Michael Raucheisen, piano (Acanta 40. 23.584).

Lieder "Edward," "Erlkönig," "Hinkende Jamben," "Odins Meeresritt" with Gerald Moore, piano, recorded on October 8, 1957, and November 18, 1957, in the EMI Studios, London (EMI AB8010).

Lieder "Hochzeitslied," "Die wandelnde Glocke," "Hinkende Jamben," "Odins Meeresritt" with Geoffrey Parsons, piano, recorded in May, 1973, in the Sofiensaal, Vienna (Decca 6.48277).

Lieder "Gregor auf dem Stein," recorded on February 7, 1944; "Die Heinzelmännchen," recorded on February 9, 1944; "Prinz Eugen," recorded on January 19, 1945; "Die verfallene Mühle," recorded on September 24, 1943; "Odins Meeresritt," recorded on September 25, 1943, with Michael Raucheisen, piano (Acanta 40 23 534).

Lieder "Edward," "Erlkönig," "Odins Meeresritt," "Die wandelnde Glocke," "Hinkende Jamben" with Gerald Moore, piano, recorded on October 8, 1957, and November 18, 1957, in the EMI Studios, London (TESTAMENT SBT 1198).

Mark Lothar
Kleine Weihnachtsgeschichte, Opus 51, with Mark Lothar, piano (Private Edition 60.531).

Franz Marschner
Hans Heiling's aria "An jenem Tag, da du mir Treue versprochen" from the opera *Hans Heiling*; Orchestra of the Städtische Oper, Berlin conducted by Artur Rother (Fono Pr 90 200).

Wolfgang Amadeus Mozart
Opera *Le nozze di Figaro* (sung in German), K 492: Irma Beilke, soprano; Helena Braun, soprano; Gerda Sommerschuh, soprano; Liane Timm, soprano; Res Fischer, contralto; William Wernigk, tenor; Josef Witt, tenor; Erich Kunz, baritone; Gustav Neidlinger, bass-baritone; Franz Normann, bass; Chorus of the Vienna State Opera, Vienna Philharmonic conducted by Clemens Krauss, recorded at the 1942 Salzburg Festival (Fono Pr 90 203).

Requiem, K. 626: Elisabeth Grümmer, soprano; Gertrude Pitzinger, contralto; Helmut Krebs, tenor; RIAS Chamber Chorus, Choir of St. Hedwig's Cathedral, Berlin, and RIAS Symphony Orchestra, Berlin, conducted by Ferenc Fricsay, recorded on March 5, 1951 (DGG 455–400–2).

Opera *Die Zauberflöte,* K. 620:

1. Antonia Fahberg, soprano; Hildegard Hillebrecht, soprano; Evelyn Lear, soprano; Lisa Otto, soprano; Roberta Peters, soprano; Rosl Schwaiger, soprano; Cvetka Ahlin, mezzo-soprano; Raili Kostia, mezzo-soprano; Sieglinde Wagner, mezzo-soprano; James King, tenor; Friedrich Lenz, tenor; Martin Vantin, tenor; Fritz Wunderlich, tenor; Dietrich Fischer-Dieskau, baritone; Hubert Hilten, bass; Manfred Röhrl, bass; Franz Crass, bass; Kurt Moll, bass; Martti Talvela, bass; RIAS Chamber Chorus, Berlin, Berlin Philharmonic conducted by Karl Böhm, recorded in June, 1964, in Berlin (DG 429 877–2).

2. Lisa della Casa, soprano; Erika Köth, soprano; Graziella Sciutti, soprano; Léopold Simoneau, tenor; Karl Dönch, baritone; Walter Berry, baritone; Kurt Böhme, bass; Chorus of the Vienna State Opera, Vienna Philharmonic conducted by George Szell, recorded at the Salzburg Festival on July 27, 1959 (Melodram Mel 007).

Modest Mussorgsky
Opera *Boris Godunov*: Martha Mödl, soprano; Hans Hopf, tenor; Lorenz Fehenberger, tenor; Hermann Uhde, baritone; Kurt Böhme, bass; Kim Borg, bass; Radio Bavaria Chorus and Orchestra conducted by Eugen Jochum, recorded between May 3 and 10, 1957, in Munich (Myto 3MCD 953.131).

Otto Nicolai
Lieder Opus 34, no. 9, WoO nos. 1, 3, and 5 with Michael Raucheisen, piano, recorded in 1942 (Acanta 40.23 542).

Carl Orff
Opera *Der Mond*: Rudolf Christ, tenor; Helmut Graml, baritone; Albrecht Peter, baritone; Karl Schmitt-Walter, baritone; Willy Rösner, narrator; Teresa Holloway, narrator; Children's Chorus, Philharmonia Chorus and Orchestra, London, conducted by Wolfgang Sawallisch, recorded in October 1958 (EMI 653–763 712–2).

Hans Pfitzner
Opera *Palestrina*: Käthe Nentwig, soprano; Franz Klarwein, tenor; Julius Patzak, tenor; Ferdinand Frantz, baritone; Albrecht Peter, baritone; Benno

Kusche, bass; Georg Wieter, bass; Chorus and Orchestra of the Bavarian State Opera, Munich, conducted by Robert Heger, recorded in 1952 (Melodram Mel 429).

"Dass nun die Andacht im Gefühle" (Borromeo's monologue) from *Palestrina,* Chorus of the Vienna State Opera, Vienna Philharmonic conducted by Rudolf Moralt (Koch 31 471–2).

Choral Fantasy *Das dunkle Reich*, Opus 38; Annelies Kupper, soprano; Cantata *Urworte, orphisch*, Opus 57; Cantata *Von deutscher Seele*, Opus 28; Clara Ebers, soprano; Gertrude Pitzinger, contralto; Walther Ludwig, tenor; Bavarian Radio Orchestra and Chorus conducted by Robert Heger, recorded in 1952 (Orfeo 273.922).

Lieder Opus 2, no. 2; Opus 7, no.1; Opus 11, no. 2; Opus 22, no. 4; Opus 29, nos. 3 and 4; Opus 30, no. 3; Opus 32, nos. 1–4 with Michael Raucheisen, piano, recorded on September 25, 1943 (Opus 2), and (Opus 2, 22, 29, no. 4), January 18 and 19, 1945 (Opus 11), and January 28, 1945 (Opus 30 and 29, no. 4), all in Berlin (Acanta 40.23.532).

Gioachino Rossini
"La calunnia è un venticello" (sung in German), Don Basilio's aria from the opera *Il barbiere di Siviglia,* Orchestra of the Städtische Oper, Berlin, conducted by Artur Rother, recorded in 1941 (Acanta DE 22.017).

Arnold Schönberg
Oratorio - *Die Gurre-Lieder:*
    1. Susan Dunn, soprano; Brigitte Fassbaender, mezzo-soprano; Peter Haage, tenor; Siegfried Jerusalem, tenor; Hermann Becht, bass-baritone; Choir of St. Hedwig's Cathedral, Berlin, Chorus of the Musikverein, Düsseldorf, and Radio Symphony Orchestra, Berlin, conducted by Riccardo Chailly (Polygram Records 30321).
    2. Eva Marton, soprano; Florence Quivar, mezzo-soprano; Jon Garrison, tenor; Gary Lakes, tenor; John Cheek, bass-baritone; New York Choral Artists, New York Philharmonic Orchestra conducted by Zubin Mehta (Sony CD 48 077).

Franz Schubert
Songs and song cycles
Lieder "Greisengesang," "Der Kreuzzug," "Wanderers Nachtlied" with Hans Dokoupil, piano, recorded 1968/69 in Vienna (Fono Pr 93 390).

Lieder "Abschied," "An die Musik," "Geheimes," "Im Abendrot," "Im Frühling," "Der Lindenbaum," "Sei mir gegrüsst," "Ständchen," "Wanderers
Nachtlied No 2" with Gerald Moore, piano, recorded in October and November 1967 in London (EMI 35583).

Lieder "Gruppe aus dem Tartarus," "Im Frühling," "Alinde," "An die Ent-
fernte," "Liebesbotschaft," "Die Stadt," "Der Doppelgänger," "Die Tauben-
post" with Geoffrey Parsons, piano, recorded in May 1973 in the Sofiensaal,
Vienna (Decca 6.482777).

Lieder "An eine Quelle," "Auf der Donau," "Dem Unendlichen," "Des Fis-
chers Liebesglück," "Du bist die Ruh," "Greisengesang," "Gruppe aus dem
Tartarus," "Prometheus," "Der Wanderer," "Der Wanderer an den Mond"
with Hans Altmann, piano, from the archives of Bavarian Broadcasting, recorded 1952 (Fono Pr 93 145).

Song cycle *Schwanengesang*, recorded on May 29 & 30, 1954; and Lieder
"Am Bach im Frühling," "An die Musik," "Geheimes," "Gruppe aus dem Tartarus," "Im Abendrot," "Im Frühling," "Meeresstille," "Sei mir gegrüsst,"
"Wanderers Nachtlied" with Gerald Moore, piano, recorded in October,
1957 at EMI Studios, London (EMI 555–565 196–2).

Lieder from the song cycle *Schwanengesang:* "Der Doppelgänger," "Die
Stadt," "Meeresstille," "Der Wanderer," "Wanderers Nachtlied" with Hermann von Nordberg, piano, recorded on November 6, 1946, in the Brahmssaal, Vienna (songs 2–4), and on April 12, 1948, and October 1, 1949, in
EMI Studios, London (EMI RLS 766).

Lieder from *Schwanengesang:* "Der Atlas," "Ihr Bild," "Die Stadt," "Am
Meer," "Der Doppelgänger" with Michael Raucheisen, piano, recorded on
August 4, 1950 (Acanta 442 117–2).

Song cycle *Die Winterreise:*
    1. With Michael Raucheisen, piano, recorded on September 24 and 25,
1943 (DG 437 351–2).
    2. With Gerald Moore, piano, recorded on May 24, 25, and 29, 1954 in
EMI Studios (EMI 555–761 002–2).
    3. With Erik Werba, piano, recorded December 15–18, 1961 in the
Brahmssaal, Vienna (DG 138 778/79).

Robert Schumann
Song cycle *Dichterliebe,* Opus 48; with Hans Altmann, piano, recorded in 1954, from the archives of Bavarian Broadcasting (Fono Pr 93 145).

Lieder from the song cycle *Liebesfrühling*: "Ich hab in mich gesogen," "Warum willst du andere Fragen" (actually by Clara Schumann, but published as part of Robert Schumann's song cycle), "So wahr die Sonne scheint," from Opus 49 "Die beiden Grenadiere," from Opus 98 "Ballade des Harfners—'Was hör ich draussen vor dem Tor'," with Michael Raucheisen, piano (Acanta 43.126), recorded on February 7, 1944 and April 29, 1943, and Gerald Moore, piano, recorded in October and November 1957 in London EMI 33 CX 1661.

Richard Strauss
Opera *Arabella,* Opus 79: Lisa della Casa, soprano; Herma Handl, soprano; Maria Reining, soprano; Rosette Anday, mezzo-soprano; Ruth Michaelis, mezzo-soprano; Julius Patzak, tenor; Horst Taubmann, tenor; Alfred Poell, baritone; Franz Szokan, baritone; Georg Hann, bass-baritone; Chorus of the Vienna State Opera, Vienna Philharmonic conducted by Karl Böhm, recorded at the Salzburg Festival on August 12, 1947 (DG 445 491–2).

Opera Capriccio, Opus 85:
   1. Ilse Hollweg, soprano; Viorica Ursuleac, soprano; Hertha Töpper, mezzo-soprano; Ratko Delorko, tenor; Emil Graf, tenor; Rudolf Schock, tenor; Hans Braun, baritone; Karl Schmitt-Walter, baritone; Georg Wieter, bass; Bavarian Radio Symphony Orchestra conducted by Clemens Krauss, recorded in 1854 in Munich (Archives of Bavarian Broadcasting).
   2. Anna Moffo, soprano; Elisabeth Schwarzkopf, soprano; Christa Ludwig, mezzo-soprano, Rudolf Christ, tenor; Nicolai Gedda, tenor; Dermot Troy, tenor; Dietrich Fischer-Dieskau, baritone; Karl Schmitt-Walter, baritone; Eberhard Wächter, baritone, Philharmonia Orchestra, London, conducted by Wolfgang Sawallisch, redorded in Kingsway Hall, London September 2–11, 1957, and on March 28, 1957 (EMI 667749 0148).
   3. Irma Beilke, soprano; Viorica Ursuleac, soprano; Hildegard Ranczak, soprano; Franz Klarwein, tenor; Carl Seydel, tenor; Horst Taubmann, tenor; Walter Höfermayer, baritone; Georg Hann, bass; Bavarian State Orchestra conducted by Clemens Krauss. recorded on October 28, 1942 (BASF 102163–3).

Opera *Elektra*, Opus 58: Astrid Varnay, soprano; Leonie Rysanek, soprano; Gertie Charlent, soprano; Helen Tetrich, soprano; Käthe Tatzmann, soprano; Käthe Molin, soprano; Jane Cook, soprano; Res Fischer, contralto; Marianne

Schröder, contralto; Trude Rösler, contralto; Ilse Ihme-Sabisch, contralto; Helmut Melchert, tenor; Hasso Eschert, tenor; Heiner Horn, bass; Leo Heppe, bass; Chorus and Symphony Orchestra of West German Radio conducted by Richard Kraus, recorded in August 1953 in Cologne (Gala GL 100 512).

Opera *Die Frau ohne Schatten,* Opus 65: Inge Borkh, soprano; Martha Mödl, soprano; Ingrid Bjoner, soprano; Jess Thomas, tenor; Bavarian State Opera Orchestra and Chorus conducted by Joseph Keilberth, recorded on November 21, 1963 (DG 138 911/14).

Opera *Salome,* Opus 54:
 1. Inge Borkh, soprano; Gertrud Ebeling, soprano; Irmgard Barth, contralto; Katja Sabo, contralto; Georg Binder, tenor; Walther Carnuth, tenor; Lorenz Fehenberger, tenor; Peter Kaussen, tenor; Max Lorenz, tenor; Karl Ostertag, tenor; Albrecht Peter, baritone; Fritz Friedrich, baritone; Carl Hoppe, baritone; Adolf Keil, baritone; Max Proebstl, bass; Rudolf Wünzer, bass; Bavarian State Orchestra conducted by Joseph Keilberth, recorded on July 21, 1951, at the Munich Opera Festival (Orfeo C 342932).
 2. Ljuba Welitsch, soprano; Elisabeth Höngen, mezzo-soprano; Set Svanholm, tenor; Brian Sullivan, tenor; Orchestra of the Metropolitan Opera, New York, conducted by Fritz Reiner, recorded in 1952 at the Metropolitan Opera House, New York (Myto 2 MCD 952.125).

Opera *Die schweigsame Frau,* Opus 80: Pierette Alarie, soprano; Hilde Güden, soprano; Hetty Plümacher, mezzo-soprano; Georgine von Milinkoviã, contralto; Fritz Wunderlich, tenor; Josef Knapp, baritone; Hermann Prey, baritone; Karl Dönch, bass-baritone; Alois Pernerstorfer, bass; Vienna State Opera Chorus and Vienna Philharmonic conducted by Karl Böhm, recorded on August 8, 1959, at the Salzburg Festival (DG 445 335–2).

Ballad "Taillefer," Opus 52: Maria Cebotari, soprano; Walther Ludwig, tenor; Singgemeinschaft Rudolf Lamy and the Berlin Radio Symphony Orchestra conducted by Artur Rother, recorded in 1943 (Fono Pr 90 222).

Lieder "Nichts," "Die Georgine," "All mein Gedanken, mein Herz und mein Sinn," "Du meines Herzens Krönelein," "Ruhe, meine Seele," " ′Nachtgang," "Ich trage meine Minne," "Sehnsucht," "Himmelsboten," "Freundliche Vision," "Wer lieben will," "Das Thal," "Der Einsame," "Gefunden," "Im Spätboot," "Mit deinen blauen Augen," "Im Sonnenschein" with Walter Klien, piano, recorded on July 27 or 28, 1967, in the Konzerthaus Studio, Vienna (Fono Pr 93 367).

Lieder "All mein Gedanken, mein Herz und mein Sinn," "Du meines Herzens Krönelein," "Ach weh, mir unglückhaften Mann" with Geoffrey Parsons, piano, recorded in May, 1973 in the Sofiensaal, Vienna (Decca 6.48277).

Lieder "Ach weh, mir unglückhaften Mann," "Ich trage meine Minne" with Gerald Moore, piano, recorded in October/November 1957 (EMI 5–60025).

Giuseppe Verdi
Opera *Aida* (selections, sung in German):
   1. Danica Illitsch, soprano; Elena Nikolaidi, mezzo-soprano; Set Svanholm, tenor; Josef von Manowarda, bass; Marjan Rus, bass; Chorus of the Vienna State Opera, Vienna Philharmonic conducted by Vittorio Gui, recorded in 1941 and 1942 in the Vienna State Opera (Ko 31 458–2).
   2. Hilde Scheppan, soprano; Margarete Klose, mezzo-soprano; Helge Rosvænge, tenor; Wilhelm Lang, bass; Wilhelm Schirp, bass; Berlin State Opera Orchestra and Chorus conducted by Artur Rother, recorded in 1942 (Fono Pr 90 239).
   3. Gloria Davy, soprano; Cvetka Ahlin, mezzo-soprano; Paul Schöffler, baritone; Chorus and Orchestra of the Vienna Volksoper conducted by Argeo Quadri, recorded in March 1942 (DG 423 872–2).

Opera *Falstaff* (sung in German):
   1. Henny Neumann-Knapp, soprano; Martina Wolf, soprano; Hedwig Fichtmüller, mezzo-soprano; Else Tegetthoff, mezzo-soprano; Peter Markwort, tenor; Philipp Rasp, tenor; Wilhelm Ulbricht, tenor; Arno Schellenberg, baritone; Gottlieb Zeithammer, bass; Chorus and Orchestra of Reich Radio, Leipzig, conducted by Hans Weisbach, recorded on April 9, 1939 (Fono Pr 90 102).
   2. "L'onore — ladri!" (Falstaff's monologue) (Fono Pr 90 200).

Opera *Otello* (selections, sung in German):
   1. "Credo in un dio crudel" (Jago's Credo), "Era la notte" (Jago's dream), Bavarian State Orchestra conducted by Heinrich Hollreiser, recorded 1943 in Munich (Fono Pr 90 250).
   2. (Same selections as CD 1), Orchestra of the Städtische Oper, Berlin, conducted by Artur Rother, recorded in 1943 (Acanta).

Richard Wagner
Opera *Der fliegende Holländer:*
   1. Viorica Ursuleac, soprano; Luise Willer, mezzo-soprano; Karl Ostertag, tenor; Franz Klarwein, tenor; Georg Hann, bass; Bavarian State Opera

Chorus and Orchestra conducted by Clemens Krauss, recorded in 1944 at the Bavarian State Opera in Munich (Fono Pr 90 250).

2. Helene Werth, soprano; Res Fischer, contralto; Bernd Aldenhoff, tenor; Helmut Krebs, tenor; Kurt Böhme, bass; North German Radio Chorus and Orchestra conducted by Wilhelm Schüchter, recorded in 1941 in Hamburg (Melodram Mel 032).

Opera *Die Meistersinger von Nürnberg:*

1. Annelies Kupper, soprano; Günther Treptow, tenor, Chorus and Orchestra of the Bavarian State Opera conducted by Eugen Jochum, recorded on December 10, 1949, in the Prinzregententheater, Munich (Melodram Mel 428).

2. Claire Watson, soprano; Lilian Benningsen, mezzo-soprano; Jess Thomas, tenor; Walther Carnuth, tenor; Karl Ostertag, tenor; Franz Klarwein, tenor; David Thaw, tenor; Friedrich Lenz, tenor; Otto Wiener, baritone; Karl Hoppe, baritone; Benno Kusche, baritone; Josef Metternich, baritone; Adolf Keil, bass; Max Proebstl, bass; Georg Wieter, bass; Hans-Bruno Ernst, bass, Chorus and Orchestra of the Bavarian State Opera conducted by Joseph Keilberth, recorded on November 23, 1963, at the festive reopening of the Nationaltheater, Munich (Eurodisc GD69008).

3. Elisabeth Grümmer, soprano; Elisabeth Schärtel, mezzo-soprano; Josef Traxel, tenor; Otto Wiener, baritone; Eberhard Wächter, baritone; Toni Blankenheim, bass; Chorus and Orchestra of the Bayreuth Festival conducted by André Cluytens, recorded at the 1958 Bayreuth Festival (Melodram Mel 582).

Opera *Parsifal:*

1. Astrid Varnay, Soprano; Set Svanholm, tenor; George London, baritone; Lawrence Davidson, baritone; Lubomir Vichegonov, bass; Metropolitan Opera Orchestra and Chorus conducted by Fritz Stiedry, recorded on April 17, 1954, at the Metropolitan Opera House, New York (Melodram Mel 442).

2. Hilde Güden, soprano; Gundula Janowitz, soprano; Anneliese Rothenberger, soprano; Elisabeth Höngen, mezzo-soprano; Christa Ludwig, mezzo-soprano; Kurt Equiluz, tenor; Erich Majkut, tenor; Fritz Uhl, tenor; Eberhard Wächter; baritone; Walter Berry, baritone; Tugomir Franc, bass; Chorus of the Vienna State Opera; Vienna Philharmonic conducted by Herbert von Karajan, recorded in 1961 at the Vienna State Opera (Pool KAR 219).

3. Irene Dalis, mezzo-soprano; Jess Thomas, tenor; George London, baritone; Gustav Neidlinger, baritone; Martti Talvela, bass; Chorus and Orchestra of the Bayreuth Festival conducted by Hans Knappertsbusch, recorded at the 1962 Bayreuth Festival (Philips Ph 416 390–2).

4. Barbro Ericsson, soprano; Jon Vickers, Tenor; Thomas Stewart, baritone; Heinz Hagenau, baritone; Gustav Neidlinger, baritone; Chorus and Orchestra of the Bayreuth Festival conducted by Hans Knappertsbusch, recorded on August 13, 1964, at the Bayreuth Festival (Melodram Mel 643).

5. Martha Mödl, soprano; Ramón Vinay, tenor; Dietrich Fischer-Dieskau, baritone; Toni Blankenheim, baritone; Josef Greindl, bass; Chorus and Orchestra of the Bayreuth Festival conducted by Hans Knappertsbusch, recorded at the 1956 Bayreuth Festival (Melodram Mel 563).

6. Christa Ludwig, mezzo-soprano; René Kollo, tenor; Dietrich Fischer-Dieskau, baritone; Gottlob Frick, bass; Zoltán Kelemen, bass; Chorus of the Vienna State Opera; Vienna Philharmonic conducted by Sir Georg Solti (Decca Dec 417 143–2 ZC).

Tetralogy Der Ring des Nibelungen:
Opera *Das Rheingold:*
1. Bruni Falcon, soprano; Maria von Ilosvay, mezzo-soprano; Ira Malaniuk, mezzo-soprano; Paul Kuén, tenor; Erich Witte, tenor; Josef Greindl, bass; Gustav Witte, bass; Ludwig Weber, bass; Orchestra of the Bayreuth Festival conducted by Clemens Krauss, recorded on August 9, 1953, at the Bayreuth Festival (Rodolphe RPC 32503.9).

2. Elisabeth Grümmer, soprano; Maria von Ilosvay, mezzo-soprano; Georgine von Milinkoviã, mezzo-soprano; Paul Kuén, tenor; Ludwig Suthaus, tenor; Gustav Neidlinger, baritone; Josef Greindl, bass; Arnold van Mill, bass; Orchestra of the Bayreuth Festival conducted by Hans Knappertsbusch, recorded on August 14, 1957, at the Bayreuth Festival (Laudis LCD34010).

3. Elisabeth Grümmer, soprano; Maria von Ilosvay, mezzo-soprano; Georgine von Milinkoviã, mezzo-soprano; Gerhard Stolze, tenor; Fritz Uhl, tenor; Theo Adam, bass; Josef Greindl, bass; Frans Andersson, bass; Orchestra of the Bayreuth Festival conducted by Hans Knappertsbusch, recorded at the 1958 Bayreuth Festival (Pool MP 441).

Opera *Die Walküre:*
1. Regina Resnik, soprano; Astrid Varnay, soprano; Ira Malaniuk, mezzo-Soprano; Ramón Vinay, tenor; Josef Greindl, bass; Orchestra of the Bayreuth Festival conducted by Clemens Krauss, recorded on August 9, 1953, at the Bayreuth Festival (Rodolphe RPC 32503.9).

2. Martha Mödl, soprano; Astrid Varnay, soprano; Georgine von Milinkoviã, mezzo-soprano; Max Lorenz, tenor; Josef Greindl, bass; Orchestra of the Bayreuth Festival conducted by Joseph Keilberth, recorded on July 26, 1953, at the Bayreuth Festival (Melodtram Mel 537).

3. Martha Mödl, soprano; Astrid Varnay, soprano; Georgine von Milinkoviã, mezzo-soprano; Ramón Vinay, tenor; Josef Greindl, bass; Or-

chestra of the Bayreuth Festival conducted by Joseph Keilberth, recorded at the 1955 Bayreuth Festival (Melodtram Mel 557).

4. Gré Brouwenstijn, soprano; Astrid Varnay, soprano; Georgine von Milinkoviã, mezzo-soprano; Ramón Vinay, tenor; Josef Greindl, bass; Orchestra of the Bayreuth Festival conducted by Joseph Keilberth, recorded at the 1956 Bayreuth Festival (Melodram 567).

5. Birgit Nilsson, soprano; Astrid Varnay, soprano; Georgine von Milinkoviã, mezzo-soprano; Ramón Vinay, tenor; Josef Greindl, bass; Bayreuth Festival Orchestra conducted by Hans Knappertsbusch, recorded on August 15, 1957, at the Bayreuth Festival (Melodram Mel 577).

6. Birgit Nilsson, soprano; Astrid Varnay, soprano; Georgine von Milinkoviã, mezzo-soprano; Ramón Vinay, tenor; Josef Greindl, bass; Bayreuth Festival Orchestra conducted by Hans Knappertsbusch, recorded at the 1958 Bayreuth Festival (Pool MP 442).

7. Régine Crespin, soprano; Birgit Nilsson, soprano; Christa Ludwig, mezzo-soprano; James King, tenor; Gottlob Frick, bass; Vienna Philharmonic conducted by Sir Georg Solti, recorded in October and November, 1965, in Vienna (Decca 414 105–2).

Opera *Siegfried:*

1. Rita Streich, soprano; Martha Mödl, soprano; Maria von Ilosvay, contralto; Paul Kuén, tenor; Wolfgang Windgassen, tenor; Gustav Neidlinger, baritone; Josef Greindl, bass; Orchestra of the Bayreuth Festival conducted by Clemens Krauss, recorded on August 10, 1953, at the Bayreuth Festival (Rodolphe RPC 32503–9).

2. Ilse Hollweg, soprano; Astrid Varnay, soprano; Maria von Ilosvay, contralto; Paul Kuén, tenor; Bernd Aldenhoff, tenor; Gustav Neidlinger, baritone; Josef Greindl, bass; Orchestra of the Bayreuth Festival conducted by Hans Knappertsbusch, recorded at the 1957 Bayreuth Festival (Laudis LCD 4.4012).

3. Dorothea Siebert, soprano; Astrid Varnay, soprano; Maria von Ilosvay, contralto; Gerhard Stolze, tenor; Wolfgang Windgassen, tenor; Frans Andersson, baritone; Josef Greindl, bass; Orchestra of the Bayreuth Festival conducted by Hans Knappertsbusch, recorded at the 1958 Bayreuth Festival (Pool MP 443).

4. Birgit Nilsson, soprano; Joan Sutherland, soprano; Marga Höffgen, contralto; Gerhard Stolze, tenor; Wolfgang Windgassen, tenor; Gustav Neidlinger, baritone; Kurt Böhme, bass; Vienna Philharmonic conducted by Sir Georg Solti, recorded in May and October, 1962 (Decca 414 110–2 ZC).

Opera *Tristan und Isolde:*

1. Martha Mödl, soprano; Ira Malaniuk, mezzo-soprano; Ramón Vinay, tenor; Ludwig Weber, bass; Chorus and Orchestra of the Bayreuth Festival

conducted by Herbert von Karajan, recorded on July 23, 1952, at the Bayreuth Festival (Pool HP 528).

2. Birgit Nilsson, soprano; Grace Hoffman, mezzo-soprano; Wolfgang Windgassen, tenor; Arnold van Mill, bass; Chorus and Orchestra of the Bayreuth Festival conducted by Wolfgang Sawallisch, recorded on August 19, 1957, at the Bayreuth Festival (Melodram Mel 575).

Opera Arias and Duets with Birgit Nilsson, soprano, Philharmonia Orchestra conducted by Leopold Ludwig (TESTAMENT Records SBT 1201).

Carl Maria von Weber
Lieder; Opus 15, nos. 1 and 2 with Michael Raucheisen, piano, recorded on March 19, 1943 (Acanta 43 126).

Hugo Wolf
Lieder to poems by Eduard Mörike, "Auf einer Wanderung," "Fussreise," "Wenn ich dein gedenke," "Wie sollt' ich heiter bleiben"; to poems by Johann Wolfgang von Goethe, "Grenzen der Menschheit," "Prometheus;" from the Italian Song Book, "Selig ihr Blinden"; from the Spanish Song Book, "Blindes Schauen, dunkle Leuchte," "Eide, so die Liebe schwur" with Michael Raucheisen, piano, recorded on January 20, 1943, and on February 9 and November 6, 1944 (Acanta 43.126).

Lieder to a poem by Eduard Mörike, "Der Tambour;" to poems by Johann Wolfgang von Goethe, "Anakreons Grab," "Ob der Koran von Ewigkeit sei," "Solang man nüchtern ist;" from the Italian Song Book, "Ein Ständchen euch zu bringen," "Schon streckt' ich aus im Bett;" to poems by Michelangelo Buonarotti, "Wohl denk ich oft," Alles endet, was entstehet," "Fühlt meine Seele" with Gerald Moore, piano, recorded on May 3, 21, and 22, 1953, in the EMI Studios in London (TESTAMENT Records SBT 1197).

Lieder to poems by Johann Wolfgang von Goethe; "Copthisches Lied" nos. 1 and 2, "Gesänge des Harfners" nos. 1–3, "Grenzen der Menschheit"; to poems by Michelangelo Buonarotti, "Wohl denk ich oft," Alles endet, was entstehet," "Fühlt meine Seele" with Gerald Moore, piano, recorded on May 3, 21, and 22, 1953, in the EMI Studios in London (EMI EAC 40099).

Index

Scheidl, Theodor, 3, 14, 15, 77, 81, 128
Schellenberg, Arno, 80
Schenk, Otto, 242
Scherchen, Hermann, 42
Schillings, Max von, 126, 128
Schipper, Emil, 45, 167
Schirach, Baldur von, 70
Schlüter, Erna, 142
Schmidt-Isserstedt, Hans, 257
Schneider-Siemssen, Günther, 133, 250,
    251, 255, 256. 257
Schoenberg, Arnold, 244, 245, 246
schöne Magelone, Die (Johannes
    Brahms), 68
Schöpfung, Die (Franz Joseph Haydn),
    116, 219
Schorr, Friedrich, 3, 22, 23
Schubert, Franz, 7, 41, 142, 149, 229, 231,
    232, 235, 237, 260
Schüchter, Wilhelm, 257
Schuh, Oskar Fritz, 64, 73, 146
Schumann, Robert, 41, 231
Schwarzkopf, Elisabeth, 82, 155, 228
schweigsame Frau, Die (Richard Strauss),
    255, 256, 257
Seaton, George, 186
Shakespeare, William, 191, 215
Shuard, Amy, 254
Siegfried (Richard Wagner), 23, 48, 49,
    62, 79, 85, 86, 93, 94, 125, 200, 221,
    251, 253
Siepi, Cesare, 179
Silja, Anja, 48, 208
Simon, John, 19
Slevogt, Max, 128
Slezak, Leo, 7, 39, 80
Smetana, Bedřich, 11
Solti, Georg, 153, 155, 230, 250, 252
Sonnleithner, Leopold, 235
South Pacific (Richard Rodgers, Oscar
    Hammerstein II), 146
Stabile, Mariano, 38
Stanislavsky, Konstantin, 110
Stein, Marion. See Lady Marion Harewood
Stevens, Risë, 185
Stewart Thomas, 253
Stolze, Gerhard, 204, 252
Strauss, Franz, 103

Strauss, Johann, 70
Strauss, Pauline, 102, 105
Strauss, Richard, 41, 48, 50, 51, 70, 86, 93,
    95, 96, 97, 98, 99, 102, 103, 104, 105,
    106, 109, 116, 121, 125, 126, 127, 129,
    134, 140, 141, 146, 148, 149, 154, 157,
    181, 230, 255, 256
Strindberg, August, 90
Svanholm, Set, 174
Swarovsky, Hans, 246
Szell, George (Georg), 7, 9, 10, 179

Tales of Hoffmann, The. See Les contes
    d'Hoffmann
Talvela, Martti, 254
Tannhäuser (Richard Wagner), 48, 257
Tauber, Richard, 7, 156, 157
Taubmann, Horst, 149
Tchaikovsky, Pyotr Ilyitch, 231
Teyte, Maggie, 39
Tieck, Ludwig, 68
Tiefland (Eugen d'Albert), 14
Tietjen, Heinz, 202
Tilden, Jane, 147
Tosca (Giacomo Puccini), 13, 146, 152, 193
Toscanini, Arturo, 7
Tristan und Isolde (Richard Wagner), 60,
    75, 124, 125, 129, 173, 174, 194, 200,
    201, 207, 220, 221, 257
Tutein, Karl, 85

Ucicky, Gustav, 100
Uhl, Fritz, 223
Ursuleac, Viorica, 90, 94, 126, 127, 128,
    129, 143, 149

Välkki, Anita, 252
Varnay, Astrid, 48, 178, 182, 183, 204
Veasey, Josephine, 254
Verdi, Giuseppe, 50, 51, 91, 92, 125, 126,
    141, 179, 187, 191, 219, 231
Vickers, Jon, 253
Vinay, Ramón, 184
Vincent, Jo, 81
Votto, Antonino, 15

Wächter, Eberhard, 223
Wagner, Cosima, 263

Wagner, Minna (Planer), 140

Wagner, Richard, 3, 16, 2, 48, 49, 60, 70,
82, 96, 125, 133, 138, 139, 141, 157, 160,
182, 187, 193, 195, 196, 198, 199, 200,
201, 203, 205, 208, 220, 225, 231, 250,
255, 257, 260, 263

Wagner, Siegfried, 40, 263

Wagner, Wieland, 40, 113, 133, 140, 196,
197, 199, 200, 202, 203, 205, 206, 208,
209, 220, 242, 250, 257

Wagner, Winifred, 202, 203

Wagner, Wolfgang, 208

Walker, Sarah Jane. *See* Mme. Charles
Cahier

Walküre, Die (Richard Wagner), 18, 22,
23, 48, 90, 110, 136, 137, 142, 157, 174,
182, 200, 207, 221, 253

Wallek, Oskar, 86

Wallmann, Margherita, 224

Walter, Bruno, 17, 18, 19, 20, 21, 80, 113,
121, 125, 129, 139, 224

Ward, David, 253, 254

Watson, Claire, 253

Weber, Ludwig, 86, 119, 143, 205

Webster, David, 157, 158, 159, 249

Webster, Margaret, 180

Wedekind, Frank, 242

Weigert, Hermann, 182

Weiss Ferdl (Ferdinand Weisheitinger),
121, 122

Welitsch, Ljuba, 181

Werfel, Franz, 11

Wessely, Paula, 7

Wiener, Otto, 256

Wilde, Oscar, 50

Willer, Luise, 13, 80, 124, 174, 228

Windgassen, Wolfgang, 204, 252

Winterreise, Die (Franz Schubert), 123,
149, 173, 233, 235, 237, 238, 239, 240

Winklmaier, Kreszentia. *See* Hotter,
Kreszentia

Wirk, Willy, 17

Wise, Patricia, 244

Wolf, Hugo, 232, 260

Wunderlich, Fritz, 84, 255, 256, 257

Zallinger, Meinhard von, 149, 230

Zaubergeige, Die (Werner Egk), 78, 257

Zauberflöte, Die (The Magic Flute), 46,
47, 133, 159

Zelter, Carl Friedrich, 232

Zimmermann, Rudolf, 176

Zindler, Rudolf, 64, 77, 81, 83, 84, 117

Zweig, Stefan, 256